GOD'S EVERLASTING COVENANT OF GRACE

Herman Hanko

Reformed Free
Publishing Association
Box 2006
Grand Rapids, MI 49501

Library of Congress Catalog Card Number 88-61707
ISBN 0-916206-34-3

PRINTED IN THE UNITED STATES OF AMERICA

To the saints of the congregation of

Hope Protestant Reformed Church

who first suggested to me the writing of this material
and who made that writing possible.

TABLE OF CONTENTS

FOREWORD

In the more than twenty years in which the author of this work and I have been co-laborers in our Protestant Reformed Theological School, we have on numerous occasions remarked upon and discussed the pervasive significance of the truth of God's everlasting covenant of grace for the entire Reformed system of truth. That this truth occupies an essential place in dogmatics, of course, goes without saying. But once one has discovered and learned to appreciate the riches of this truth from a dogmatical viewpoint, he discovers greater and greater treasures of truth in the entire rank of theological studies and, in fact, in our entire Reformed world-and-life view. About this Prof. Hanko and I talked many times in connection with our seminary teaching.

Another aspect of this truth which we frequently discussed was that which I would call the interdependence of the truth of sovereign grace and the truth of God's everlasting covenant of grace. On the one hand, it is ultimately impossible to maintain the truth of sovereign grace – with sovereign predestination at its heart – without a consistently Scriptural and Reformed understanding of the covenant. On the other hand, it is equally impossible to maintain the truth of God's everlasting covenant of grace apart from a thorough-going understanding and maintenance of the Reformed doctrine of sovereign grace. How often in our discussions we remarked about this fact I would not venture to say.

The author therefore has done his readers a favor by developing the truth of the covenant of grace in a manner consistent with the truth of sovereign grace. This is not merely a book for professional theologians; it is written for the broad readership of God's people. In fact, the book began many years ago as a series of popular-style pamphlets. It is readily digestible by the Christian reader.

I count it an honor to recommend Professor Hanko's work in this Foreword and to express the hope that many of God's people will be spiritually edified by it.

– Homer C. Hoeksema

INTRODUCTION

Anyone who is acquainted with the history of the development of doctrine since the time of the Protestant Reformation will understand the importance of the truth of God's everlasting covenant of grace. As the truths of the Calvin Reformation developed both in England and on the continent, the doctrine of the covenant occupied an extremely important place. Almost every theologian of note paid attention to it.

Yet there is one remarkable feature about the development of this doctrine: almost never were theologians who paid attention to it able to bring this truth into harmony with the truths of sovereign grace in general and with the truth of sovereign predestination in particular. Look where you will among Presbyterian and Reformed theologians, and you will find tension between these two great truths of God's Word. If the truths of sovereign grace and double predestination were emphasized (and there were many who did this) the truth of the covenant was pushed into a relatively small corner of their theology. If, on the other hand, the central emphasis of a theologian lay on the doctrine of the covenant (such as, e.g., Cocceius), the truths of sovereign grace and double predestination received, at best, short shrift.

Why was this? We are convinced that the answer to this question lies in the fact that almost without exception the doctrine of the covenant was, in the main, defined in terms of an *agreement* between God and man. The essence of the covenant was defined in terms of such an agreement, and both the establishment of the covenant and its continuation were dependent upon the mutual stipulations, conditions, provisions, and promises which are inherent in an agreement. Here lay the problem. A covenant which is an agreement is a covenant which is conditional. And a covenant which is conditional depends for its realization upon man. When in any sense the work of salvation depends upon man, the truths of sovereign grace suffer accordingly.

This is not to say that every theologian taught a salvation which depended upon man. This is far from the truth. Both in English and continental theology there were many who defended vigorously and consistently the truths of sovereign grace. But when such was the case, either the covenant of grace was not integrated into the whole system of theology set forth by these men, or a kind of "happy inconsistency" led theologians to hold to both. The fact is that a conditional covenant and sovereign grace cannot be harmonized.

This problem quite naturally is closely related to the whole question of infant baptism. If the covenant is an agreement and therefore conditional, little children cannot, in the deepest sense of the word, belong to that covenant; they are unable to fulfill the conditions until such a time as they are mature. This has led throughout the years to sometimes bitter controversies over the question of infant baptism. Sometimes the debate has raged between the defenders of infant baptism and those who hold to believers' baptism. This debate has intensified the last few decades, probably in part because many who hold to a "baptist" position have, at the same time, adopted a certain Calvinism which emphasizes the doctrines of grace. They are Calvinistic Baptists in distinction from Arminian or Free Will Baptists. Going back to Charles Spurgeon, and even beyond, there is a stream of thought among Baptists which holds to the central truths of sovereign grace while continuing to deny infant baptism.

These "Reformed" or "Calvinistic Baptists" have sparked a renewal of the debate, or at least have generated a degree of greater intensity in the debate because those who hold to the truth of infant baptism have generally maintained that the ideas of believers' baptism and sovereign grace are mutually exclusive, and that those who hold to these two positions hold a contradictory view of salvation. Baptists have, of course, repudiated this charge, and the debate goes on.

But even within the circles of those who hold to infant baptism there is controversy. Many who have been historically Reformed and who have, from their Reformed position, held to the doctrine of infant baptism, are no longer able to defend their position over against the energetic and forceful apologetic of the Baptists. The result is that many Reformed people who wish to cling to the doctrines of sovereign grace have been influenced by Reformed Baptists and have gone over to that position. It is our conviction that this inability to defend the doctrine of infant baptism is rooted in an incorrect conception of the truth of the covenant, namely that the covenant is an agreement resting on certain conditions.

By making the covenant an agreement – which, obviously, little children are not able to enter – the ground has been taken away from the truth of infant baptism. It is true that various solutions have been proposed to this problem, as we shall see later, but these solutions have proved unsatisfactory and without Scriptural foundation. Much of the debate within Reformed circles has centered in this question: what is the ground for infant baptism? The various answers which have been given have led to much controversy within Reformed circles, controversy which has as yet not died down completely. The difficulty is always that the controversy has been carried on within the limitations of a covenant defined as an agreement, bilateral and conditional. And the controversy will not be solved until these ideas are laid to rest once and for all and the Biblical idea of the covenant is clearly set forth.

But another problem has intruded into any discussion of the covenant. I refer to the fact that much of the work done in theology in our day is man-centered. Theology begins with man and ends with man. It is concerned with man's well-being and man's happiness. Man stands at the center of all the church's thinking, and man becomes the chief object of consideration.

While it is certainly true that the Scriptures deal with men, it is also true that men are not the Scriptures' chief concern. Emphasis on man is really a form of religious humanism, and such humanism, with all its grave evils, has become the object of theological reflection. This is a sad and dangerous error. Man is not the chief concern of the Scriptures at all. Nor ought it to be ours. The emphasis of the church on man is not the emphasis of the Bible. The Scriptures have to do with God. The Scriptures start with God and end with God. All of the Scriptures are the revelation of God and have their chief concern in God and His glory. God is foremost and supreme. Whatever happens to man, or what is said of man is of secondary importance. God is first and last. All things begin with Him and end in Him. God is central and transcendently important in any discussion of the truth. We deny this fundamental emphasis or ignore its truth at our own peril.

How often does not the apostle Paul break forth into a mighty and soul-stirring doxology of praise as he contemplates the truth revealed to him – a doxology of praise to God Who alone is worthy of all praise and glory? After discussing, e.g., the great truths of election and reprobation, especially as they apply to the salvation of Jews and Gentiles in Romans 9-11, he concludes it all by saying: "O the depth of the riches both of the wisdom and knowledge of God; how unsearchable are his judgments, and his ways past finding out! For who hath known the mind of the Lord? or who hath been his counselor? Or who hath first given to him, and it shall be recompensed unto him again? For of him, and through him, and to him, are all things; to whom be glory for ever. Amen" (vss. 33-36).

And what was true of Paul was true of all the other authors of the Scriptures. David, in the Psalms, seems as if he cannot speak often enough and long enough about the great glory of God. Taken up in the ecstasy of God's greatness, he calls upon the heavens and the earth, the sea and the stars, and all this vast creation to join him in a song of praise to Him Who is great and greatly to be praised. The book of Revelation heaps doxology upon doxology and anthem upon anthem of praise and glory to Him Who alone is worthy of the honor of all the universe. Indeed, the whole of the Scriptures can rightly be called one beautifully glorious hymn of praise to God alone.

This must be uppermost in our hearts and minds when we attempt to solve any of the problems that confront us or attempt to determine the truth of God's Word. There is perhaps nothing quite so difficult for sinful man than to lose sight of himself and see only the glory of God. But such is nevertheless essential. And this is pre-eminently true of the doctrine of the covenant of grace.

And so in our discussion of the truth of the covenant, we must begin with God and end with God. If we do this, as the Scriptures do, it will give to us an entirely different perspective on this truth, and will enable us to see our way clear through the tangle of problems which the controversy over the covenant has generated through the years. It will lead us to the Scriptures so that our discussion may be based on the Scriptures and on the Scriptures alone. And such a study will show us that the truth of the covenant pervades the whole of the Scriptures. It is not an exaggeration to say that not only does the covenant of grace run like a golden thread through the whole of the Scriptures, but that it is in fact the Scriptures' dominant theme. And if this truth is the Scriptures' dominant theme, it is also the fundamental truth of all theology. There have been theologians in the past who have developed theology from the viewpoint of the covenant. We need only mention such men as Cocceius and Witsius. This approach, we believe, is correct and Biblical. And this we shall attempt to show.

In order to do this we shall treat the truth of the covenant, not topically, but historically. While it is beyond the scope of this book to deal with the whole of the Scriptures from Genesis to Revelation, and treat every passage presented to us, we shall nevertheless follow the broad lines of the historical development of the covenant in the Old Testament to show how the idea of the covenant was revealed by God to His people in that dispensation, and then relate it to the new to show how it all was fulfilled in Christ. We believe that this historical approach will help to make the truth of God's covenant clear.

We believe that this historical approach, along with an emphasis on the centrality of God and His glory, will bring the great truths of sovereign grace and God's everlasting covenant into perfect Biblical harmony.

Chapter 1

GOD, A COVENANT GOD

God is a covenant God. The deepest ground for the covenant of grace must be found in the truth that God lives a covenant life in Himself even apart from the creatures He has created.

God is triune. That is, God is one in essence and three in person. This central and all-important doctrine of the church has stood as the immovable rock upon which all of the truth is based. And this trinity is the deepest reason why God is a covenant God and lives a covenant life within Himself. Without the reality of the trinity, the covenant would be impossible.

That God is one in essence means that there is only one God, one divine Being, one divine essence. There is in God only one mind and one will, one divine nature, one divine life. All the attributes of God are attributes of the essence and therefore of God Himself.

Yet, while God is one in essence, he is also three in person. Within God are three distinct Egos, three that say "I." These three persons are the Father, the Son, and the Holy Spirit.

We must not be left with the false impression that these three are not entirely distinct one from another as far as their personal characteristics and attributes are concerned. The Father is personally distinct from the Son and the Holy Spirit, and the Son is personally distinct from the Father and the Holy Spirit. And what may be said of the Father and Son may equally be said of the Holy Spirit. It is true that they live in one unity of essence. It is true that they have together but one mind and one will. But the Father thinks as Father; the Son thinks as Son; the Holy Spirit is personally distinct from Father and Son in His thinking and willing. And yet they think and will the same thoughts and desires. Their life is one; their joy is one; their purpose is one; there is only one God.

On this truth of the trinity rests the truth of the covenant life which God lives in Himself.

God is not the Mohammedan Allah who is only an impersonal, static force with which one must reckon. God is triune. And because He is triune, He is the living God, living a perfect and complete life within Himself. This life He lives is full and blessed. He needs none other, not even the creature, to make His life fuller or richer. The creation cannot add to His glory and happiness. No creature can enrich Him Who is all-sufficient. He is perfect, holy, eternally blessed, purely happy in all His life.

This is true because He lives a covenant life within Himself. And this covenant life which God lives within Himself is the fellowship and communion which He enjoys within Himself in the *unity* of essence and *trinity* of person of the Godhead. There is and can be perfect fellowship only because there is a perfect unity of essence underlying God's life. But at the same time, there is and can be fellowship and communion only because there is a trinity of person. If God were one in essence and one in person, such communion would be impossible, for communion implies a plurality of person. If, on the other hand, God were three in person and three in essence, fellowship would also be less than perfect, for the difference in essence would make full fellowship impossible. But, on the contrary, each of the three persons knows the other two perfectly and completely. And in this unity of essence there is a communion of essence and nature, a fellowship of life and love, a transcendent happiness that characterizes God's fellowship as the three persons rejoice in their mutual communion. This fellowship, supreme happiness, communion of life and love is God's own covenant life.

As we said, this life of God is full and perfect. Man cannot enrich God's life in any way. God is not incomplete without man. It would be the height of folly and the apex of sinful pride to say that the only true and living God, the Sovereign of heaven and earth, the only One Who is infinitely glorious and eternal, has need of man to complete or perfect His glory. His happiness is full; His life and love are complete; His glory is perfect. God has no need of us; we only have need of Him.

This truth is clearly set forth, e.g., in Isaiah 40:12-18: "Who hath measured the waters in the hollow of his hand, and meted out the heavens with the span, and comprehended the dust of the earth in a measure, and weighed the mountains in scales, and the hills in a balance? Who hath directed the Spirit of the Lord, or being his counsellor hath taught him? With whom took he counsel, and who instructed him, and taught him in the path of judgment, and taught him knowledge, and showed to him the way of understanding? Behold, the nations are as a drop of a bucket, and are counted as the small dust of the balance; behold, he taketh up the isles as a very little thing. And Lebanon is not sufficient to burn, nor the beasts thereof sufficient for a burnt offering. All nations before him are as nothing; and they are counted to him less than nothing, and vanity. To whom then will ye liken God? or what likeness will ye compare unto him?"

If we would ask ourselves at this point, why it is that God created man and established His covenant with His own people, then we touch on the very heart of our relation to God in all our life. The answer to which we come is an answer that can only prostrate the child of God in dust and ashes before the greatness of the Almighty. It is only because of the deepest sovereign goodness of God that can never be adequately explained in human language or understood by mere finite minds that God has seen fit not only to create the worlds, but also to create a people to love Him and to participate in His glory and goodness. God willed to do it! More than this we cannot say.

Here we touch upon an essential point in our understanding of the doctrine of the covenant of grace.

God cannot be known by any efforts which man would put forth. Because He is so great and so infinitely exalted above all that is of this creation, He is also unknown to man – apart from revelation. The infinitely deep and wide chasm that separates God from man is a chasm that cannot possibly be bridged by man nor crossed by the efforts of the creature. God dwells in a light unto which no man can approach. He is the invisible One Who alone is greatly exalted. The heavens are His throne and the earth is His footstool. If, therefore, He is to be known by the creature, He is known only because He makes Himself known through His own revelation. If it is possible for us to know Him at all, it is only because He has revealed Himself unto us in a way that we can both understand and appropriate for ourselves.

In other words, if God is to be known at all, it can only be by the amazing wonder of a revelation that at once reveals the truth of the infinite God, and yet reveals it in such a way that man can understand it. Not by our powers of reason and intellect, nor by the strength found in man; not by man's scientific investigation, nor by man's best efforts can God ever be known. The only way is for man to bow in humility before the Word of God and pray that his earnest efforts to penetrate the wonders of that Word may be blessed by his Father in heaven. In that Word is contained all the truth of the trinity, the truth of all God's glorious perfections, the truth of His own glorious covenant life, the truth of the everlasting covenant of grace.

And so to speak of the covenant of grace is to speak of revelation. All revelation is God speaking about Himself. Whether now we are talking about God's "revelation" in creation, in Christ, or in the Scriptures as the infallible record of God's revelation in Christ, it is always God speaking. And God speaks only of Himself. Thus it is too with His revelation of the covenant of grace. This revelation is God speaking of Himself, particularly of the covenant life which He lives in Himself. When God reveals His own covenant life to man, then and then only is the covenant of grace established with man.

We must remember, however, that this is not simply a revelation in words. It is that too; but it is more. When God establishes His covenant with His people, He does so not only by telling them about the covenant life which He lives within Himself, but He reveals His covenant life which He lives within Himself to His people by taking them into His own covenant life. He causes men to share in the joy and happiness of His own fellowship. He gives to man to taste the greatness of that communion and fellowship which He enjoys in Himself.

Perhaps a figure will make this clear. God's covenant life which He lives within Himself is a "family" life. The triune God is a "family" God. This "family" life is reflected in our own family lives where there is truly covenant fellowship. Such a family is usually composed of a father, a mother, and their children. This family enjoys the fellowship and communion of a unity of nature and a distinction of persons. This family life, blessed by God, is happy and peaceful. If this family should be walking down the street of one of our larger cities, they might come across a small waif, a little girl who has been abandoned by her family. This girl has no parents, no home, no friends, no fellowship with any one. She is poor and starving. Her belly is swelled by malnutrition. Her clothes are rags. Her hair is lice-filled and matted. Her body is covered with sores filled with pus. The passing family might take pity on her and say among themselves that it is certainly very sad that this girl has no idea of the joy of family life. At that point they could do one of two things. They could, in their desire to acquaint her with the joys of family life, take her aside and tell her all about their own home. This would surely give the girl some idea of what a blessing family life can really be. But it would do the girl absolutely no good. They might also say among themselves that the only way to make this girl understand fully what a blessing family life can be is to take her home with them and make her a part of their own family. So they then would lead her to their home, wash her thoroughly in a tub of hot water, put healing salves on her sores, clean and comb her hair, bring her to their table where she could have a place with the other children, make her their very own daughter who would share in a real way in all the joys and blessings of the family. When she would really know with all her heart that she is loved and cared for, a true member of the family, then she would also know exactly what the blessedness of family life is all about.

This is the revelation of God's own covenant life to us. It is a wonder that is almost past finding out. God takes His people into His own triune family life. He delivers them from their sins, washes them from their corruption, feeds them with heavenly bread, makes them His sons and daughters – as their very own heavenly Father – and decrees that they shall be the heirs of His own everlasting inheritance. They are taken into God's triune covenant life. Peter is so bold as to say that we actually become partakers of the divine *nature* (II Peter 1:4).

But it must be remembered that this covenant life which God lives in Himself is a life of fellowship and friendship. When by His covenant of grace God takes us into that fellowship and friendship of His own trinity, this is the covenant of grace established with us through Jesus Christ. And thus this covenant is that bond of fellowship and friendship which God establishes with us through His own dear Son.

To enter into God's own life of fellowship will stand eternally as the incomprehensible wonder of our salvation.

Chapter 2

THE IDEA OF THE COVENANT

Throughout the history of the development of the doctrine of the covenant, almost always the covenant was considered as some kind of agreement between God and man, which bilateral or two-sided agreement included various stipulations, conditions, obligations, and promises to which both parties in the covenant bound themselves.

It is not completely clear how this conception of the covenant entered into the thinking of theologians. Most probably this idea arose chiefly because the word "covenant" in the Scriptures had consistently been translated in the Latin *Vulgate* by the word *foedus.* This Latin word meant in classical and medieval Latin: a league, a treaty, a covenant, a stipulation between two or more, an agreement. When applied to human covenants made between men, this word can aptly be used. For example, when a husband and wife enter into the covenant of marriage, there must of necessity be an agreement between them. Likewise, when two nations enter a covenant of peace, this must necessarily take on the form of an agreement. Each nation makes certain promises and assumes certain obligations to which it binds itself; and only when these conditions are met and maintained is the agreement in force.

The trouble was that this same idea was then applied to the covenant of grace which God establishes with man. In every theologian who spoke of the covenant at all since the time of the Reformation, this idea held sway. It is true that if one reads the works of these theologians, one can sometimes find certain ones who held to the idea of the covenant as a bond of friendship. Olevianus, e.g., a theologian of the 16th century and one of the authors of the Heidelberg Catechism sometimes spoke of the covenant as *Bund und Freudshaft* (bond and friendship). But even he did not escape the idea of the covenant as an agreement with a certain bilateral character.

In defining the covenant in this fashion, the idea was promoted that God and man together enter into an agreement by which the covenant is realized. Both enter into mutual consultation and arrive at an agreement satisfactory to them. It is true, as many theologians maintained, that God takes the initiative and comes to man with the first propositions, but the covenant is not in force nor obligatory on both parties until both have entered into the agreement by which they bind themselves.

If you ask how this works, the answer is: God comes to man with the proposition, through the preaching of the gospel, that He will save man and give to man all the blessings of salvation merited in the cross of Jesus Christ. But this promise of God is of no real effect until man agrees to it and assumes certain conditions that must be fulfilled. These conditions attached to this promise are obligatory upon man and are primarily that man must agree to accept the promise as his own, must agree to walk faithfully in the midst of the world, and must keep fidelity to God's covenant. Only when these conditions have been agreed to and successfully met can the covenant be realized and the blessings of the covenant become the possession of man.

To whom is this promise made? Different answers have been given to this question. Some say that the promise is made to all who hear the preaching of the gospel. The gospel then is described in terms of an offer of salvation which comes to all who hear and which expresses God's intention and desire to save all who hear. Wherever the gospel goes, to whomever it comes, there comes also the promise of God that He will certainly bless them provided that they will accept the conditions of the promise and enter into this agreement.

Others, while not opposing this position, tend to stress more the place of infants in the covenant. They emphasize, therefore, that at baptism the promise of God comes to all who are baptized without distinction. If, however, the promise is ever to become the treasured possession of the one being baptized, this can come about only when such a child grows older and accepts that which once was offered or promised to him in his infancy at the moment of baptism.

While these differences and others of a more minor sort may separate various views, the fact remains that all agree to the conception of the covenant of grace as a bilateral and conditional agreement.

The Scriptures, however, do not speak of the covenant in this way. Many serious objections can be brought against this view. The following are the most important.

If it is true that the promise of God to establish His covenant comes to all who are baptized, or in the broader sense of the word to all who hear the gospel, then it follows that all the blessings of salvation merited by Christ on the cross are promised to all who come into contact with the gospel in any form. And this is exactly intended to be the idea with those who promote these views. Now it is a patent fact that many, and in reality, most of those who hear the gospel are not saved. In fact, it is also true that many infants who are baptized are not saved. What does this mean? It means that God promises to a certain man something which that man never receives. And the only reason he does not receive it is because he himself is able to frustrate the promises of Almighty God.

But the question is not merely whether the promise of God comes to all men; the question is also whether or not Christ died for all these men to whom the promise comes. If God promises the blessings of the cross of Christ to all men, Christ died for all men. Indeed, this would certainly be the solution to the problem, for how could God promise something – blessings of the cross of Calvary – to men for whom these blessings of the cross were never intended? But then we are forced into the heresy of universal atonement, a heresy which Arminians willingly espouse, but which has always been sharply repudiated by those who believe the Scriptures. For if Christ died for all men and all men are not saved, the cross of Christ is of no effect. Calvary is a sham. There is then no power in the blood nor efficacy in the cross. Christ's intense sufferings under the wrath of God were futile for a great number of men for whom Christ died but who are never saved.

It may, however, be objected that Christ indeed died only for His elect people, while the promise of the blessings of Christ come to all men. But this is not a solution at all. Is it then true that God promises something to mankind which was never merited by Christ? Does God promise to man a salvation which was never merited? Can God promise heaven to one for whom there is no room beyond the gates of the new Jerusalem? Can God offer the magnificent blessings of a place in His house of many mansions when no such place actually exists? And how can such a place exist for a man if Christ did not merit that place for him? This is the grossest mockery of the cross imaginable, and, in fact, borders on the blasphemous.

Again, it may be objected that although the promise of the covenant of God hinges upon these conditions and the acceptance of certain obligations, nevertheless God gives the grace to fulfill these conditions and meet the requirements which He makes. But while this solution has often been proposed as an attempt to preserve both the conditionality of the covenant and the sovereignty of grace, this answer will not do. It sounds rather pious to introduce at this point some statement to the effect that the conditions are filled only by grace, but this can never change the matter. If the covenant is an agreement, man must have his place in such an agreement. If the promise comes to all who hear the gospel, the fulfillment of the promise hinges upon man's work alone. This is the awful dilemma from which there is no escape. Either mockery is made of the promise of God or a retreat must be ordered into the camp of the Arminians. The latter has usually been the sad result in the church of Jesus Christ.

Arminianism is the plague of the church and the scourge of sound doctrine. It is really the theological refinement of the lie which Satan spoke to Eve when he tempted her to eat of the forbidden tree: "Ye shall not surely die: for God doth know that in the day ye eat thereof, then your eyes shall be opened, and ye shall be as gods, knowing good and evil" (Genesis 3:4, 5). This lie has been perpetuated through the ages in the lives of man as man strives "to be as God."

This is the terrible sin of pride. Pride is the curse of man, the one sin which lies at the root of all man's iniquity. In pride man exalts himself to the throne of God and makes himself equal with the Most High. He seizes for himself attributes which belong to God alone, gives to himself honor which is due to God, and boasts in himself while completely ignoring his Creator.

There is perhaps no other way in which men have shown their pride more than by robbing God of His sovereign power. In their arrogance and vicious hatred of humility before the Lord, they make themselves equal with and often greater than God when they make themselves powerful beyond the power of the Almighty. They rob the Most High of sovereignty that belongs to Him alone and claim for themselves that which belongs to their Creator.

Nowhere has this evil of man become more apparent than in his beliefs concerning salvation. Rather than humbly confess that God alone saves and that all the power to save belongs to Him, man claims for himself a power equal with or even greater than the power of God: a power of man's will which can do something which God cannot do – save a sinner; a power which must first come into action by man's initiative before the work of salvation can be accomplished. God, so it is said, waits for man. Man, so it is said, must accept Jesus Christ as his personal Savior; must make a personal commitment to Christ and demonstrate a willingness to belong to Christ before it is possible for God to save him. And should he refuse to accept Christ, refuse to yield to the earnest entreaties with which he is assailed, God is completely unable to save him and to bring him into the blessedness of life eternal.

Consequently, there has been a terrible travesty of the ministry of the gospel. Those who claim to preach the gospel of redemption do not any longer preach the sovereign power of the cross, but rather bombard the ears of any audience with earnest pleas and heart-rending cries that do nothing less than present the Almighty God as a beggar Who must stoop so low from His lofty throne that He must plead with men to accept His salvation. Men's efforts, so they seem to think, are only crowned with success when men are moved so intensely that in a spasm of emotional passion they answer the "altar call."

This view has had a long, an almost uninterrupted, history in the church. Augustine, the great church father of the 5th century, already faced it when he did battle with Pelagius. This learned but superficial monk taught that all men come into the world free from sin or moral blot. Their natures and their lives are clean and spotless; they have no tendency to sin and are capable of living a life of perfect and unblemished holiness. The stark fact that men do actually sin is not to be ascribed to some defect in their nature, but only to the bad example of their fellow men with whom they come into contact and whose habits they pick up and emulate. Sin is, therefore, not rooted in the corruption and depravity of the nature, but is a mild sickness that pervades man only with tendencies of habit towards moral wrong, but is comparatively easy to cure. Such being the character of sin, man is able to overcome these habits and defects of his nature by repeated attempts to walk in holiness, occasionally assisted somewhat by divine grace. Then men earn their own salvation.

But in such a view there is no room for the guilt of sin and the depravity of a fallen human race. There is no room for the cross, for grace, for God's work of salvation.

Augustine fought this view bitterly. He held, on the basis of the Scriptures, that such a superficial view of sin is not the teaching of the Bible nor in harmony with reality. He taught that the sin of our first parents Adam and Eve in Paradise was a sin so grievous in the sight of God that He immediately punished that sin with death as He had said He would do.

This death which came upon Adam and Eve was spiritual death which can best be described by the well-known words "total depravity." Their death made them entirely incapable of doing any good in the sight of God. But this death was passed on to all men so that it is the state of the human race to live in a condition in which it is impossible to do anything but sin from life's first breath until the moment of death.

Already in his lifetime, Augustine faced a modified form of Pelagianism called Semi-Pelagianism. This heresy was basically adopted by the Romish Church and resulted in its teaching of salvation by faith and works.

Although the Reformation restored the truths of sovereign grace to the church, not many years passed before the old Pelagian heresy was resurrected in the teachings of Arminius. He spoke of man, although afflicted by the results of sin in his nature, as still possessing the ability to will the good. He could, if he chose, turn to God and accept Christ. He could, if this was his desire, forsake his sin and cast himself on the cross of Calvary. But, in fact, salvation could only come into the possession of a man if he first of all would exercise his will in such a fruitful way. The initial step was left to man. Salvation had to be begun by man. God stood helpless in His work until man had agreed to come to God and reach out his hand to that which was freely offered him.

Such have been the subtle attempts to undermine the truth of God's sovereign grace and power.

But it is this very heresy which has inextricably intertwined itself with the doctrine of the covenant when the covenant is presented as a bilateral and conditional agreement. Once again, we do not want to imply that all who have held to the covenant as an agreement have been Arminian in their thinking. This is far from the truth. But the fact remains that those who have taught strongly the truth of sovereign grace have not been able to integrate these truths with the doctrine of the covenant as long as it has been maintained that the covenant is such an agreement. The history of the doctrine of the covenant has been a history of an unsuccessful attempt to harmonize the truths of sovereign grace and double predestination with the doctrine of the covenant. And, while sometimes as a result, the doctrine of the covenant was not given prominent place in the thinking of these theologians (cf., e.g., Turretin, with his strong emphasis on sovereign grace, but relatively meager treatment of the covenant), as often as not the truths of sovereign grace were brushed aside and a form of Arminianism took over in the thinking of the church.

Over against all this, the clear teaching of the Scriptures is quite different. The Scriptures nowhere speak of the covenant as being an agreement between two parties. As true as this may be with respect to covenants made between men, this is far from true with respect to the covenant of grace. It may be that any covenant between men is an agreement between two parties, for, after all, men are equals. But God's covenant is not between equals, but between the living God and man. God is God. There is none like Him. He is infinitely great and glorious, far exalted above all His creation. What is man when all the nations of the earth are less than a drop of the bucket and less than the dust of the balance? And if God is so infinitely exalted above us, it is incredible that we should ever attempt to place man on such a footing with God that the two can enter into an agreement.

The Scriptures, we insist, nowhere speak of such a covenant. They do not speak of a promise which is made to all the children who are baptized or to all those who hear the gospel preached. They do not speak of conditions which must be met by man before the covenant can be realized. They do not speak of the covenant as being bilateral. They do not speak of parties in the covenant. Exactly the opposite is true. The Scriptures are one long and gloriously beautiful anthem of praise to the sovereign Lord of heaven and earth Who is absolutely sovereign in all of salvation as well as in the establishment and maintenance of the covenant of grace.

This then is the covenant. It is God's work of grace; a work in which there is no cooperation of man; a work that in itself must always be a revelation of God as the God of our salvation through Jesus Christ, to Whom belong all praise and glory forever and ever.

Thus we come to a parting of the ways in the idea of the covenant. Arminianism begins with man; and, doing this, it will also end with man. On quite a different note, the Scriptures begin with God and end with God. This must be our emphasis, too, as we seek to understand what the Scriptures teach concerning the covenant of grace.

If we begin with God in our discussion of the character and nature of the covenant, we must maintain first of all that the covenant is the revelation of God in which He makes known the covenant life which He lives within Himself. He does this by taking those with whom He establishes His covenant into His own fellowship as the triune God.

Because of this, the essence of the covenant of grace is this same covenant fellowship which God lives in Himself. Always all God's works are reflections of what God is in Himself. All His works reveal Himself: His life, His attributes, His glory, His praise, His wondrous majesty. All that He does is done in order that God may reveal Who He is and what He does.

Originally, when He formed the heavens and the earth and all that they contain, He formed them in such a way that they revealed perfectly the glory and power of His own divine Being. "The heavens declare the glory of God and the firmament showeth His handiwork" (Psalm 19:1). All the creation was one glorious reflection of the glory of the Creator. As Augustine expressed it so eloquently: "And what is this? I asked the earth; and it answered me, 'I am not He;' and whosoever are in it, confessed the same. I asked the sea and the deeps, and the living creeping things; and they answered, 'We are not thy God, seek above us.' I asked the moving air; and the whole air with his inhabitants answered, '. . . I am not God.' I asked the heavens, sun, moon, stars; 'Nor (say they) are we the God whom thou seekest.' And I replied unto all the things which encompass the door of my flesh; 'Ye have told me of my God, that ye are not He; tell me something of Him.' And they cried out with a loud voice, 'He made us.' " (*Confessions of St. Augustine,* Book X, Section 9).

The Belgic Confession of Faith speaks in this same vein when it remarks in Article II: "We know (God) by two means: first, by the creation, preservation and government of the universe; which is before our eyes as a most elegant book, wherein all creatures, great and small, are as so many characters leading us to contemplate the invisible things of God, namely, his power and divinity."

But if the works of God in the creation of the universe are revelations of Himself and His glory, the same is true of God's work of salvation. The highest possible and most beautiful revelation of God is through Jesus Christ His Son in all His works of suffering, dying, rising from the dead, and being exalted at God's right hand. The central aspect of this work of salvation is the establishment of the covenant of grace. This covenant of grace is therefore also a revelation of God's own covenant life which He lives in Himself.

Thus this covenant is also a communion of friendship and fellowship between God and His people. All the emphasis must fall on this idea of a bond which is characterized by fellowship, friendship, and communion. In the covenant of grace God becomes the Friend of His people, makes them His friends, takes them into the companionship of friendship and lives with them in this blessed relationship.

It is always in this way that the Scriptures speak of God's covenant. The Scriptures describe the relation between God and His people in the covenant as being a relation in which God reveals His secrets to man, gives to His people the fellowship of His life, causes them to walk in the truth and do the good. He describes His covenant as dwelling with His people by putting His own dwelling place in their midst and taking them under one roof with Him. Always covenant fellowship with God is the intimacy of walking and talking with God in perfect communion.

Enoch, Noah, and Abraham are said in the Scriptures to have walked with God and to be the friends of God (Genesis 5:22; 6:9; James 2:23). While no special mention is made in these connections of the covenant, the idea is clearly there, for we read in the Scriptures that God established His covenant with Noah (Genesis 8:9) and with Abraham (Genesis 17:7); and Amos speaks of the fact that two cannot walk together unless they be agreed (3:3).

In Psalm 25 we have what almost amounts to a definition of God's covenant: "What man is he that feareth the Lord? him shall he teach in the way that he shall choose. His soul shall dwell at ease; and his seed shall inherit the earth. The secret of the Lord is with them that fear him; and he will show them his covenant" (12-14). If we remember that Hebrew parallelism is used here, namely, that the two clauses of the text explain one another, it is clear that the definition of God's covenant given by verse 14 is: "The secret of the Lord is with them that fear Him."

That the covenant is a work of God whereby He takes His people into His own family is evident from the fact that repeatedly the Scriptures call God's people sons and daughters of God Who is their Father. One example of this is II Corinthians 6:16-18: "And what agreement hath the temple of God with idols? for ye are the temple of the living God; as God hath said, I will dwell in them, and walk in them; and I will be their God, and they shall be my people. Wherefore come out from among them, and be ye separate, saith the Lord, and touch not the unclean thing; and I will receive you, and will be a Father unto you, and ye shall be my sons and daughters, saith the Lord Almighty."

In keeping with this, the emphasis always falls on the fact that God establishes His covenant with His people. "Incline your ear, and come unto me: hear, and your soul shall live, and I will make an everlasting covenant with you, even the sure mercies of David" (Isaiah 55:3). "For I the Lord love judgment, I hate robbery for burnt offering; and I will direct their work in truth, and I will make an everlasting covenant with them" (Isaiah 61:8). "And I will make an everlasting covenant with them, that I will not turn away from them, to do them good; but I will put my fear in their hearts, that they shall not depart from me" (Jeremiah 32:40). "Moreover I will make a covenant of peace with them; it shall be an everlasting covenant with them: and I will place them, and multiply them, and will set my sanctuary in the midst of them forevermore. My tabernacle also shall be with them: yea, I will be their God, and they shall be my people. And the heathen shall know that I the Lord do sanctify Israel, when my sanctuary shall be in the midst of them forevermore" (Ezekiel 37:26-28).

As is evident from the last text, the tabernacle and temple were an old dispensational type of the covenant, for these edifices were pictures of God dwelling in the midst of His people in covenant fellowship. This idea is emphasized throughout the Scriptures and the final salvation of God's people in heaven is pictured in this same way: "And I heard a great voice out of heaven saying, Behold, the tabernacle of God is with men, and he will dwell with them, and they shall be his people, and

God himself shall be with them and be their God. And God shall wipe away all tears from their eyes; and there shall be no more death, neither sorrow, nor crying, neither shall there be any more pain: for the former things have passed away" (Revelation 21:3, 4).

There is an earthly picture of this relationship of fellowship and friendship in the marriage bond. Necessarily, this earthly relation is a limited and imperfect picture, but the Scriptures do teach that husband and wife live together as a picture of the covenant established in Christ. For husband and wife are one flesh in that covenant of marriage and as such enjoy a unity and communion of life and love. Thus Paul writes: "Wives, submit yourselves unto your husbands, as unto the Lord. For the husband is the head of the wife, even as Christ is the head of the church: and he is the saviour of the body. Therefore as the church is subject unto Christ, so let the wives be to their own husbands in everything. Husbands, love your wives, even as Christ also loved the church, and gave himself for it; For no man ever hated his own flesh; but nourisheth and cherisheth it, even as the Lord the church; for we are members of his body, of his flesh, and of his bones. For this cause shall a man leave his father and mother, and shall be joined unto his wife, and they two shall be one flesh. This is a great mystery: but I speak concerning Christ and the church" (Ephesians 5:22-26, 29-32).

In the marriage relation there is an intimate fellowship between husband and wife which grows with the years they spend together. There is the fellowship of their mutual love and life. There is the communion they experience in the problems they face and solve, the burdens they mutually carry, the needs they bring together before the throne of grace. There is the intimacy in their life of the mind and will in which they seek and pursue the same goals, cherish and desire the same ideals, reveal to one another the secrets of their hearts and the thoughts of their minds. They become "one flesh" in their life. And in this they reflect Christ and His church.

It is not surprising therefore that the Scriptures often present the covenant relation between God and His people in terms of marriage. Especially in the prophets this relation is described as one which God's people have broken. They are now an adulterous people who live in fornication because they have forsaken their God and turned to other lovers to whom they give their allegiance. They sin against their God and walk in all the lusts of their own carnal and wicked lives. They are wilful and perverse, constantly breaking the bond of marriage and trampling under their feet God's covenant.

But God is a faithful Husband Who keeps His covenant always. In His infinite and eternal love for His people through Jesus Christ, He comes to them to save them. And when He reveals to them His love, He makes them to be His own bride once again, His covenant people. He embraces them with arms of love, speaks to them comforting words of His grace, tells them of the forgiveness of all their sins, makes known to them the glorious life which He has graciously prepared for them in the life to come, and restores them to the intimacies of His heavenly marriage. In this intimacy of marriage He reveals to them all the secrets of His heart, makes them to know and taste of the power and glory of His own covenant life that He lives within Himself. In their trouble He cares for them; in their sorrows He comforts them with His promises; in their sins He forgives them wondrously and graciously; in their distress He points them to His power to sustain them in every need; in their cares He cares for them; in their afflictions He whispers in their hearts of His love and assures them that all things work together for their good for they are the called according to His purpose. When they cry to Him, He always and again hears them. His ears are never closed to their anguished sobs, their heart-rending pleas. He walks by their side. He preserves them from evil and temptation. And even though they walk through the valley of the shadow of death, they need fear no evil, for His rod and His staff comfort them. Surely goodness and mercy shall follow them all the days of their life till finally they dwell in the house of the Lord forever.

For such passages in the Scriptures we need only look to Hosea 1 and 2, Jeremiah 31:31-34, Jeremiah 3, especially verse 14, and many similar passages.

It stands to reason that this covenant fellowship is imperfect and incomplete on this side of the grave. For even believers do not lose their sin and sinful natures as long as they live here below. Nevertheless, in its glorious beginning already here they experience fellowship with God. And the night of sin is soon enough over. The day comes ere long when they lay down the weapons of their spiritual warfare to exchange them for the palm branch of victory; when the noise of the battle which they must fight against sin and temptation is quieted in death, and they awake to hear only the beautiful song of Moses and the Lamb sung by the choir of heaven. It is but a short time here below that they travel as pilgrims and strangers; for before long they fold up their tent for the last time and go to the house of many mansions in heaven. The end of their life here is the last triumph over the last enemy, death. There they shall change their hideous and filthy rags of sin and iniquity for the white robes of the righteousness of Christ. There in glory shall the covenant be perfectly realized. There shall be life and joy forever.

To be partaker of this covenant is the greatest blessing which can befall a man. To represent God's covenant in the midst of the world is a privilege and calling than which there is none higher. To look forward in eager anticipation to the day when this covenant is finally perfected is the hope that sustains the people of God all their life. This is the hope that inspires them to press on in faithfulness towards their everlasting reward. When the vision of that glorious day shines in their eyes, they suffer persecution and mockery, the taunts and derision of wicked men with stedfast courage. This blessedness sustains them in the hours of their need, in their weary pilgrimage here below, and finally in the hour of their death. For the high calling of this covenant, they march unwaveringly and unflinchingly to the stake, the cross, the scaffold, the lions, daring all the powers of men to rob them of their faith and hope. With the sweet song of the promises of their Father ringing in their hearts, they face privation and hardship; and with the blessed knowledge that death is their gain, they lay down their weary heads on death's pillow in the sure knowledge that they pass on to their eternal rest.

Chapter 3

THE COVENANT WITH ADAM

God's covenant was first established with Adam. That is, God first revealed the blessings of His own covenant life to Adam in Paradise before he fell.

When God formed the heavens and the earth, He created a beautiful garden in the east of Eden known in the Scriptures and throughout time as the first Paradise. In this beautiful garden God placed man. "And the Lord God planted a garden eastward in Eden; and there he put the man whom he had formed. . . . And the Lord God took the man, and put him into the garden of Eden to dress it and to keep it" (Genesis 2:8, 15).

Man was the highest of all God's creatures. He was not only created from the dust of the earth, but God breathed into his nostrils the breath of life. And by means of this creative act of God, "man became a living soul" (Genesis 2:7).

It is undoubtedly true that from a certain viewpoint the creation of man resembled the creation of the animals. Just as was true of all the animals, man was taken from the dust of the earth. He was of the earth earthy. He was created from the earth in such a way that he knew only this creation. He lived in the midst of the earth, was connected to and dependent upon it, and could see, hear, smell, taste, and touch only the things of this earthly creation. God also created heaven where the angels dwell; but man had no contact with this creation. He was a creature of the physical and material universe. He had to eat and drink as well as breathe the air about him to continue his life.

But man was also created with higher faculties and powers which raised him far above the beasts of the field. He was endowed with the powers of mind and will. He could know and perceive; he could reason and remember; he could meditate and think; he could will and desire. By means of these extraordinary powers, he could transcend the limitations of time and space. With his mind he could go back into the distant past or penetrate the hazy future. He could soar high over the barriers of space and be transported in his mind to places other than the area in which he lived. But, above all, he could know his Creator through the creation, understand Who and What God is, live in a personal relationship to God. In all the vast heavens, in the wonder of the deep, in the treasures of the earth, he could hear God speak and know God as the One Who had formed him and upon Whom he was dependent. Creation was an elegant book which spoke on every page of the mysteries of the Almighty.

Besides, man was created in the image of God. We read in Genesis 1:26, 27, "And God said, Let us make man in our image, after our likeness: and let them have dominion over the fish of the sea, and over the fowl of the air, and over the cattle, and over all the earth, and over every creeping thing that creepeth upon the earth. So God created man in his own image, in the image of God created he him; male and female created he them."

That man was created in God's image meant that God gave man the gifts of the true knowledge of God, perfect righteousness and unblemished holiness. (See Colossians 3:10, Ephesians 4:23, 24.) Man was without sin, able to serve his Creator perfectly. He was able to love the Lord his God with all his heart and mind and soul and strength. He was king over the creation, but he was king in order that he might rule over God's world in the service of his Maker. He was royalty, made by God as such; but he was also servant, created to serve the God Who had made him king. All his life, his talents, his work, his powers were laid on the altar of perfect consecration to God.

All this was necessary for Adam to live in God's covenant. Only a creature with mind and will, capable of knowing his Creator; only one who was perfect and holy could live in fellowship with the Lord. Only one who could love his God, see the glory of God in the creation, enjoy the blessings of the world which God formed could live a covenant life with God. No stone, tree, animal, or bird could possibly enjoy this blessedness. One to whom God could speak, one who could understand and respond in love to this speech is the only one who could live in God's covenant.

What was the nature of that covenant?

It has been a long tradition in the line of European federal theology to define this covenant as a "covenant of works." It is probably correct to say that the germ of the idea goes back as far as Olevianus and Cloppenburg, theologians of the 16th and early 17th centuries. Throughout succeeding centuries this idea was developed more extensively until today most theologians accept some sort of covenant of works as the kind of covenant in which Adam lived before he fell.

The idea is that, shortly after Adam's creation, God entered into an agreement with Adam. God, on His part, promised to give Adam life eternal on the condition of Adam's perfect and continued obedience. He added to this promise the threat that Adam would surely die if Adam disobeyed God, particularly by eating of the forbidden tree. Adam was on probation. Exactly how long this probationary period was intended to last, the defenders of the covenant of works have never been able to say. But the point is that, if Adam remained obedient for a given period of time, he would be transferred from this earthly creation to heaven and given life eternal. But if Adam disobeyed God and ate of the forbidden tree, he would be killed by God and deprived of eternal life.

Adam agreed wholeheartedly with these stipulations and promised to live in obedience to God, expecting then from God's hand the promised reward. By virtue of all this the covenant was in force. It was a covenant which contained a promise, a threat, a condition and which was ratified at that point where Adam agreed to the provisions of it.

We might insert here the fact that this idea of the covenant of works was developed especially among Dutch Reformed theologians. It does, however, also find a place in the Westminster Confession of Faith and has been generally maintained by most Presbyterian theologians. The article in the Westminster Confession reads: "The first covenant made with man was a covenant of works, wherein life was promised to Adam, and in him to his posterity, upon condition of perfect and personal obedience." From the article itself and from the Scriptural references appended to the article, it is not clear whether the Westminster divines considered the covenant as an *agreement* between God and Adam, and whether the promise was of *eternal* life in heaven in distinction from perpetual *earthly* existence in an uncursed world. At any rate, the idea of the Westminster Confession is slightly different from the view commonly held in Reformed churches. Nevertheless, it is interesting to note that the conception of the covenant of works held by Reformed theologians never entered the creeds of the Reformed churches and has no confessional status in these churches.

But this idea of a covenant of works has serious objections.

In the first place, it is clear that nowhere in the record of Genesis 1 and 2 does one find any mention of such a covenant as described above. It is true, of course, that Adam was to eat of the Tree of Life. It is also true that God specifically commanded him not to eat of the Tree of Knowledge of Good and Evil. And the penalty for eating of the forbidden tree was surely death: "The day thou eatest thereof thou shalt surely die." But this is far from a covenant. It all hinges on the presupposition that the covenant can be defined in terms of an agreement. Now even if this were true, we read nothing of such an agreement in the Genesis narrative. God gave Adam certain commands; and surely obedience to God was to be followed by life. But of any kind of an agreement or pact of any sort, we read nothing. Nevertheless, as we learned earlier, the simple fact is that the covenant cannot anywhere in the Scriptures be construed as an agreement; it is rather a relationship of friendship and fellowship with God.

In the second place, while it is true that Adam's obedience was surely the way in which Adam would have continued to live, we read nothing of a promise of *eternal life*. It is probably true that Adam would have lived perpetually in the garden if he had not fallen and had refrained from disobeying the command of God, although it is also true that the Scriptures tell us of no arrangement which God made for the possibility of perfect obedience in Paradise. But perpetual life here upon earth is quite different from eternal life. The latter is a life which is given only through Jesus Christ and has as its essential characteristic life in heaven. It is not a life which is earned and merited through good works and obedience but is merited only through the perfect work of our Savior. Jesus makes this clear shortly before He raised Lazarus from the dead when He told the sorrowing Martha: "I am the resurrection and the life: he that believeth in me, though he were dead, yet shall he live: and whosoever liveth and believeth in me shall never die" (John 11:25, 26). Also in His highpriestly prayer Jesus says, "And this is life eternal, that they might know thee the only true God, and Jesus Christ, whom thou hast sent" (John 17:3).

If it be objected that these words of our Lord were spoken the way they were because the fall intervened and made life eternal impossible, the answer is that we must not forget that Adam was created of the earth, earthy. He was material and physical as far as his body was concerned. It was true for Adam as it is always true that, "The first man is of the earth, earthy: the second man is the Lord from heaven. As is the earthy, such are they also that are earthy: and as is the heavenly, such are they also that are heavenly. And as we have borne the image of the earthy, we shall also bear the image of the heavenly. Now this I say, brethren, that flesh and blood cannot inherit the kingdom of God" (I Corinthians 15:47-50). For Adam to receive eternal life would have involved a change, even before the fall, in his entire nature which is possible only through the death and resurrection of Jesus Christ.

In close connection with all this, the whole idea of a covenant of works necessarily implies the idea that man can merit with God. If Adam had been faithful for a certain length of time, he would have merited by this faithfulness a higher life than that which he enjoyed in Paradise. But the whole of the Scriptures is opposed to any idea of merit. There is never any way for man to merit with God. Even Adam in Paradise owed his life and existence to his Creator. How could he merit with Him Who held his life in His hands? Jesus makes this clear when He says, "So likewise ye, when ye shall have done all those things which are commanded you, say, We are unprofitable servants: we have done that which was our duty to do" (Luke 17:10).

But there is still another objection which, if possible, is more serious than the foregoing. If it was God's intention that Adam continue in a state of righteousness and earn through his obedience the life of heaven for himself and his posterity, it follows from this that God's intention was severely frustrated by the combined efforts of Satan who came to tempt man and man who bent his ears to the voice of the serpent. What God had decided to do as revealed to Adam was now impossible. God suffered a defeat. God was forced to fall back on an alternate plan to bring men to heaven, a plan which included the work of Christ; a plan which now becomes second best, conceived in desperation to undo what man had done. There is no other way to explain this conception. But it does despite to God, Who knows all His works from the beginning of creation.

Finally, this view of the covenant of works becomes some sort of addition to Adam's original state. Adam was not created in a covenant relation to God; rather, the whole covenant, if a covenant of works, was added to Adam's existence. Thus, the covenant becomes a feature of Adam's life in Paradise which was "tacked on" by God after Adam was formed. It was not inherent in Adam's creation. As he came from the hands of his Creator, he lacked an important ingredient to his full blessedness: the covenant had still to be added.

But God's covenant with Adam was quite different from all this.

The covenant fellowship in which Adam lived was a fellowship and communion with God which was his by virtue of his creation. It was a blessed relationship of friendship which he enjoyed the moment he opened his eyes and saw the wonders of God's world and heard the speech of his Maker in all the things which were made. He was immediately in full possession of the blessings of fellowship with God. At the moment he heard God speak, a song of praise and adoration welled up in his heart. God spoke to him and he responded with praise: "My God, I love Thee." And in this consciousness of fellowship with God, he lived and walked, worked and sang. In the cool of the day, as another day was passed with the dying of the sun in the distant west, God appeared to Adam. There they communed together as God made known to Adam the secrets of His will and spoke to him as a friend speaks to a friend.

God caused Adam to taste the rich blessing of the covenant life which God lives in Himself. God lives a covenant life within Himself. But in great condescending grace He was pleased to take Adam into that life of blessedness. He said as it were, "This is the life that I live in Myself. This is the covenant that I eternally enjoy. Come with Me into the intimacies of this life and, enjoying it, praise Me as God forever." God could have created a man who would be capable of understanding intellectually the covenant life of God. But this revelation of God's covenant is more intense and full. God took Adam into that life. He filled Adam with the joy of it. The life of that covenant vibrated throughout Adam's whole being. It filled his soul, thrilled his heart, overwhelmed his mind, and caused him to taste of it in conscious and daily experience.

So Adam did not merit this in any way. It was given to him graciously and without merit. Adam did nothing and could have done nothing to merit it; no work could earn it. It was grace and grace alone.

But at the same time, it was not God's intention nor purpose to glorify Himself through Adam's perfect life in covenant fellowship with God. God had determined some better thing: the blessedness of covenant fellowship with Himself in Jesus Christ. Adam was only the first Adam, but not the last. "The first Adam was made a living soul; the last Adam was made a quickening spirit" (I Corinthians 15:45). The first Adam was a type of the last Adam. The first Adam was blessed; but the last Adam, our Lord Jesus Christ, is the fountain of all blessing for His elect people. For as the first Adam was a picture of Christ, so was the first Paradise a shadow and type of the Paradise which shall come at the end of the ages when our Lord returns. This heavenly Paradise is life eternal when God's everlasting covenant is completed and perfected.

Chapter 4

THE COVENANT AND THE FALL

The covenant in which Adam stood by virtue of his creation was only of short duration. Adam fell.

Previous to Adam's fall, a fall into sin had also occurred in heaven. God had created angels to inhabit heaven, and a large number of this world of angels had fallen under the leadership and instigation of Satan. They had rebelled against God, coveting His glory and attempting to occupy His throne. Banished from their blessed estate in glory because of their sin, they were doomed to roam the earth in preparation for the time when they would finally be punished in hell.

These devils, with Satan at their head, determined to enlist man in their conspiracy to defeat the cause of God. Using the serpent as his instrument, Satan came into the garden of Eden and persuaded first Eve, then Adam to eat of the Tree of the Knowledge of Good and Evil. In this way he persuaded them to rebel against God and to join with him in his conspiracy to banish God from His world and make this world the kingdom of Satan.

This fall of our first parents had the most disastrous consequences for themselves and for the whole human race.

As far as they themselves were concerned, Adam and Eve were expelled from the garden and banished from the Tree of Life. To Eve it was said that she would have sorrow in childbirth and that her desires would be to her husband. To Adam God said that he was sentenced to a life of toil, working by the sweat of his brow to force the sin-cursed ground to produce enough to support his frail existence.

But the most dreadful punishment which came upon them was the sentence of death. God had said, "In the day that thou eatest thereof, thou shalt surely die." And die they did. Oh, it is true that they did not fall dead immediately at the foot of the tree from which they ate. From a merely human standpoint, it might have been better if they had. But they died spiritually and physically. They became guilty before God's bar of justice for their awful sin of rebellion, and the punishment for their crime was a spiritual death which destroyed completely their spiritual life. This spiritual death permeated the whole of their nature and inflicted upon them a punishment which would ever call to mind the horror of their sinful deed.

This spiritual death was God's punishment for their sin. They became guilty before Him and were sentenced to this death. Included in it were different sorrows.

In the first place, they lost the image of God in which they had been created. No more did they possess the knowledge of God, righteousness and holiness. Their knowledge was turned into the lie; their righteousness into unrighteousness, and their holiness into the filth and pollution of sin.

In the second place, they were deprived of all the excellent gifts which they had received. Over against the errors of Arminianism, the Canons of Dordt expressed this truth this way: "Man was originally formed after the image of God. His understanding was adorned with a true and saving knowledge of his creator, and of spiritual things; his heart and will were upright; all his affections pure; and the whole man was holy; but revolting from God by the instigation of the devil, and abusing the freedom of his own will, he forfeited these excellent gifts; and on the contrary entailed on himself blindness of mind, horrible darkness, vanity and perverseness of judgment, became wicked, rebellious, and obdurate in heart and will, and impure in his affections" (III & IV, 1). Even his will was so corrupted that he not only *could* no longer do the good, but he was totally incapable even of *willing* to do the good. He had no longer the power to want to seek God, nor to be saved from his sin. His whole being revolted against God and all that is holy and just and good. He was filled with revulsion against all that is of God and God's purpose. Nothing he did could meet with God's approval; nothing he did could secure God's favor; he could not even *want* this favor any longer. He was spiritually dead.

This is commonly called the truth of total depravity. Throughout the ages men have attempted to find various ways to soften this truth somewhat. They have said, e.g., that man did not really become as bad as he could have because God remained gracious towards him with some common grace. They have said that a distinction must be made between total depravity and absolute depravity; the former meaning only that Adam became corrupt in all parts of his nature though not thoroughly so, the latter meaning that every part of his nature was completely corrupted. Adam was only totally depraved, not absolutely depraved. Others have argued that if God had not come in common grace to Adam, he would have become an animal; that he did not is evidence of the fact that some good remained in him.

But all these efforts to soften the truth of total depravity are contrary to the Scriptures. It was not grace that kept Adam from becoming an animal after the fall. He was created as a man and he fell as a man. His fall did not and could not change this manhood. Hence, he also remained a rational and moral creature, with mind and will, who could still see God's speech in the creation and who could still know it to be his duty to serve and worship God. Even these natural powers were sharply reduced by the corruption of his nature, but he always remains without excuse. Nor do the Scriptures ever speak of the difference between total depravity and absolute depravity. Just as it is absurd to speak of a man who is totally dead, but not absolutely dead, so it is absurd to speak of the natural man as totally depraved, though not absolutely so. The sinner is dead in trespasses and sins. As a man, his nature is as bad as it can possibly be. Not all the sin and corruption of that nature comes to manifestation immediately, of course. Throughout the centuries of history, as man gradually subdues the earth for his own sinful purposes, that sinful nature comes to fuller expression. But the Scriptures teach, and we must believe, that the natural man is incapable of doing any good whatsoever.

Finally, death was also physical. Although Adam did not drop dead at the foot of the tree, the seeds of death were sown in his body so that the grave was the end. Irrevocably, death summoned him to its corruption. From the grave there was no escape. He might live one hundred years or he might be snatched by the cold hand of death; but death remained his master and was his final conqueror. The grave waits with yawning mouth to gulp man down. And the grave is the door out of this creation into hell. God created man to represent God's cause in God's world. If man refuses to do this, there is no place for man in God's world any more. God, in fury and rage, drives man out, through the grave into everlasting hell. "For dust thou art, and unto dust shalt thou return" (Genesis 3:19).

But these terrible consequences of sin were not simply a harvest which Adam reaped for himself; they were also the fruit of the fall to be reaped by every man which followed him.

Adam was not created as a lone individual in complete separation from the rest of mankind. He was created as the head and first father of the whole human race. He was united to the rest of mankind by a bond both legal and organic. He was the representative of the human race, and from him sprang the multitude of men who live. Both of these are important.

Adam was the covenant and representative head of all men. As he stood in the covenant in Paradise, he represented the human race as a whole. Sometimes this relation is called a judicial or legal relation because it has to do with the legal relation in which men stand to God. What Adam did in relation to God's commands he did as one responsible for the whole human race. His fall, therefore, was the responsibility of the whole human race. The result of this is evident. When Adam became guilty for eating of the forbidden tree, this guilt was directly imputed to all men. All, including ourselves, became guilty for the one sin which Adam committed. On the basis of this one sin, we also are justly heirs of eternal punishment, and for this one sin we all need the redeeming blood of Jesus Christ. All men are worthy of hell irrespective of any sins which they may commit in their own lives. If it could be imagined that a man would live without sin, he would still be worthy of hell because he is guilty in Adam.

But because all men become guilty before God, all men are also worthy of death. This sentence comes on all men as God's just judgment. This sentence is carried out upon all men through Adam's organic relation to all men. He is the father of all. His nature became polluted and corrupted, but this corrupt nature he passed on to all those who came from him. Death comes upon all through the death that came upon Adam.

This truth is clearly set forth in Romans 5:12-14: "Wherefore, as by one man sin entered into the world, and death by sin; and so death passed upon all men, for that all have sinned: (For until the law sin was in the world: but sin is not imputed when there is no law. Nevertheless, death reigned from Adam to Moses, even over them that had not sinned after the similitude of Adam's transgression, who is the figure of him that was to come." This text clearly teaches that sin entered into the world through Adam's transgression; and through this transgression, death came upon all men. This is not, according to the text, because of each man's individual sin, but it is because of the sin of Adam: "For all have sinned," i.e., in Adam. Death reigned even over them that had not sinned after the similitude of Adam's transgression. This can only be because all men stand guilty before God for the sin which Adam committed. And this can in turn be true only because Adam was the representative head of the whole human race.

And so the corruption of Adam's sin became the corruption of all men. Total depravity is the lot of all. There is no good thing which any man is able to do. With the horrible malady of this corruption we come into the world. It is God's righteous judgment upon us for our own guilt which we incurred in Adam's sin. David speaks of this in Psalm 51:1-5: "Have mercy upon me, O God, according to thy lovingkindness: according unto the multitude of thy tender mercies blot out my transgression. Wash me thoroughly from mine iniquity, and cleanse me from my sin. For I acknowledge my transgressions: and my sin is ever before me. Against thee, thee only, have I sinned, and done this evil in thy sight: that thou mightest be justified when thou speakest, and be clear when thou judgest. Behold, I was shapen in iniquity; and in sin did my mother conceive me."

All of this is denied today in almost every quarter. How rarely does one hear anything, e.g., concerning the guilt which was imputed to the whole human race because of Adam's sin. It is a doctrine all but unheard of. And even the truth of total depravity is softened and even openly denied, for Arminianism has gained the day. Yet these very truths are fundamental to the truth of sovereign grace, for it is only because we are totally depraved and unable to do or will any good that salvation is by grace alone.

But these truths stand closely connected to our discussion of the doctrine of the covenant.

It must never be forgotten that Adam fell as covenant head. He was himself the covenant friend of God, but he stood as representative and first father of the whole human race in that covenant. When he fell, therefore, he fell in that position in which God had placed him. Thus, not only did he become a covenant breaker, but the whole human race in him also became covenant breakers. He and all his posterity, through his sin, departed from the ways of God's covenant and lost all right and claim to the blessedness of that covenant. As far as man was concerned, that was the end of the covenant.

Nevertheless, God always maintains His covenant. He is always faithful to it and never turns His back upon His own work. He maintained His covenant already in Paradise, when, after announcing His judgment upon man's sin, He spoke to them the words of His promise: "And I will put enmity between thee and the woman, and between thy seed and her seed; it shall bruise thy head, and thou shalt bruise his heel" (Genesis 3:15).

It must be remembered that the fall of man was not a mistake, an unexpected defeat of God's purpose, a turn of events which God had not anticipated and which required of Him an alternative plan. God's purpose from all eternity had been to realize the full blessedness of His covenant only through Jesus Christ. The creation of the first Adam, the fall of Satan, and the fall of Adam were all the means which God had ordained to achieve a higher and greater purpose in His own Son, our Lord and Savior. The first Adam had to make room for the second Adam, and the fall into sin had to take place in order that the riches of grace in Christ might become manifest.

While the first creation was indeed a remarkable and blessed revelation of God's perfect covenant life, the realization of that covenant in Jesus Christ is higher and more blessed. There are several reasons why this is true.

In the first place, Adam could know God and have fellowship with Him in the covenant only through the creation itself. And while this was no doubt wonderful, it cannot compare with fellowship with God through Christ Jesus, God's own Son, our Mediator. We shall have occasion to discuss this more fully somewhat later.

In the second place, while also in the first Paradise God revealed Himself as merciful and gracious, in the work of redemption in Christ these attributes are revealed in a far higher way, for they are now revealed against the backdrop of our sin and unworthiness. Grace and mercy, love and longsuffering – all are revealed to sinful and undeserving sinners, sinners who cannot do anything of themselves but hate God and rebel against Him. God's covenant established in grace is a covenant given to desperately wicked people.

In the third place, because God's grace is revealed only to those whom He has chosen from all eternity, His wrath and displeasure are revealed to all the wicked. Thus, what was not possible in Paradise in a very clear way is possible now: the revelation of God as holy and just, the Avenger of all wickedness, the God Who hates sin and punishes the sinner because of His own great moral perfection.

Finally, while the covenant with Adam would only, in the way of obedience, result in perpetual life in this world, God's covenant with His people in Christ is realized finally in glory when all things shall be made new in the new heavens and the new earth. This revelation of glory, now combined in one heavenly creation, far excels the first Paradise. All God's glory shines most brightly through Christ – and because of the fall.

Does all this mean that also the fall is within God's purpose and will? Of course it does. Who can deny it and still be faithful to the Scriptures? God also determined the fall in His counsel so that this too might serve His eternal purpose which He had planned from before the foundation of the world. This in no way subtracts from the responsibility of Adam or of ourselves, but it preserves intact the absolute sovereignty of God.

Chapter 5

THE COVENANT IN THE OLD TESTAMENT

Having discussed in some detail the fall of Adam and its implications for the human race, it is now necessary to discuss the covenant of grace as this was revealed to Adam, to the saints in the old dispensation and to us who live in the end of the ages.

This covenant is established by God with His people through Jesus Christ Who is the Head of the covenant, and Who was eternally appointed to be the Mediator of the covenant. Yet this must not be construed as meaning that there was no covenant in the old dispensation. For even then God established His covenant with His people. The difference is that in the old dispensation God revealed to His people the truth of the covenant in such a way that this truth was clothed in types and shadows. It was not until the dawning of the new dispensation with the coming of Christ that the shadows fled away and that the reality of the shadows was clearly revealed. For only with the coming of Christ could the reality of that covenant be clearly seen and understood, and the full blessedness of that covenant become the inheritance of the church.

But this in turn does not mean that the old dispensation is of no value to us. For in a concentrated study of the old dispensation, and by allowing the light of the New Testament Scriptures to shine upon its shadows, we find a tremendous wealth of truth revealed to us concerning the character and significance of the covenant of which we speak. And therefore we do well to turn our attention first of all to this wealth of material, composing more than half of our Bible, found in the Old Testament Scriptures to ascertain what our God has revealed to us there concerning His covenant.

But before we enter into a more detailed study of several aspects of the Old Testament history, it is well to make a general survey of the old dispensation to lay down some principles which we must follow in our discussion.

There are several truths which we ought to notice.

First among these is the truth that immediately after the fall, while our first parents were still in Paradise, God preached the gospel to them. This gospel is found in the words spoken to Satan: "And I will put enmity between thee and the woman, and between thy seed and her seed; it shall bruise thy head, and thou shalt bruise his heel" (Genesis 3:15). This Word of God contains the seed of the entire gospel and the promise of salvation. All that God would reveal throughout the ages and finally and fully reveal in Christ was contained in these words uttered so soon after sin entered the world. This is, so to speak, the bud which would unfold into the whole glorious flower of the promise of God. Every truth concerning God's covenant, concerning the plan of redemption, concerning the wonder of grace was principally implied and contained in these words. It is the "mother promise," the principal description of the entire work of God. Everything else revealed would be only a further explanation and development of these words.

This was also true of the history of the old dispensation. Only, we must remember that God did not reveal the truth of His promise and the promise of His covenant to His saints in old times in the same way in which He reveals them to us. He reveals them in the form of shadows or types. This means, significantly enough, that the history of the old dispensation itself is the revelation of God's promise. God revealed the truth of salvation typically and symbolically through the history that the church lived and by means of the history which that church experienced. All of *sacred* history is sacred exactly because it revealed the truth of God. This history includes the actual events and circumstances of the lives of the saints and of the nation of Israel; it includes the wonderful things that happened to them; the economy under which they lived – the law, the tabernacle and temple, the ceremonies of Israel's religious life, the political aspects of their life and all that pertained to their existence. Through all these things God spoke to Israel concerning His promise and covenant. As our Heidelberg Catechism so beautifully expresses it: "Whence knowest thou (thy Mediator)? From the holy gospel, which God Himself first revealed in Paradise; and afterwards published by the patriarchs and prophets, and represented by the sacrifices and other ceremonies of the law; and lastly, has fulfilled it by his only begotten Son" (Lord's Day VI, 19).

Nor must we fall into the temptation of belittling or underestimating the spiritual understanding of the old dispensational saints. It is true, of course, that they did not clearly see the promise in all its implications. They could not, for they looked at the promise of God's covenant in the form of types and shadows. But this does not mean that they believed that the types were really their only hope and salvation. They did not fasten their hope on the earthly land of Canaan, nor on the earthly temple which Solomon built; they did not believe that all the bloody sacrifices that were offered in the outer court of the temple actually took away sin. It was rather as if Jesus Christ was in heaven where He could not as yet be seen. The shadows of the old dispensation were the long shadows cast from heaven by the Sun of Righteousness. And although Israel could only see the shadows and not the Sun, they nevertheless knew that somewhere the Sun was shining, that the shadows could be cast only because that Sun shone, and that presently a new day would dawn when the Sun of Righteousness would appear to banish the shadows and bring the day of the full realization of the promise.

Of this truth we read more than once in the Scriptures. When Jesus was debating with the Pharisees about who were the true children of Abraham, He tells these hypocritical enemies of the church who claimed to be Abraham's children, but did not believe in Christ: "Your father Abraham rejoiced to see my day: and he saw it, and was glad" (John 8:56). Even though Abraham walked as a pilgrim and stranger in the land of Canaan, and even though the Lord had promised Abraham that land for an inheritance, nevertheless we read in Hebrews 11:8-10: "By faith Abraham, when he was called to go out into a place which he should after receive for an inheritance, obeyed; and he went out, not knowing whither he went. By faith he sojourned in the land of promise, as in a strange country, dwelling in tabernacles with Isaac and Jacob, the heirs with him of the same promise: for he looked for a city which hath foundations, whose builder and maker is God." And this same author of the epistle to the Hebrews, in summing up the lives of the patriarchs in his call of the role of the heroes of faith, speaks of them as those who all "died in faith, not having received the promises, but having seen them afar off, and were persuaded of them and embraced them, and confessed that they were strangers and pilgrims in the earth. For they that say such things declare plainly that they seek a country. And truly, if they had been mindful of that country from whence they came out, they might have had opportunity to have returned. But now they desire a better country, that is, an heavenly: wherefore God is not ashamed to be called their God: for he hath prepared for them a city" (Hebrews 11:13-16). The same was true of David, who saw, though dimly, the resurrection of Jesus Christ, of which he wrote prophetically in Psalm 16 when he said, "Therefore my heart is glad, and my glory rejoiceth: my flesh also shall rest in hope. For thou wilt not leave my soul in hell; neither wilt thou suffer thine Holy One to see corruption" (verses 9, 10). That this was indeed prophetic of Christ is evident from the fact that Peter later quoted this very passage in his powerful Pentecostal sermon as referring to Jesus (Acts 2:25-28). And who can deny that the ancient prophet Isaiah, also living in the dispensation of shadows, nevertheless stood in prophecy almost at the foot of Calvary when he penned the beautiful words of Isaiah 53? Israel understood, and it seems, better than some people today, that the types and shadows were but faint images of better things to come.

In all the history of the ancient patriarchs and of Israel as a nation, there was constant progression and development in the revelation of the truths of God's promise. God did not reveal all the truth immediately. It is true that all the truth was principally contained in the bud of the "mother promise," but it took many centuries of history for this bud to unfold into the glorious blossom of the Christ. The church saw it gradually develop and become richer as time went on until finally it was fully manifested when the Word became flesh. Thus we can easily trace the development of the promise. To Adam and Eve was revealed, as we have said, only the bud. But a millennium and a half later God revealed to Noah, and through Noah to the church, that the flood was a picture of more of the riches of the promise. When the promise came fully, the world of sin would be destroyed; the destruction of the world would also be the salvation of the church; the church would, through its salvation, inherit a new creation, for God's creation is universal, established with all the creation as well as with God's elect people.

But there were even more riches to this promise. God told Abraham that although God's people walk in the earth as Abraham walked in Canaan, as pilgrims and strangers, nevertheless presently God would give the land of Canaan for an inheritance; only it would be the heavenly Canaan when heaven and earth become one and the church is brought to the glory of the new creation. Besides, it was revealed to Abraham most dramatically that God alone establishes His covenant, and that sovereignly, and that this covenant is established in the line of generations with Abraham's spiritual seed – a seed brought forth by a wonder of grace.

And so it continued. Israel was in Egypt, but was also delivered by signs and wonders. And again God shed more light on the promise and made it plainer to His people. For the promise evidently meant that Egypt was a picture of the bondage of sin and death, and that in it God's people were also enslaved. But it was also true that God taught His people then and now that it was only the blood of the Lamb that separated the church from the world when judgment came; that when the church is delivered, it is by the strong hand and stretched-out arm of Jehovah; that it is by mighty signs and wonders of grace that the church is brought through the wilderness of this present life into the glory of the heavenly Canaan where all enemies are defeated and the people of God are given a land flowing with milk and honey.

When David ascended Israel's throne, the Lord taught His people that the promise also included the truth that Christ came to establish a kingdom which would take the place of all the kingdoms of the earth and in which the people of God would live as citizens in obedient submission to the Lord of lords and King of kings Who is most blessed forever. And when finally David went to his grave, Solomon his son sat upon the throne. But through the glorious reign of Solomon God taught His people to look for a kingdom that would exceed in beauty Solomon's earthly kingdom in blessedness, wealth, and prosperity, but that the center of that kingdom was to be the temple of God in which He would dwell in covenant fellowship with His people forever. For the real temple, of which the temple of Solomon was but a figure, was the body of Jesus Christ as our Lord Himself says (John 2:18-22). And in the temple of the body of Christ, by faith, the people of God are taken into fellowship with their God to dwell under one roof with Him forever.

And finally the fullness of time came and God sent forth His Son. Then all these types and shadows fled away. Jesus Christ went to the cross, rose again on the third day, ascended to heaven where He was highly exalted at the Father's right hand. From this position of greatest authority and power, Christ rules to work out the counsel and will of God in order that all the fullness of God's covenant and promise may be perfectly realized in the day of His second coming when the tabernacle of God shall be with men. To Him the shadows pointed; in Him they are all gloriously realized; and He is the One indeed Whom we, who live in the end of the ages, see by faith.

Although a detailed discussion of this subject would carry us too far afield, we ought to note at least in passing that one basic error of dispensationalism, in whatever form it appears, is the failure to recognize the true typical nature of the Old Testament. Because these Scriptures reveal the truth of salvation in typical form, they have their fulfillment only in the spiritual realities of salvation in Christ for one church composed of Jews and Gentiles. Failure to reckon adequately with this truth leads dispensationalists to speak of a temporal and earthly fulfillment of these very types and shadows. This should become more clear as, in subsequent chapters, we pay closer attention to the way in which these types and shadows spoke of God's covenant.

For the present it is sufficient for us to see that all the revelation of God's covenant was in the form of types and shadows because Christ Jesus, the Reality, had not yet come. And because He had not yet come, the church of the old dispensation did not receive the Spirit of Christ in full measure.

There are two points which need to be noticed here.

In the first place, all the revelation of God is through Christ and by the Spirit of Christ in the hearts of His people. The Spirit applies the objective truth of God's revelation to the hearts of God's people in such a way that they are given eyes to see that truth and ears to hear and faith to believe. But the Spirit always works in connection with and never apart from that objective revelation. Thus the saints in the old dispensation also possessed the Spirit. That Spirit regenerated and converted them, gave them faith to believe and applied the blessings of salvation to their hearts by His efficacious work. But because the revelation of God's covenant was through types and shadows, and because the Spirit worked with that typical and shadowy revelation, the people of God did not understand it in all its glory and beauty. Their understanding was limited to the mode of revelation, the types. The difference can perhaps be explained by a comparison between seeing someone's colored slides of Yellowstone National Park, shown on a screen in the living room of one's house, and actually visiting the park to see the vast panoramas of beauty, feel the breezes blow, hear the sighing of the wind in the pines and back away from the mighty roar of Old Faithful. The slides are nice and their beauty cannot be questioned, but the reality is far better.

In the second place, because the reality came with Jesus Christ, the Spirit Who was poured out on Pentecost could give to His church an understanding of the full truth of the reality only when Christ ascended into heaven. Then His work of fulfilling all the types and shadows was completed. The reality to which all the types pointed had now come. And the Spirit of the exalted Christ, given to the church, revealed the full riches of God's truth of His everlasting covenant of grace in full measure. Sent from Christ and poured out within our hearts, the Spirit gives us all the riches of this truth in a way in which the Old Testament saints could never understand it.

But all of this does not mean, as we said, that the Old Testament Scriptures are of no significance. If, before going to Yellowstone, one sees his friend's slides of the park, he knows what to look for, what to expect, what to anticipate. The slides serve him well as he for himself explores the wonders of this corner of God's creation. Undoubtedly he will say to himself, "The half has not been told me. The reality is so much more beautiful than I had anticipated." But he will also thank his friend for introducing him to these wonders through the slides because his appreciation for and understanding of the reality will be all the greater. The old adage remains true: "The New is in the Old contained; the Old is in the New explained."

Chapter 6

THE DAYS BEFORE THE FLOOD

Perhaps the one word which best describes the history of the world from the time of the fall to today is the word "warfare." And while it is true that this word can refer to the battles which have raged between the nations, we refer especially to the spiritual battle of faith that has been fought with such fierce intensity between the seed of the serpent and the seed of the woman. This is the real battle of the ages.

If one would inquire into the deepest cause of this battle, one would have to find his answer in the words of God spoken to our first parents in Paradise. The Lord had said that He would put enmity between the seed of the woman and the seed of the serpent. This enmity is the reason for the great battle of the ages.

If one would inquire further how God put this enmity into the world between these two seeds, the answer of the Scriptures is that the enmity comes from the grace of God. This may perhaps strike us as strange – that grace could result in enmity; but this is nevertheless the case.

How is this possible?

The answer to this lies in the fact that the seed of the woman to which the Lord referred is a seed created by the sovereign grace of God. When our first parents fell into sin, God came to them in grace and immediately saved them. Adam and Eve fell into the arms of Christ, Who stood behind them, the promised Seed Who would make atonement for sin. On the basis of this promise, He saved them from the misery and death of sin. The devil was perfectly aware of the implications of this. In fact it is more than likely that he understood these implications better than did our first parents. Filled with rage at the possibility that his awful work would still be destroyed by the promise of God, he determined to destroy the seed of the woman, to frustrate the operation of grace, and to prevent the Christ from coming to shed His blood.

The battle was joined; the issue was clearly defined; the world has rung ever since with the noise and tumult of that terrible struggle.

Immediately after the fall this battle was begun.

Adam and Eve had children. When Eve carried her first child in her arms and named him Cain, it seems she must have thought that already the Lord had sent Christ; for in naming him, she said, "I have gotten a man from the Lord" (Genesis 4:1). How disappointing it must have been to her and her husband when it soon appeared that not only was Cain not the promised Savior Whom they expected, but that he also proved to be of the seed of the serpent.

Yet this does not mean that already the Lord had forgotten His promise and that He did not send the seed of which He had spoken; God gave to Adam and Eve another son whom they called Abel. And so appeared already in the family of our first parents the two seeds of which God had spoken, and the enmity between these two seeds, and enmity which would continue throughout history.

When Adam and Eve after their fall knew they were naked, the Lord had prepared for them coats of skins of animals (Genesis 3:21). In doing so, the Lord clearly taught our parents that the nakedness of their sin could only be covered through the shedding of blood. With that clear lesson, the early saints were instructed in the truth that only in the way of the shedding of blood could sin be forgiven, and man be restored to the favor of God.

This Abel understood and believed. This Cain understood and hated. And so when a day came in which the two brothers brought their sacrifices, Cain came with the firstfruits of the ground; Abel came with the best lamb that he could find in his flock. Cain, knowing that the Lord required the shedding of blood, chose to ignore the Lord's command and brought of his vegetables that he had raised in order to prove that he needed not the shedding of blood, the blood of atonement. Abel, in the consciousness of his sin, brought a lamb. How beautiful is the simple and expressive commentary of Hebrews 11:4: "By faith Abel offered unto God a more excellent sacrifice than Cain, by which he obtained witness that he was righteous, God testifying of his gifts: and by it he being dead yet speaketh."

When Cain saw that the Lord was pleased with Abel's sacrifice, but that He was angry with the mocking sacrifice of Cain, he was furious. In his anger and resentment against all that God had said, and against the righteousness of his brother, he killed Abel, destroying his testimony in the earth.

The seed of the serpent had succeeded in destroying the seed of the woman.

And behind it all lurked the devil with his hatred for God.

We must not see in this murderous deed of Satan simply the passing emotion of the moment; the blind rage that ended in tragedy. Then there would be no point in this story being recorded in Holy Writ. The devil saw in Cain his ally. But he saw also in Abel the seed of the woman of which the Lord had spoken. Satan knew that if he could destroy this seed of the woman, the promised Christ could never come and atonement could never be made for sin. Then his evil purposes would certainly be successful. The need for Satan was the destruction of Abel. And in this he was successful.

The first battle was fought. It seemed as if the devil had won. A terrible sadness entered the home of our first parents.

But the hatred of Satan and Cain towards Abel, concentrated in Abel's sacrifice of a lamb, was due to God's grace in Abel. Abel was also born a sinner, totally depraved. If he had remained such, Cain would never have hated him. But God had saved Abel and worked His work of grace within Abel's heart so that Abel saw his sin, confessed it before God, and expressed this confession in the sacrifice of a lamb which pointed ahead to the Lamb of God. It was this which filled Cain and Satan with fury. (See I John 3:12.)

But God could not allow the seed of the serpent to be successful. For although Abel went to heaven where he dwelt alone for a while with the angels, God gave to Adam and Eve another seed, Seth, in whose loins was the Christ Who was to come.

And so the history preceding the flood is the history of the struggle between these two seeds.

On the one hand, Cain, cursed of God, went out from the country where his parents lived and built a city which he named after his son. There, in that city, Cain also produced seed, and the seed of the serpent increased. There was Enoch the son of Cain. There was Lamech who married two wives and had three sons: Jabal, Jubal, and Tubal-cain. The interesting thing about these men and their descendents was that they increased in knowledge and culture. They were inventors and men of renown. They were the intellectual giants of their day; men of science and technology; men of culture and the arts. But while they increased in knowledge and invention, they also increased in sin. They were horribly corrupt and fearfully wicked. So terrible was the development of their sin that in the short span of 1,600 years they filled the cup of iniquity and became ripe for judgment.

On the other hand, there was the seed of the woman. This seed is traced for us in the Scriptures through Seth, Enos, Cainan, Mahalaleel, Jared, Enoch, Methuselah, Lamech, Noah. There are several points of interest concerning this seed of the woman which we must note.

In the first place, they were God-fearing men who walked in the paths of righteousness. God preserved His truth and continued His covenant through them. They were men who, by grace, feared God, men who "walked with God" (Genesis 5:24; 6:9), men who preserved the truth of Paradise and the fall as well as the truth of God's promise, men who called upon the name of God (Genesis 4:26), and who worshipped with blood sacrifices.

In the second place, many of them were preachers of righteousness. They preached the truth of God to God's church, but they also condemned the seed of the serpent for all its wickedness. They were men of courage and conviction, fearless and brave in the cause of God's covenant. Of this we read, e.g., in Jude 14, 15: "And Enoch also, the seventh from Adam, prophesied of these, saying, Behold, the Lord cometh with ten thousands of his saints, to execute judgment upon all, and to convince all that are ungodly among them of all their ungodly deeds which they have ungodly committed, and of all their hard speeches which ungodly sinners have spoken against him." Or again, we read in II Peter 2:4, 5: "For if God spared not the angels that sinned, but cast them down to hell, and delivered them into chains of darkness, to be reserved unto judgment; and spared not the old world, but saved Noah the eighth person, a preacher of righteousness, bringing the flood upon the world of the ungodly."

In the third place, and because of the upright walk of the saints and their condemnation of the world, these days prior to the flood were days of severe persecution. The wicked world with Satan as their captain, was desperately intent on destroying the church. The devil could not and would not rest until the seed of the woman was destroyed so that Christ could not come.

There are several indications of this already in the narrative of

Genesis. We read of Lamech, e.g., that he composed a song in which he celebrated his triumph of killing the people of God and challenged the Lord to punish him for it: "Hear my voice; ye wives of Lamech, hearken unto my speech: for I have slain a man to my wounding, and a young man to my hurt. If Cain be avenged sevenfold, truly Lamech seventy and sevenfold" (Genesis 4:23, 24). Or again, Enoch was evidently not taken to heaven because he was more righteous than those who were also of the church at that time; rather the fact that Enoch condemned the world filled the seed of Cain with fury so that they were intent on killing him. But God snatched him out of their hands in order that they might not touch him. This is indicated by a careful consideration of Hebrews 11:5: "By faith Enoch was translated that he should not see death; *and was not found,* because God had translated him: for before his translation he had this testimony, that he pleased God."

Besides, the Scriptures point more than once to the fact that the days preceding the flood were days that prefigured the final days of this world's history just before the coming of the Lord. Jesus Himself calls our attention to this in Matthew 24:37-39: "But as the days of Noe were, so shall also the coming of the Son of man be. For as in the days that were before the flood they were eating and drinking, marrying and giving in marriage, until the day that Noe entered into the ark, and knew not until the flood came, and took them all away; so shall also the coming of the Son of man be." Peter mentions this same truth in his second epistle, chapter 3:1-7.

In the fourth place, the seed of the woman became very small in those days. Gradually, through this terrible persecution, the church decreased until at the time of the flood, there were only eight people left in the church, while the world must have numbered in the millions.

However, this smallness of the church of Jesus Christ was not due only to persecution; it was due also to a terrible apostasy that raged through the church. Many fell away from the truth. Although they were born and raised in the line of the covenant, they were not the true seed of the woman, but soon manifested themselves as seed of the serpent. This is indicated in the history recorded in the early chapters of Genesis. We read in Genesis 6:1-6: "And it came to pass, when men began to multiply on the face of the earth, and daughters were born unto them, that the sons of God saw the daughters of men that they were fair; and they took them wives of all which they chose. And the Lord said, My spirit shall not always strive with man, for that he also is flesh: yet his days shall be an hundred and twenty years. There were giants in the earth in those days; and also after that, when the sons of God came in unto the daughters of men, and they bare children to them, the same became mighty men which were of old, men of renown. And God saw that the wickedness of man was great in the earth, and that every imagination of the thoughts of his heart was only evil continually. And it repented the Lord that he had made man on the earth, and it grieved him at his heart."

Finally, from all this it is evident that in spite of all the attempts of the devil to destroy the seed of the woman so that Christ could not be born, God nevertheless preserved that line so that the devil and his satanic seed could never destroy those who bore the Christ within them. And this is indeed true not simply because our God is stronger than Satan and all his hosts, but because the Almighty holds even Satan in His hands so that without the will of our Father in heaven he cannot do anything to God's people.

In this we also who must fight the same battle may take courage. For although at times all is dark and dreary, although it may appear as if the forces of evil march on from victory to victory, nevertheless God and His Christ reign supreme in the heavens to give to us the victory. Faith is the victory that overcomes the world.

Chapter 7

THE COVENANT WITH NOAH

In a study of the events surrounding the flood, we will find a wealth of material which has to do with the truth of God's covenant.

We need not spend a great deal of time on the history itself, for it is well known. It is evident from the Scriptures that until the time of the flood it had never rained upon the earth. We read in Genesis 2:5b, 6: "For the Lord God had not caused it to rain upon the earth, and there was no man to till the ground. But there went up a mist from the earth, and watered the whole face of the ground."

One can imagine the surprise of the inhabitants of the earth when Noah began to build the ark. The people watching Noah beginning to build perhaps inquired as to what he was building. He must have informed them that he was building a boat to sail on the water. This would no doubt have seemed to them highly peculiar and even extremely funny, for Noah was building his boat in the middle of the land. But Noah explained to them that this was not at all strange, for God was going to send a flood in which rain would fall and all the world would be destroyed. The ark was intended to save Noah and his family from the flood. Such nonsense these wicked men could scarcely imagine. They laughed and scoffed while Noah, year after year, patiently went on with his work. And, in fact, it was a great act of faith that prompted him to build a boat when he had never seen rain. So we read in Hebrews 11:7: "By faith Noah, being warned of God of things not seen as yet, moved with fear, prepared an ark to the saving of his house; by the which he condemned the world, and became heir of the righteousness which is by faith."

After 120 years had expired and Noah had completed his ark, the Lord sent to him animals of all kinds which Noah led into the ark: two of each kind of unclean animals and seven of each kind of clean animals. Food had also to be put into the ark; and when all the preparations were completed, Noah and his family of eight also entered.

The flood which came upon the earth was from every point of view a miracle. Evidently it rained then such as it has never rained since. The rain that fell in forty days and forty nights was not simply a shower that gradually increased the depth of water upon the earth, but heaven and earth were torn apart. The windows of heaven were opened and the fountains of the great deep gushed with water. Raging and howling torrents tore the earth open to its bowels. We read in Genesis 7:11: "In the six hundredth year of Noah's life, in the second month, the seventeenth day of the month, the same day were all the fountains of the great deep broken up, and the windows of heaven were opened."

But no less of a miracle was the preservation of Noah and his family with the animals in the ark of gopher wood as it was carried above the raging torrents of water and as it safely protected the church of God from that which destroyed the world. Every living creature outside the ark perished in the flood.

Although the rain was upon the earth for forty days and forty nights, nevertheless it was a year and ten days before Noah finally left the ark to receive the cleansed creation from the hand of God.

These are, briefly, the facts. But they have tremendous implications for the truth of God's covenant.

We mentioned in the last chapter that the days before the flood were days that picture to us the evil days which will precede the end of the world. At that time there was terrible wickedness in the world so that the cup of iniquity was filled and the world had become ripe for judgment. So shall it be before our Lord returns. Then, before the flood, the church had become very small through persecution and apostasy. It shall be no different in the days preceding the return of Christ. In fact, for the elect's sake the days shall be shortened. Before the flood, the people of God faithfully preached judgment against the world and spoke of the coming of judgment in the flood. But Peter tells us that "there shall come in the last days scoffers, walking after their own lusts, and saying, Where is the promise of his coming? For since the fathers fell asleep, all things continue as they were from the beginning of the creation" (II Peter 3:3, 4).

But even as the days before the flood were days which prefigured the evil days before the Lord's return, so was the flood itself a picture of the final destruction of the world. Then wicked men were destroyed by the waters of the flood while the church was saved in the ark. Then the church was given a new and cleansed creation for its inheritance; while after the final judgment the church shall receive the new heavens and the new earth in which righteousness shall dwell. In the passage quoted above, Peter goes on to explain this: "For this they willingly are ignorant of, that by the word of God the heavens were of old, and the earth standing out of the water and in the water: whereby the world that then was, being overflowed with water, perished: but the heavens and the earth, which are now, by the same word are kept in store, reserved unto fire against the day of judgment and perdition of ungodly men. . . . But the day of the Lord will come as a thief in the night; in the which the heavens shall pass away with a great noise, and the elements shall melt with fervent heat, the earth also and the works that are therein shall be burned up" (II Peter 3:5-7, 10).

That these days are even now near no one can deny. For as in Noah's day there were scoffers that mocked and said God could never send a flood even though they were surrounded by water, so also today men mock and say that the world shall endure forever, even though the world is surrounded by fire. Nevertheless, God's Word shall surely be fulfilled. As then the flood came and destroyed the world, so presently shall the fire of judgment come and burn this world in which we live. But even as Noah and his family were saved in the ark, so shall the righteous also be saved at the end.

In other words, through the means of the flood, God explained further the promise which He had given to Adam and Eve, that the crushing of the head of the serpent and his seed implied the full salvation of the church in glory. The words of Peter come to us in all their force: "Seeing then that all these things shall be dissolved, what manner of persons ought ye to be in all holy conversation and godliness, looking for and hasting unto the coming of the day of God, wherein the heavens being on fire shall be dissolved, and the elements shall melt with fervent heat? Nevertheless, we, according to his promise, look for new heavens and a new earth, wherein dwelleth righteousness. Wherefore, beloved, seeing that ye look for such things, be diligent that ye may be found of him in peace, without spot, and blameless" (II Peter 3:11-14).

But this is not all that God revealed through the flood. This ought to be evident from the fact that we have said nothing yet concerning the seed of the woman which is principally Christ. Was there no mention or pre-figuration of Christ in the flood? Is it not Christ that crushes the head of the serpent and saves His people? Does He not do this through the blood of the cross? What did the flood reveal concerning what Christ did on Calvary?

The answer to these questions is that the Scriptures plainly teach us that the water of the flood was a picture of the blood of Christ. And, furthermore, because the water of the flood was a picture of the blood of Christ, the water of the flood was a picture of the water of baptism. Noah and his family were baptized in the flood and received the sign of the cleansing from sin through the blood of atonement.

That the Scriptures plainly teach this is obvious first of all from I Peter 3:18-21: "For Christ also hath once suffered for sins, the just for the unjust, that he might bring us to God, being put to death in the flesh, but quickened by the Spirit: by which also he went and preached unto the spirits in prison: which sometime were disobedient, when once the longsuffering of God waited in the days of Noah, while the ark was a preparing, wherein few, that is, eight souls were saved by water. The like figure whereunto even baptism doth also now save us (not the putting away of the filth of the flesh, but the answer of a good conscience toward God,) by the resurrection of Jesus Christ." Apart now from what this somewhat difficult passage may mean in detail, it is obvious that Peter teaches that the waters of the flood were a type of baptism. For although Noah was certainly saved from the wicked world through the water of the flood, the text nevertheless considers this of secondary importance. The point is that Noah was saved not by the ark, but by water. And if he was saved by water, then his salvation consisted in his deliverance from the wicked and corrupt world that was destroyed in that water. This the text says is a picture of baptism.

The water of baptism is a sign and seal of the blood of Christ. Or, to put it a little differently, the water of baptism is a sign and seal of the power of the cross of Christ to save from sin and death. To be baptized means to be baptized in the blood of Christ, or to receive the blessings and benefits of His suffering and death. Paul writes of this in Romans 6:3-11: "Know ye not, that so many of us as were baptized into Jesus Christ were baptized into his death: Therefore we are buried with him by baptism into death: that like as Christ was raised up from the dead by the glory of the Father, even so we also should walk in newness of life. For if we have been planted together in the likeness of his death, we shall be also in the likeness of his resurrection: knowing this, that our old man is crucified with him, that the body of sin might be destroyed, that henceforth we should not serve sin. For he that is dead is freed from sin. Now if we be dead with Christ, we believe that we shall also live with him: knowing that Christ being raised from the dead dieth no more; death hath no more dominion over him. For in that he died, he died unto sin once: but in that he liveth, he liveth unto God. Likewise reckon ye also yourselves to be dead indeed unto sin, but alive unto God through Jesus Christ our Lord."

The figure is clear. On the far side of the flood Noah and his family lived in that wicked and corrupt world of which they were a part. Through the waters of the flood, however, they were saved from that wicked world and taken out of it. By those same waters of the flood the world was destroyed. Carried on the tide of the flood Noah and his family were transferred into a new creation which God had given them for their inheritance.

In like manner also the blood of Christ, symbolized in baptism, is the power to save. On this side of the blood of Christ, we are conceived and born in sin, a part of this wicked and corrupt world in which we live and to which we belong. But God takes us on the powerful and cleansing tide of the blood of Christ out of this world into His new and heavenly creation. For, carried on the tide of the blood of Christ, we are carried to Calvary where we die with Christ, are buried with Him, but also rise again with Him into the glory of God's heaven. On this side of the blood of Christ is sin and death, corruption and the curse. On the other side is holiness and life, joy and happiness in God's fellowship. For through the blood of the cross, the power of Satan and sin and death has been destroyed and the head of the serpent crushed.

The Baptism Form in use in our churches speaks of this in the prayer: "Almighty and eternal God. . . who hast according to thy severe judgment punished the unbelieving and unrepentant world with the flood, and hast according to thy great mercy saved and protected believing Noah and his family. . . by which baptism was signified. . . ."

This is not perfected in our lives as long as we are here upon earth. It is begun in our hearts, but its final victory and perfection come only when we are presented without spot or wrinkle in the assembly of the elect in life eternal. Then shall the wicked world be finally destroyed. Then we shall be perfectly redeemed.

But baptism is a sign and seal of God's covenant, and we might expect, therefore, that the covenant is also discussed in the narrative of the flood.

This covenant idea was already expressed before the flood when we read that God walked with Noah. Here, as we noticed before, the emphasis is surely not on a covenant which is some mechanical pact or agreement, but is rather on a bond of friendship. God walked with Noah as a friend walks with a friend. To Noah He revealed the secrets of His heart and will. To him He gave words of encouragement and comfort in the bitter and difficult struggle against the wicked around him. God assured Noah of the faithfulness and unchangeableness of His promise when things looked so black and hopeless. God told Noah of the coming of the seed of the woman Who would destroy forever all the wicked. He told Noah of His grace and mercy towards Noah, an undeserving sinner. And, reciprocally, Noah talked to God as they walked together, pouring out his heart to his God, speaking of all his doubts and fears, his worries and cares; but also expressing his thankfulness for all that God had done for him.

This was especially true after Noah emerged from the ark and entered the creation which God had given. The first thing which Noah did was take one of each clean animal and offer it to God as a sacrifice of praise. And it was at this moment that God spoke of His covenant.

It is true, God had spoken specifically of His covenant already before the flood. When God commanded Noah to build the ark because God would destroy the whole world, God had added: "But with thee will I establish my covenant; and thou shalt come into the ark, thou, and thy sons, and thy wife, and thy sons' wives with thee" (Genesis 6:18). But after the flood God spoke of this covenant more in detail in Genesis 9:8-17: "And God spake unto Noah, and to his sons with him, saying, And I, behold, I establish my covenant with you, and with your seed after you; and with every living creature that is with you, of the fowl, of the cattle, and of every beast of the earth with you; from all that go out of the ark, to every beast of the earth. And I will establish my covenant with you, neither shall all flesh be cut off any more by the waters of a flood; neither shall there any more be a flood to destroy the earth. And God said, This is the token of the covenant which I make between me and you and every living creature that is with you, for perpetual generations: I do set my bow in the cloud, and it shall be for a token of a covenant between me and the earth. And it shall come to pass, when I bring a cloud over the earth, that the bow shall be seen in the cloud: and I will remember my covenant, which is between me and you and every living creature of all flesh; and the waters shall no more become a flood to destroy all flesh. And the bow shall be in the cloud; and I will look upon it, that I may remember the everlasting covenant between God and every living creature of all flesh that is upon the earth. And God said unto Noah, This is the token of the covenant, which I have established between me and all flesh that is upon the earth."

The question is: what is specifically revealed concerning God's covenant in this passage? It cannot help but strike our attention that the emphasis throughout falls upon "every creature" and "all flesh." Not only is the sign of the covenant a rainbow, something in the creation itself, but no fewer than ten times is reference made to all the creatures on the earth.

In order to understand the significance of this, we must first of all remember that when Satan originally tempted our first parents to sin, he had a larger purpose in mind than just to persuade Adam and Eve to transgress God's commandment. Satan wanted Adam and Eve to disobey because he wanted this creation to be his possession over which he could rule. He was interested in robbing God of all that belonged to Him, of ascending the throne of the universe, and of taking from the hands of the Creator this vast and beautiful creation. In order to accomplish this, he knew he would have to gain man as his ally because man was the representative of God in the world, placed in the world as king, able to rule over the creation and subdue it. But Satan himself is a spirit and has no access to this material and physical creation. He had to get man to agree to be his representative instead of God's so that he could rule through man with man his willing slave.

In connection with this, while Satan surely accomplished his purpose and man became his willing and obedient servant, God promised Christ Who would crush the head of the serpent and foil his foul plots. So

Satan, who seemed momentarily to gain the victory, had now also to see to it that Christ could never come. If Christ after all came, all he had set about to do would be a failure.

No wonder then that when Christ did come and the devil tempted Him in the wilderness, Satan offered Christ all the kingdoms of the earth, if only Christ would bow down to him.

But now God reveals to Noah that the devil will never be successful. God's purpose in sending the seed of the woman would also mean that God would not allow Satan to take this creation out of God's hand. God would establish His covenant not only with Noah and with his seed, but also with the whole creation. Not only will the people of God be taken into this covenant of grace, but also the entire creation will be included in it. This present creation, even though under the curse now because of the fall of Adam its head, must be God's and will be God's. And, while the devil now claims it as his own, it is still true that the earth is the Lord's and the fullness thereof.

One can readily see the connection. When man fell as the head of the creation, the punishment for sin fell not only upon man but also upon the creation itself: "Cursed is the ground for thy sake; in sorrow shalt thou eat of it all the days of thy life; thorns also and thistles shall it bring forth to thee; and thou shall eat the herb of the field" (Genesis 3:17, 18). Even Lamech named his son Noah because, "This same shall comfort us concerning our work and toil of our hands, because of the ground which the Lord hath cursed" (Genesis 5:29).

But God promised a second Adam, our Lord Jesus Christ, Who would be not only the Head of all His people, but also the glorious Head of the creation itself. It, too, is destined to be rescued from the curse; the blood of atonement is shed not only for the elect, but also for the whole creation. So often in our altogether proper concern for the salvation of the people of God, we nevertheless fail to see the vast scope of God's work. We become wrapped up in ourselves and are so narrow-minded that we cannot see anything but the salvation of the church. But God's plan of redemption far transcends our boldest conceptions. It is proper that we not lose sight of the fact that we are not the sole objects of God's favor and grace. He takes not only us into the fellowship of His covenant, but He includes in it the whole creation: the birds, the fish, the animals, the lofty firmament studded with stars, the spreading maple, the arching elm, yes, the entire creation about us. He destines this creation also to be a means to reveal and reflect the glory of His own being. In Christ, and for the sake of the elect, this creation also is to be redeemed.

This God revealed to Noah through the new creation which God gave him. Of this universal scope of God's covenant, God gives the rainbow as a sign. Through the waters of the flood God had led Noah and his family. Into a new creation He had brought them. Now, as they stood and gazed at the glorious rainbow, spanning heaven and earth, scintillating in all its majesty of color, it spoke (and still speaks today) of the universal scope of God's covenant of grace. God saves and redeems His creation.

But just as man, delivered from sin and death, is not brought back to the old Paradise, but given a much higher and richer salvation in Christ, so also this creation is not restored to the original pre-fall creation, but is reformed into a new heavens and a new earth.

The Scriptures speak of this in many places.

That Christ, by His death, died for the whole creation and restored it to the fellowship of God's covenant is taught by Paul in Colossians 1:14-20: "In whom we have redemption through his blood, even the forgiveness of sins: Who is the image of the invisible God, the firstborn of every creature: for by him were all things created, that are in heaven, and that are in earth, visible and invisible, whether they be thrones, or dominions, or principalities, or powers: all things were created by him and for him: and he is before all things, and by him all things consist. And he is the head of the body, the church: who is the beginning, the firstborn from the dead; that in all things he might have the preeminence. For it pleased the Father that in him should all fulness dwell; and, having made peace through the blood of his cross, by him to reconcile all things unto himself; by him, I say, whether they be things in earth, or things in heaven." It is almost as if Paul does not want us to be mistaken about what he means by Christ having reconciled *all things* unto himself; he repeats: "whether they be things in earth, or things in heaven."

That the brute creation itself expects this deliverance into which it presently shall enter is found in Romans 8:19-22: "For the earnest expectation of the creature waiteth for the manifestation of the sons of

God. For the creature was made subject to vanity, not willingly, but by reason of him who hath subjected the same in hope, because the creature itself also shall be delivered from the bondage of corruption into the glorious liberty of the children of God. For we know that the whole creation groaneth and travaileth in pain together until now."

A prophetic picture of this glorious redemption of the entire creation is found in Isaiah 11:1-9: "And there shall come forth a rod out of the stem of Jesse, and a Branch shall grow out of his roots: and the spirit of the Lord shall rest upon him, the spirit of wisdom and understanding, the spirit of knowledge and of the fear of the Lord; and shall make him of quick understanding in the fear of the Lord; and he shall not judge after the sight of his eyes, neither reprove after the hearing of his ears: but with righteousness shall he judge the poor, and reprove with equity for the meek of the earth: and he shall smite the earth with the rod of his mouth, and with the breath of his lips shall he slay the wicked. And righteousness shall be the girdle of his loins, and faithfulness the girdle of his reins. The wolf also shall dwell with the lamb, and the leopard shall lie down with the kid; and the calf and the young lion and the fatling together; and a little child shall lead them. And the cow and the bear shall feed; their young ones shall lie down together: and the lion shall eat straw like the ox. And the suckling child shall put his hand on the cockatrice's den. They shall not hurt nor destroy in all my holy mountain; for the earth shall be full of the knowledge of the Lord, as the waters cover the sea."

The final glory of this is seen by the apostle on Patmos and is recorded for us in Revelation 21:1-4: "And I saw a new heaven and a new earth: for the first heaven and the first earth were passed away; and there was no more sea. And I John saw the holy city, new Jerusalem, coming down from God out of heaven, prepared as a bride adorned for her husband. And I heard a great voice out of heaven saying, Behold, the tabernacle of God is with men, and he will dwell with them, and they shall be his people, and God himself shall be with them, and be their God. And God shall wipe away all tears from their eyes; and there shall be no more death, neither sorrow, nor crying, neither shall there be any more pain: for the former things are passed away."

This then is the covenant with Noah. It is a covenant established with Noah only figuratively and typically. Noah did not inherit the real new creation, only a type. Noah did not receive a perfect earth, much less heaven, for the curse was still there. It was not as if there was no sin anymore in Noah and his family; they were still wicked. It was not the final destruction of the world, for wickedness soon again appeared on the earth. But it was a type. And as a type, it spoke of better things to come. These were symbolized in the rainbow. Presently God will establish His covenant with Christ as the new Head over all. In Christ God will finally crush the head of the serpent and his seed. In the blood of the cross the seed of the woman will finally be saved – of which the water of baptism was only a picture. In the glory of Christ's mighty victory the new heavens and the new earth will be built. Christ as Head and Lord over all will take the entire creation to Himself with His people and into the fellowship of God where we may rest forever in the arms of our everlasting Father.

Now the wicked seem to be victorious. They seem to have gained God's creation for themselves to do with it what they will. But God's promise can never change. Presently the meek shall inherit the earth. Our God's salvation includes His whole creation.

Chapter 8

THE COVENANT WITH ABRAHAM

There is no stronger proof in the Old Testament that God alone establishes His covenant sovereignly than the history of the patriarch Abraham. We have often pointed out that the absolute sovereignty of God is the fundamental principle of the revelation of the mystery of salvation. This principle must necessarily also be applied to the establishment of the covenant if we are to stand solidly upon the truth of the Scriptures. It is wrong to interject into our discussion of the covenant the element of man's cooperation. If the covenant is nothing other than a pact or agreement between two parties, then of course the result is that God is helpless to establish the covenant which He willed to reveal until man agrees to cooperate. Man is then, in the final analysis, the determining factor. Without his consent and agreement no covenant will ever be realized. Without his earnest efforts to aid the Lord of heaven and earth, all that God does is futile and vain. But inasmuch as men sacrifice the truth of God's sovereignty by such a distortion of the truth, they have also made their own idol of Jehovah and destroyed the glory of the God of heaven and earth.

In Genesis 11 Scripture traces the covenant line from Shem to Abraham. For the time being (the time of the old dispensation) God limited the covenant line to the generations of Shem, Noah's son. Of Ham Noah had prophesied: "Cursed be Canaan; a servant of servants shall he be unto his brethren" (Genesis 9:25). Of Japheth the Lord had said through Noah that the blessings of the covenant would be withheld from Japheth until a future era: "God shall enlarge Japheth and he shall dwell in the tents of Shem; and Canaan shall be his servant" (Genesis 9:27). But of Shem God had said, "Blessed be the Lord God of Shem; and Canaan shall be his servant" (Genesis 9:26). Further history makes plain that during the entire old dispensation the establishment of the covenant was limited to these generations of Shem, and it would not be until the fullness of time when Christ came to perform His work that Japheth would enter into Shem's tents to receive this blessing with Shem.

But this does not mean that all the generations of Shem were included in the line of the covenant. Undoubtedly for a time this was true – and then not only for Shem but also for Japheth. But rapidly that covenant line was narrowed down until it was limited to Abraham. In Genesis 11 the line of the covenant is traced from Shem through Arphaxad, Salah, Eber, Peleg, Reu, Serug, and Nahor. Then we read: "And Nahor lived nine and twenty years, and begat Terah: and Nahor lived after he begat Terah an hundred and ninteen years, and begat sons and daughters. And Terah lived seventy years, and begat Abram, Nahor, and Haran. Now these are the generations of Terah: Terah begat Abram, Nahor, and Haran; and Haran begat Lot. And Haran died before his father Terah in the land of his nativity, in Ur of the Chaldees. And Abram and Nahor took them wives: the name of Abram's wife was Sarai; and the name of Nahor's wife, Milcah, the daughter of Haran, the father of Milcah, and the father of Iscah. But Sarai was barren; she had no child" (Genesis 11:24-30).

All the other generations of Shem are forgotten in the sacred narrative, and the Scriptures concentrate their attention upon Abraham with whom God chose to establish His covenant.

Although we will reserve our discussion of the miraculous birth of Isaac, Abraham's son, for later, it is important that we see that this miraculous birth, which foreshadowed so wondrously the birth of Christ, was always the central event in the life of Abraham. He had no children until he was very old. Again and again the Scriptures call this to our attention. Again and again Abraham returns to his complaint that God had given him no seed. The point, repeatedly emphasized, is that the full realization of the covenant hinged upon Abraham's having children. Without children the covenant meant nothing at all and could not be realized. But God had closed Sarah's womb; she was barren; she and her husband did not know the joys of parenthood. It appeared to be forever impossible that Sarah would be instrumental in continuing the lines of God's covenant; and it appeared to be impossible, therefore, that God's covenant would ever be realized.

That Abraham and Sarah could have no children was not due only to Sarah's barrenness; but when Abraham arrived finally in the land of Canaan after his early life in Ur of the Chaldees and a brief sojourn in Haran, Abraham had already reached the ripe old age of seventy-five.

Besides, Sarah was sixty-five years old, well beyond the age of child-bearing. In their sojourn in the promised land, therefore, it seemed too late now to think of having any children to be their heirs and to perpetuate their name. And yet the whole promise of God and the enduring reality of His covenant hung upon their having a child. It is in the light of all this that the life of Abraham must be explained.

It was this problem which Abraham brought to God's attention in Genesis 15. The Lord had come to His servant with the reassuring words: "Fear not, Abraham: I am thy shield, and thy exceeding great reward." But to Abraham this was not the real problem. He had no child. And so the patriarch suggests an alternative: that one born in his house, the son of his steward, be his heir and the child of the promise: "And Abraham said, Lord God, what wilt thou give me, seeing I go childless, and the steward of my house is this Eliezer of Damascus? And Abraham said, Behold, to me thou hast given no seed: and, lo, one born in my house is mine heir." But this alternative would never do. God assured Abraham that his own son would be his heir: "And, behold, the word of the Lord came unto him, saying, This shall not be thine heir; but he that shall come forth out of thine own bowels shall be thine heir. And he brought him forth abroad, and said, Look now toward heaven, and tell the stars, if thou be able to number them; and he said unto him, So shall thy seed be" (Genesis 15:4, 5).

Added to this promise of a multitude of seed which Abraham would receive, the Lord added another promise: "I am the Lord that brought thee out of Ur of the Chaldees, to give thee *this land to inherit it*" (verse 7). Canaan was to be the inheritance of that seed. But once again the problem for Abraham was: How is this possible since I have no children? "Whereby shall I know that I shall inherit it?" (verse 8)

It was in answer to this question that the Lord formally established His covenant with Abraham. The beautiful words of this establishment are found in Genesis 15:9-21.

Abraham was instructed to take a heifer of three years old, a she goat of three years old, a ram of three years old, a turtledove, and a young pigeon. Further, he was to divide the animals in half and lay the halves over against each other, while the birds were not to be divided. This ritual, strange to us, was commonly used in the days of Abraham to signify the agreement of a pact or treaty between two men. After an animal or animals had been cut in half, the two men who were concluding some sort of agreement would walk together between the pieces. By doing this they would solemnly assure one another that rather than break the provisions of the agreement, they would prefer to be cut in pieces themselves and have all their possessions destroyed.

This same form the Lord Himself uses. One would expect that now both Abraham and God would walk between the pieces together and thus solemnly conclude the covenant which God purposed to establish with Abraham. And if the covenant is a bilateral agreement in which both God and man participate, this would undoubtedly have happened. But this is exactly what did not happen. When the sun was going down, Abraham fell into a deep sleep and a horror of great darkness came upon him. While Abraham was sleeping the Lord appeared to him in a vision and established His covenant. But in the establishment of it, *God alone walked between the pieces.* We read in verses 17, 18a: "And it came to pass, that, when the sun went down, and it was dark, behold a smoking furnace, and a burning lamp that passed between those pieces. In the same day the Lord made a covenant with Abram." And in connection with this covenant God also speaks of His promises: "Know of a surety that thy seed shall be a stranger in a land that is not theirs, and shall serve them; and they shall afflict them four hundred years; and also that nation, whom they shall serve, will I judge: and afterward shall they come out with great substance. And thou shalt go to thy fathers in peace; thou shalt be buried in a good old age. But in the fourth generation they shall come hither again: for the iniquity of the Amorites is not yet full" (verses 13-16). "And unto thy seed have I given this land, from the river of Egypt unto the great river, the river Euphrates" (verse 18b).

What does all this mean?

It is evident in the first place that the emphasis here strongly falls on the fact that the covenant which God established with Abraham was God's work alone. The establishment of the covenant was not of the nature of an agreement, a covenant bilaterally put into force. God alone established His covenant. God passed through the pieces alone. Abraham was sound asleep. He witnessed the vision, but did not actively participate in it. He was completely passive. The covenant is therefore completely unilateral in its establishment; it is God's work,

His revelation of His sovereign purpose, made to Abraham without any cooperation or assistance.

This does not mean that the covenant now for the first time is established. Already Adam and the prediluvian saints, as well as the sons of Shem, were included in that covenant. But now God establishes His covenant with Abraham in such a way that He reveals for all time that this work is the work of God alone. He is sovereign also with respect to His covenant. He determines it eternally in His counsel; He brings it to pass in time; He establishes it with His people.

In the second place, it is also evident that God's promises are closely connected to the covenant which He establishes. Although God told Abraham that his seed would dwell in a strange land as slaves for four hundred years until the iniquity of the Amorites was full, nevertheless, clearly the Lord assured Abraham that he will receive a seed and that some day that seed will inherit the land of Canaan upon which Abraham was lying. This promise is an integral part of the covenant. God will bless Abraham with a son; that son shall become a mighty seed; that seed shall inherit the promised land. This, too, emphasizes the unilateral character of the covenant, for it is God Who makes all the promises; Abraham makes none at all, agrees to no provisions, supplies no promises of his own, establishes no stipulations, and assumes no obligations upon which the establishment of the covenant hinges. He is all the while sleeping. God alone makes the promises of the covenant. God, as it were, says to Abraham: "This is my covenant and these are my promises which I graciously give to you."

But this promise is made very certain by the ritual itself. God in passing through the pieces and by this act assuming full responsibility for the covenant in its realization and fulfillment seals this all with a mighty oath. God assures Abraham that the promise of the covenant is so certain that He Himself would rather be cut into pieces (as the animals are cut) than that His covenant should fail. That is, God sealed His promise with the solemn oath that the certainty of the promise hinged upon His own very existence as God. "Either," God said, "My covenant shall stand into all eternity, or I am not the true and living God." The certainty of God keeping covenant is rooted in the certainty of His own divine existence.

That God should say this by passing through the pieces is full of implications. It ought to be evident to any one who reads these amazing Scriptures that this is exactly what also happened in Jesus Christ. In order to maintain and realize His covenant, God was indeed "cut into pieces" when in the person of His Son Jesus Christ, He suffered and died on the cross to make the covenant possible. God would even go so far as to give His only begotten Son to the bitter and shameful death of the cross to make His covenant possible. If such a great suffering for Christ is necessary, God would not even shrink back from this. What amazing grace and love!

And so God bases the surety of His own promise on the certainty of His existence as the only true God. God swears with an oath that He will, as surely as He is Jehovah, perform what He had said. It may appear absolutely impossible to Abraham that he ever have a son. That makes no difference. Solemnly God assures Abraham that such will nevertheless be the case.

This remarkable fact is further corroborated by other passages of the Scriptures. We read, e.g., in Hebrews 6:16-20: "For men verily swear by the greater: and an oath for confirmation is to them an end of all strife. Wherein God, willing more abundantly to shew unto the heirs of promise the immutability of his counsel, confirmed it by an oath: that by two immutable things, in which it was impossible for God to lie, we might have a strong consolation, who have fled for refuge to lay hold upon the hope set before us: which hope we have as an anchor of the soul, both sure and steadfast, and which entereth into that within the veil; whither the forerunner is for us entered, even Jesus, made an high priest forever after the order of Melchisedec."

God assures us of the faithfulness of His promise by the oath which He swears by Himself. Although surely the unchangeableness of His own being would be sufficient, nevertheless, because of the weakness and frailty of our faith and in order that we may have an anchor for our souls that is sure and stedfast, God binds Himself to an oath that we may be assured by these two immutable things.

And so God's promise is an integral part of the covenant. We may therefore distinguish two aspects of the promise. From a formal point of view that promise of God is His oath which He swears by Himself so that we may be assured of the certainty of what He says. From a material point of view, the promise has as its content that God will surely establish His covenant with Abraham and his seed, and that this will be realized in Christ, God's own Son, Whom God gives to the suffering of the cross that the covenant may in fact be perfected.

What a great comfort this also is!

This comfort is rooted first of all in the fact that God alone establishes His covenant. He is the sovereign Lord also in the work of salvation. He saves by His power alone. Upon Him we are completely dependent. The comfort of this ought to be evident to anyone who has come to know the depths of his sin. Such a one knows that salvation for him is absolutely hopeless. If the fulfillment of the promise and the realization of the covenant depend in any way upon him, it is forever out of reach. If we must cooperate with God in the work of the covenant, it lies eternally outside our grasp. If we must be willing and agreeable before such a covenant can be established, we shall forever be left outside. If that glorious covenant is only concluded when the sinner has agreed to its provisions, he shall never find peace for his troubled soul. But God establishes His covenant with His people. He takes them into it without their aid and effort, and only by His grace. He simply brings His people into it, makes His promises to them and fulfills them by His power. Because this is the sovereign work of God alone apart from our help, we who cry out under the burden of sin know that the power of our deliverance is the power of an almighty God. We cling to Him alone, for He saves.

Besides, this comfort of the believer is based upon the surety of God's promise. The promise which God made to Abraham is a promise that rings down the centuries of time. It comes to all the people of God throughout all history. True it is, of course, that it was given to Abraham cloaked in the typical language of the Old Testament. But its essence remains the same. That God is Abraham's God means that God is our God also. The promise essentially has not changed. God promised to Abraham a seed. That seed is Christ. Christ is ours. God promised to Abraham the land of Canaan. That earthly land was but a picture of the heavenly. The heavenly Canaan is promised to us.

But this assurance of God's promise we desperately need. We live in a hostile world. So often it seems as if the kingdom of God goes down to defeat. Darkness and sin run rampant; iniquity prevails. God's promise seems far away and heaven recedes in the distance. Besides, we are very wicked. Our faith is weak; doubts and fears storm over our soul; we are tossed about on the restless seas of time. The day grows blacker and hope fades.

But the promise of God stands immutable in the heavens. As surely as God Himself is God, so surely does His promise stand. Nothing can ever alter it. Nothing can prevent its fulfillment. God will surely give it to us. And this promise is the anchor of our souls both sure and steadfast. We who have fled for refuge to Christ have this strong consolation. With souls anchored by this promise of God, we are safe in the harbor of eternity where all is serenity and peace.

Chapter 9

ABRAHAM AND HIS SEED

A question which has stirred up considerable discussion over the years is the question of who are the seed, the true children of Abraham.

To this important question many different answers have been given. And, according to the varied answers that have been given, different solutions have been found to other vexing problems related to this question – problems such as: What is the significance of the Old Testament sign of circumcision administered to Isaac? What is the significance of the sacrament of baptism? To whom should baptism be administered?

Anyone who has at any time pondered these questions is undoubtedly aware of the controversy that any discussion of these questions can initiate.

We mention here a few of the answers that have been given to the most basic question of all: Who are the true seed of Abraham?

There are those who answer that only the natural Jews constitute this seed. This was true in the Old Testament not only, but it remains no less true in the New. The Jews are indeed, for a time, dispersed throughout the world during this dispensation while God gathers the fullness of the Gentiles; but God will return again to His chosen people and restore the Jews to Canaan establishing the commonwealth of Israel once again, restoring the throne of David and bringing the people of Israel from their captivity. These are the premillennialists who find in the Scriptures the doctrine of a literal one thousand-year reign of Christ with the Jews on Mount Zion in the Palestine of the Middle East.

Others answer this question by insisting that not only are the Jews the true children of Abraham, but the children of Abraham include both Jews and Gentiles. But here also one finds a wide divergence of opinion among those who hold to this view.

There are some who maintain that only those who give proof of being born again by manifesting the faith of Abraham are Abraham's true seed. Evidence of being Abraham's seed is found in a personal testimony of the influence of the Holy Spirit within them and a profession of faith. These maintain that, whether Jew or Gentile, the sacrament of baptism is to be administered only to those who, upon arriving at years of discretion (when these years are is not clearly stated) make a testimony of their faith. Circumcision (of infants) belongs only to the old dispensation; baptism is only for believers.

Others maintain that the true seed of Abraham is composed of both Jews and Gentiles, but that this seed is made up not only of believers, but also of their seed. The children of believers as well as believers themselves belong to this seed of Abraham. But here again differences of opinion arise. There are some who believe that all the children of believers without exception belong to this seed of Abraham; that they all must be baptized as a sign of the covenant; that through baptism they all receive the promises of God as the blessings of that covenant; that however, they may, in process of time, reveal themselves to be covenant breakers and fall away from the covenant, ultimately to go lost. Others insist that only the elect children of believers are the true children of Abraham; that, although all children must be baptized, only the children of election belong to this true seed; that they are the exclusive heirs of God's promises and the true members of the covenant of grace.

At first glance, these questions may seem to be somewhat abstract. They may appear to be the speculations of "ivory tower" theologians that do not have any real bearing on the practical life of the Christian. Nothing could be farther from the truth. It remains a fact, of course, that any question involving the truth of the church of Christ is an important question worthy of our consideration. But it is also true that this question is filled with practical implications for the calling and comfort of believers. The question involves the important point of who truly make up the church of Christ. Who constitute the true membership of that church? Who are they who belong to this body of Christ that always exists on this earth? Besides, the question deals with our own children. There are no closer relationships of life than the relationships of parents and their children. Any God-fearing parent loves his children for God's sake. And the fact remains that sometimes these children are taken from us by God in the earliest years of their life. The question presses for an answer: Are these children saved? Or again, both parents and the church have a very serious calling with respect to the children born to them within the church. And the question must be answered: What is this calling which the church and believing parents have? On what basis does this calling take on urgency? Or to look at a different aspect of the problem: there is no greater grief to believing parents or to the church than that children walk in the ways of the world. The question is: what is the explanation for this? And, are there any statements of the Scriptures concerning this which can bring peace and comfort to both parents and the church of Christ?

These questions are answered by the Scriptures in connection with the Scriptural data on the establishment of the covenant with Abraham. The proper place to begin is with the history of Abraham himself as recorded for us in the Bible. There we will learn much of what the Scriptures have to say on these matters. And, having learned from the Genesis narrative what the Scriptures have to say about these things, we will then have to turn our attention to other parts of the Scriptures, especially the New Testament, to discover what light the Scriptures as a whole shed on these fundamental questions.

Turning then to the Genesis narrative (the reader ought to consult chapters 12-25), we find that Isaac was born to Abraham and Sarah in their old age. Repeatedly, this matter of the birth of a child had been of deepest concern to the ancient patriarch and his wife. God had given them the promise of inheritance in the land of Canaan and of a seed that would be as great as the number of stars in the heavens. And Abraham and his wife understood full well that these promises were but typical, pointing ahead to the promise of a heavenly kingdom in a heavenly Canaan that would come to them through Christ. But all these promises hinged upon their receiving a child. And they had none. If no child was given them, as now seemed to be the case, Canaan could never be theirs and Christ could never come.

Besides, it is rather striking that although God had promised Abraham a seed, He had not specifically told Abraham that he would be the father, even though this was to be expected. Only finally in chapter 15 do we read that Abraham was assured that this son would be his own. Even then, nothing was said of Sarah as the mother. This did not take place until Abraham was 99 years old. (See chapter 17.)

No wonder then that Abraham and his wife considered various possibilities of helping the Lord in getting a child for themselves. After all, both of them were well past that time of life when they could expect to have children. Already when they went from Ur of the Chaldees to the land of Canaan, they were seventy-five and sixty-five years old respectively. Really, all hopes of having children were past. One does not expect to produce seed in the twilight of life. Besides, all her life Sarah had been barren. It was beyond her natural ability to produce offspring. It seemed utterly hopeless.

We are not surprised to find Abraham and Sarah proposing various solutions to the problem. Abraham originally had suggested that perhaps the son of Eliezer, the faithful steward of his house could be considered as his son and heir. But the Lord had emphatically said that this was impossible; only one born of Abraham himself could be the heir.

It seems that Sarah suggested another approach to the problem. She had an Egyptian slave named Hagar who could perhaps be considered as the one to bear Abraham this promised seed. Because of the fact that Hagar was a slave, Sarah could justly claim the child as her own and the problem would be solved. All Abraham had to do was make Hagar his concubine, and the requirement of God would be fulfilled. So ideal did the solution appear that Abraham did not even ask the Lord about it but proceeded with the matter. The result was that in due time the plan was accomplished and Hagar bore Ishmael. But this was no solution after all, and problems were the result. When Sarah claimed the child as her own, Hagar would not part with him. And this was the beginning of a series of troubles in the home of the patriarch that finally culminated in the departure of Hagar and Ishmael from the household of Abraham. All this trouble was brought on by a lack of faith and the sinful conduct of Abraham and Sarah; and it resulted only in bringing forth a child who was not the true seed of Abraham and was instead a child of the flesh and a picture for all time of children of the flesh. So Paul writes in Galatians 4:22-25: "For it is written, that Abraham had two sons, the one by a bondmaid, the other by a freewoman. But he who was of the bondwoman was born after the flesh; but he of the freewoman was by promise. Which things are an allegory: for these are the two covenants; the one from mount Sinai, which gendereth to bondage, which is Agar. For this Agar is mount Sinai in Arabia, and answereth to Jerusalem which now is, and is in bondage with her children."

No wonder either when God announced again in the plains of Mamre that Sarah would indeed have a son that she laughed. We can understand that this was more than she was capable of believing when all these years had passed (Genesis 18:9-14).

But God was faithful to His promise. Indeed, God waited till Abraham was one hundred years old and Sarah ninety. Then not only Sarah was beyond the years of childbearing, but Abraham was also. The birth of the seed from every conceivable human point of view was impossible. Only then did God fulfill His promises and give to them Isaac. The theme running through the whole narrative is: what is impossible with man is possible with God.

The apostle Paul expresses this in Romans 4:16-21: "Therefore it is of faith, that it might be by grace; to the end the promise might be sure to all the seed; not to that only which is of the law, but to that also which is of the faith of Abraham; who is the father of us all, (As it is written, I have made thee a father of many nations,) before him whom he believed, even God, who quickeneth the dead, and calleth those things which be not as though they were. Who against hope believed in hope, that he might become the father of many nations, according to that which was spoken, So shall thy seed be. And being not weak in faith, he considered not his own body now dead, when he was about an hundred years old, neither yet the deadness of Sarah's womb: he staggered not at the promise of God through unbelief; but was strong in faith, giving glory to God; and being fully persuaded that, what he had promised, he was able also to perform."

Concerning this there are several points to consider.

1) The child of the promise was a child born of Abraham and Sarah, as God had said. Ishmael was not the heir, nor was the child of Eliezer; but one born of Abraham and Sarah themselves.

2) This child was born when it was humanly impossible for him to be born. It was, of course, true that Isaac was the child of Abraham and Sarah, but these two old saints were like two dead tombs. The birth of Isaac was therefore a miracle. It was accomplished by an act of God "Who quickeneth the dead, and calleth those things which be not

as though they were." Isaac was born by a wonder of grace. This is important. Isaac was the promised seed whose birth was miraculous; but this is the only way the promised seed can ever be born. Normal conception and childbirth result in producing children that are not the promised seed, but are children of the flesh as Ishmael was. The true promised seed of the covenant are those who are born by a miracle, i.e., by a spiritual and heavenly birth wrought miraculously by God. A wonder of grace is required to produce the seed of the promise. This fact remains true for all time. To this we must return presently.

3) The child was, from the moment of birth on, a child of the covenant. He was the child that God had promised not only; but through his birth the promise of God's covenant could be fulfilled – the promise of inheritance in the land of promise; the promise of Christ.

4) That all these things pointed ahead to Christ ought to be clear. This was not only objectively true; it was a fact that lived in the consciousness of Abraham. Abraham saw that all that happened to him was only type and shadow; that therefore the full reality must await the coming of Christ. We read of the ancient heroes of faith and of Abraham in particular that, "These all died in faith, not having received the promises, but having seen them afar off, and were persuaded of them and embraced them, and confessed that they were strangers and pilgrims on the earth. For they that say such things declare plainly that they seek a country. And truly, if they had been mindful of that country from whence they came out, they might have had opportunity to have returned. But now they desire a better country, that is, an heavenly: wherefore God is not ashamed to be called their God: for he hath prepared for them a city" (Hebrews 11:13-16).

Nevertheless, this is not all.

Although Isaac was born by a wonder of grace, and was, consequently, a child of the promise, he was still only figuratively the true seed of Abraham. God made His promises to Abraham and his seed. And the question still remains: who is this seed of Abraham? Granted that it was Isaac in the old dispensation (and Isaac's generations – Jacob, Judah, David, Solomon, etc.), is this really the full answer to the question?

Paul answers this question in the negative. He writes in Galatians

3:16: "Now to Abraham and his seed were the promises made." We might be inclined to conclude that Paul means here that God made the promises of His covenant to Abraham and his son Isaac – and to Isaac's generations, the nation of Israel. Then these promises are only of Jewish validity and significance, as the premillennialists maintain. But this is not Paul's argument here. He calls our attention to the fact that when God made His promises to Abraham and his *seed,* God spoke of *seed* in the singular, and not of *seeds* in the plural. This might seem to us a minor point, but upon this use of the singular, Paul rests an important truth. If the promise was made to Isaac and the nation of Israel as a whole, God would have given His promise to the many *seeds* of Abraham. But Paul writes: "He saith not, And to seeds, as of many; but as of one, And to thy seed." But when the question immediately arises: who then was this one seed to whom the promises were made? the answer is, "And that seed is Christ!"

This is an important truth. Isaac was, after all, only a type of Christ. Christ was the true seed of Abraham. The birth of Isaac was also therefore a picture of the birth of Christ. Isaac was born by means of a miracle because his birth was humanly impossible. But this was especially true of Christ. That birth of Christ was emphatically humanly impossible. How often did not this become evident throughout the old dispensation! On the one hand, there were always barren women in the line of the promise that was to produce Christ. Sarah was not the only one. But on the other hand, there were constant attempts of the devil to destroy that promised line so that Christ could never be born. Sometimes the devil used the very subtle means of apostasy to lead Israel away from the worship of God so that they would be lost among the nations that served idols. Again and again wicked people and wicked kings were in that line of Christ. One need only think of Ahaz, Manasseh, Jehoiakim, and others. Other times he deliberately tried to wipe that seed from the face of the earth. This was after all behind Pharaoh's attempt to destroy the baby boys of the Israelites. This was Athaliah's intent when she slew all the seed royal except for Joash, who was rescued. This was basically Haman's plot to kill all the Jews because of his anger with Mordecai. In the background lurked the devil who tried in various ways to prevent the Christ from being born. Only because God preserved that line did it continue until Christ came.

Yet all of this was nothing compared with the fact that at last the royal line of David from which Christ was to be born ended in a virgin. The line came to a dead end. It came to a dead end in a virgin who could never by herself bring forth the promised seed. This is undoubtedly the meaning of Mary's word to the angel that announced to her that she was to be the mother of Christ: "How shall this be, seeing I know not a man?" If ever the hope of the fulfillment of the promise seemed impossible, it was then. If ever it was humanly out of the question that man bring forth the seed of the promise, it was when Mary stood alone at the end of the line.

Yet, what is impossible with man is always possible with God. For Christ was born not by the will of men, but by the power of God. "The Holy Ghost shall come upon thee, and the power of the Highest shall overshadow thee; therefore also that holy thing which shall be born of thee shall be called the Son of God" (Luke 1:34, 35). This was the wonder of the ages, the central miracle of all time, the great miracle of grace. Christ was born. He was born not by the will of man, for it was impossible for man to bring Him forth. He was born not in a natural and earthly way, for His birth was outside the scope of human activity. He was born from a virgin, through the power of the Most High acting on the womb of Mary apart from any human father. It was the mystery of the incarnation, the wonder of Bethlehem, God with us, Immanuel.

This Christ is the Heir of the promises of God – the exclusive Heir of all of them. He is the true Seed of Abraham of which there is none other. Centrally and principally Christ alone stands as the Seed of the promise, the Heir of the inheritance.

These promises He also received as His own. He received them because He was the obedient Servant of Jehovah, Who, while on earth accomplished all the Father's will. He walked the lonely and desolate way of the cross. He entered the portals of hell and made His own life a perfect sacrifice upon the altar of God's wrath. He went to the bottom of hell where the waves of wrath poured over His soul and consumed Him. He came to do God's will and accomplished it. And because He accomplished it all, He was raised from the dead and exalted in the highest heavens. He was given a place of honor and power at the Father's right hand. He was made in heaven the Heir of all the promises of God. He inherited the heavenly Canaan as His own and was filled with all the blessings of salvation as His own possession. He was made rich and glorious beyond compare. "God, who at sundry times and in divers manners spake in time past unto the fathers by the prophets, hath in these last days spoken to us by his Son, whom he hath appointed heir of all things. . ." (Hebrews 1:1, 2).

But the Scriptures go on to tell us that also those who belong to Christ are the true children of Abraham and heirs of the promise.

We bring forth many children as the believers have done throughout all the ages of time. But we can never bring forth the children of God. This is for us as it was for Abraham a human impossibility. We can only bring forth children such as ourselves who are dead in trespasses and sins. We bring forth children who carry in them the depravity of Adam's fall, who are children of the world, citizens of the kingdom of darkness, a generation that is under the power and influence of the hosts of hell, who are destined in themselves to spend eternity in hell. This is all we can ever do. Nothing else is possible for us. The true seed of the promise, the heirs of salvation we can never bring forth ourselves.

And so, the fact still remains that what is impossible with man is possible with God. The seed of the promise is born by a wonder of grace.

Several points are important in this connection.

1) If Christ is the Heir of the promise of God *par excellence*, then only those are the heirs who are in Christ: that is, those who belong to Christ are heirs with Christ of the same promises. They are those who are chosen in Christ from before the foundation of the world and given to Christ as His own possession. These are the elect, the chosen of God. "The Spirit itself beareth witness with our spirit, that we are the children of God: and if children, then heirs; heirs of God, and joint heirs with Christ; if so be that we suffer with him, that we may be also glorified together" (Romans 8:16, 17).

2) If Christ became the Heir of the promise through His work on the cross, those are the heirs of the promise for whom Christ died. This must not be separated from election. There are those who would do this. They claim that Christ died for all men. But this must inevitably lead to a denial of election. For the cross is rooted in election; it has its foundation in the eternal and immutable decree of God. Those whom

God chose are given to Christ. For them He died. And through the cross they, and they alone, are the heirs of the blessings of that cross.

3) The elect are heirs because they are children of God. They are children of God because they are born again by a wonder of grace – as Isaac was born; as Christ was born. This wonder of grace is that regeneration spoken of repeatedly in the Scriptures. Their natural birth leaves them children of darkness, dead in sin and burdened with guilt. But this spiritual birth is from above. It is the birth of the wonder of grace. It is a miraculous work of God whereby He gives to His elect people the new resurrection life of Christ Jesus. Yes, this work also is through Christ. For it is by the Spirit of Christ which imparts this resurrection life that the elect are born again. "Blessed be the God and Father of our Lord Jesus Christ, which according to his abundant mercy hath begotten us again unto a lively hope by the resurrection of Jesus Christ from the dead" (I Peter 1:3). "But as many as received him, to them gave he power to become the sons of God, even to them that believe on his name: which were born, not of blood, nor of the will of the flesh, nor of the will of man, but of God" (John 1:12, 13).

4) Implied in this new birth is the gift of faith. For faith is that bond which unites the elect to Christ. Through that bond of faith flows the life of Christ into the hearts of Christ's people. That faith places the people of God in abiding communion with their Savior. As the Heidelberg Catechism expresses it: "Are all men then, as they perished in Adam, saved by Christ? No; only those who are *ingrafted into him*, and receive all his benefits, by a true faith" (Lord's Day VII).

That faith is called into consciousness by the power of the gospel so that consciously the people of God believe in Christ and lay hold on Him and on all the blessings of the cross. This faith is not the work of man as the proud heresy of Arminianism maintains; it is the work of God, for "by grace are ye saved through faith; and that not of yourselves, it is the gift of God" (Ephesians 2:8). Therefore the heirs of the promise are called in the Scriptures believers. Those who believe are the heirs of the promise, for they receive the promise by faith. They who possess this faith are the true children of the promise, the true seed of Abraham. It was through faith that Abraham laid hold on the promise of God and saw it afar off. But this same faith is also the faith that lives in the hearts of all those who are the true seed of Abraham.

This is emphasized in the Scriptures. To quote but a few texts will serve our purpose. In Galatians 3:7-9 we read: "Know ye therefore that they which are of faith, the same are the children of Abraham. And the scripture, foreseeing that God would justify the heathen through faith, preached before the gospel unto Abraham, saying, In thee shall all nations be blessed. So then they which be of faith are blessed with faithful Abraham." Or, in the same chapter, verses 26-29 we read: "For ye are all the children of God by faith in Christ Jesus. For as many of you as have been baptized into Christ have put on Christ. There is neither Jew nor Greek, there is neither bond nor free, there is neither male nor female; for ye are all one in Christ Jesus. And if ye be Christ's, then are ye Abraham's seed, and heirs according to the promise."

This then is the beautiful chain of the Scriptures: Christ is the Heir of the promises and the Seed of Abraham. Election in Christ, atonement by Christ's work, regeneration through Christ, faith to believe and lay hold on Christ – all of these are the work of God's sovereign grace. And through Christ, those who are elect and redeemed, regenerated and given faith to lay hold on Christ are the heirs of the promises of God.

Chapter 10

BELIEVERS AND THEIR SEED

In the last chapter we discussed the question: who is the true seed of Abraham? This question we answered in a threefold way.

1) Typically and figuratively Isaac was the seed of Abraham, the child born by a wonder of grace, the child of the promise.

2) Centrally and antitypically, Christ is the Seed of Abraham and the Heir of all the promises of God. For, "to Abraham and his seed were the promises made. He saith not, And to seeds, as of many; but as of one, And to thy seed, which is Christ" (Galatians 3:16).

3) But finally, all those who are in Christ are also the true seed of Abraham and the heirs of the promises of God. Those who are in Christ are those who are chosen in Christ from all eternity, the elect; those who are redeemed in the blood of Christ; those who are engrafted into Christ by faith; and those who, by this power of God-given faith, believe in Christ. For, "If ye be Christ's, then are ye Abraham's seed, and heirs according to the promise" (Galatians 3:29).

We must now discuss various other views concerning those who constitute the seed of Abraham; and these views must be put to the test of the Scriptures.

There are first of all then, those who hold to premillennial or dispensational views. It is not our purpose to enter into a detailed discussion of these views – especially as these views touch upon such matters as the return of Christ, the rapture, the millennium, etc. It is more our interest to point out that the dispensationalists err in their conception of who constitute the true seed of Abraham. This view, in brief, holds that we must make a distinction between the Old and New Testament, the old and new covenant, and therefore also between the Jew and Gentile. Only the natural Jews are the true children of Abraham and the true people of God. These Jews were the people of God in the old dispensation, the true kingdom people, but are temporarily forsaken by God when they crucified their Messiah. They are, during this dispensation, in "captivity" while God gathers an "interim people," the church gathered from the Gentiles. But when the fullness of the Gentiles is brought in, God will return again to the Jews to deal with them as of old. He will gather them again to the promised land of Canaan, restore to Israel the theocracy, establish the throne of David, give to the natural Jew the inheritance of Canaan and send Christ to reign with them on Mount Zion for one thousand years.

Those who maintain these views are very insistent that these things are taught in the Scriptures, and that, in fact, there are any number of Old Testament prophecies that will never be fulfilled if these literal events do not take place.

But the fundamental point is nevertheless whether there is such a distinction between the Old and New Testaments and therefore between the Jew and Gentile. If it can be shown from the Scriptures that the prophecies of the Old Testament have their fulfillment in the New; if it can be demonstrated that there is no *essential* difference between the two dispensations even while there are differences of outward form; then the whole structure of dispensationalism falls away.

And this is not difficult when we are willing to follow the principle that the Scriptures interpret the Scriptures. Although it will, of course, be impossible to look at all the texts in the Old Testament which are supposed to refer to a reign of Christ with the Jews on Mount Zion and which are thus supposed to teach that the Jews are a separate people and the true seed of Abraham, a few examples will suffice if we remember that these are keys to the interpretation of them all.

In the first place, crucial to the dispensational position is that a distinction must be made between the "kingdom people" and the church. It is maintained that the Jews alone constitute the kingdom people, while the church is a term limited to the Gentiles who are gathered during the interim. It is even maintained that the New Testament word for "church," *ecclesia,* is never used for the Jews, but is reserved specifically for the Gentiles. But this is manifestly not true. Stephen in his address before the Sanhedrin, in talking of Moses, says: "This is he, that was in the *church* in the wilderness with the angel which spake to him in the mount Sina, and with our fathers: who received the lively oracles to give unto us" (Acts 7:38). Here the evangelist specifically calls the Old Testament people of God "church," *ecclesia,* and by doing so immediately creates a fundamental unity between the church in the old dispensation and the new. This by itself establishes the fundamental principle that there is only one church throughout history composed of both Jews and Gentiles.

Secondly, we call attention to Hosea 1:10, 11: "Yet the number of the children of Israel shall be as the sand of the sea, which cannot be measured nor numbered; and it shall come to pass, that in the place where it was said unto them, Ye are not my people, there it shall be said unto them, Ye are the sons of the living God. Then shall the children of Judah and the children of Israel be gathered together, and appoint themselves one head, and they shall come up out of the land; for great shall be the day of Jezreel." Now it will readily have to be admitted that this text seems to teach indeed that God will deal with Israel separately by bringing them from all the nations of the earth in which they are scattered and establishing them as a theocracy once again in earthly Canaan. And, in fact, it is this text and others like it which the dispensationalists are fond of quoting to prove their point.

The trouble with this interpretation, however, is that it contradicts what Paul teaches in the new dispensation. Paul does not at all find that this passage has its fulfillment in some future dealings with the Jews. Rather, he finds the fulfillment in the gathering of the *Gentiles* throughout this entire dispensation. In speaking in Romans 9 of the profound truth of election and reprobation, the apostle is precisely concerned with the question of whether God had permitted His Word to be of none effect when the nation of Israel was rejected. But this is not true. God's Word is surely fulfilled. He has promised to save Israel. That will certainly take place. But in connection with his discussion of this truth, Paul calls attention to the fact that one church is gathered which consists of both Jews and Gentiles. And this is the fulfillment of the prophecy of Hosea. He writes: "What if God, willing to shew his wrath, and to make his power known, endured with much longsuffering the vessels of wrath fitted to destruction: and that he might make known the riches of his glory on the vessels of mercy, which he had afore prepared unto glory, even us whom he hath called, not of the Jews only, but also of the Gentiles? As he saith also in Osee, I will call them my people, which were not my people; and her beloved, which was not beloved. And it shall come to pass, that in the place where it was said unto them, Ye are not my people; there shall they be called the children of the living God" (verses 22-26). And Peter applies the same passage from Hosea to the Gentiles in his first epistle, 2:10.

It is very clear that the apostles, under the inspiration of the Holy Spirit, find the fulfillment of Hosea's prophecy in the gathering of the Gentiles during the new dispensation and not in the establishment of a thousand-year reign of Christ with the Jews in earthly Palestine.

Another favorite passage of the dispensationalists is Amos 9:11-15: "In that day will I raise up the tabernacle of David that is fallen, and close up the breaches thereof; and I will raise up his ruins, and I will build it as in the days of old: that they may possess the remnant of Edom, and of all the heathen, which are called by my name, saith the Lord that doeth this. Behold, the days come, saith the Lord, that the plowman shall overtake the reaper, and the treader of grapes him that soweth seed; and the mountains shall drop sweet wine, and all the hills shall melt. And I will bring again the captivity of my people of Israel, and they shall build the waste cities, and inhabit them; and they shall plant vineyards, and drink the wine thereof; they shall also make gardens, and eat the fruit of them. And I will plant them upon their land, and they shall no more be pulled up out of their land which I have given them, saith the Lord thy God."

If ever there was a passage that seems to point to the coming of some future Messianic and earthly kingdom in Palestine for the Jews, this is the one. But this cannot possibly be the case, for the Jerusalem Council in the new dispensation was discussing the problems of salvation for the Gentiles and whether they were obligated to keep the law, particularly that of circumcision. James was the one who insisted that this was not necessary inasmuch as the new dispensation is the fulfillment of the old, and God had prophesied of the salvation of the Gentiles. To prove this James quotes precisely this text from Amos: "And to this agree the words of the prophets; as it is written, After this I will return and will build again the ruins thereof, and I will set it up: that the residue of men might seek after the Lord, and the Gentiles, upon whom my name is called, saith the Lord, who doeth all these things" (Acts 15:15-17).

This is striking. It is not only striking that James should quote this passage from Amos as proof for the fact that God gathers a church from Jews and Gentiles, but that the Council in Jerusalem evidently saw immediately the force of the argument. They understood better than today's premillennialists the force of this passage in Amos. And it must therefore be granted that either this passage, which seems to speak of the establishment of a millennial kingdom, in fact does not, or that James and the Jerusalem Council misinterpreted badly this Word of God. The latter would, of course, deny the inspiration of the Scriptures and the words of the Council itself: "It seemed good to the Holy Spirit, and to us. . ." (Acts 15:28).

It must be remembered that we have here a fundamental principle of Scriptural interpretation. These passages are not merely rare instances of a unique interpretation given to a few select Old Testament Scriptures. The point is that the Scriptures themselves set forth a rule according to which all similar passages must be interpreted. This is clear from the fact that the early church, under the guidance of the Spirit, followed this method of interpretation and this follows from the words of James: "And to this agree the words of the prophets. . . ."

But there are other passages of the Scriptures which literally speak of the fact that the children of Abraham are both Jews and Gentiles in both the old and the new dispensations. "For he is not a Jew, which is one outwardly; neither is that circumcision, which is outward in the flesh: but he is a Jew, which is one inwardly; and circumcision is that of the heart, in the spirit, and not in the letter; whose praise is not of men, but of God" (Romans 2:28, 29). "For the promise, that he should be the heir of the world, was not to Abraham, or to his seed, through the law, but through the righteousness of faith. For if they which are of the law be heirs, faith is made void, and the promise made of none effect: because the law worketh wrath: for where no law is, there is no transgression. Therefore it is of faith, that it might be by grace; to the end the promise might be sure to all the seed; not to that only which is of the law, but to that also which is of the faith of Abraham; who is the father of us all" (Romans 4:13-16). Or again, "Know ye therefore that they which are of faith, the same are the children of Abraham. And the Scriptures, foreseeing that God would justify the heathen through faith, preached before the gospel unto Abraham, saying, In thee shall all nations be blessed. So then they which be of faith are blessed with faithful Abraham" (Galatians 3:7-9). Again and again the Scriptures teach that there is in the new dispensational church no longer any difference between Jew and Greek; they are all one. (Cf., e.g., Galatians 3:27-29; Ephesians 2:11-16, etc.)

The conclusion is that those who limit the children of Abraham only to the natural seed of Abraham and look to some future dealings of God with the Jews in some future millennium greatly err. This is a view which is certainly not in the Scriptures. Rather, the Scriptures teach that the church of all ages is one. True, it was limited in large measure to Israel in the old dispensation, but that was the dispensation of types and shadows. The church is all one, united only in Christ Jesus. Christ is centrally the seed of Abraham; and those also are the seed who are in Christ, whether Jew or Gentile, whether from the old dispensation or the new.

There are others who maintain that the true children of Abraham are only those who, upon coming to years of discretion, can give some evidence of the new birth by a confession of their faith and by a promise of a godly walk. Whether these be Jews or Gentiles now makes no difference. The point is that only *believers* can be counted as seed. Infants and children, not having arrived at the point where they can speak consciously and intelligibly about their own personal salvation, are excluded. Only adults and mature young people who give evidence of salvation are considered children of Abraham.

Those who maintain this hold, with perfect consistency, to the view that baptism should be administered only to adults or mature young people who can give account of their salvation.

The question is, therefore, whether children and infants also belong to the children of Abraham. If they do, then they also are included in the covenant of grace and as such ought to bear the sign of the covenant, the seal of baptism.

The proof for infant baptism in the Scriptures rests primarily upon four points.

1) In the first place, the doctrine of infant baptism rests upon the fact that the Scriptures teach that the church in the old and the new dispensations is one. We have discussed this above in connection with the views of dispensationalists, and it is sufficient for our purposes to note now that it is rather striking and also for the most part historically true that Baptists, to be consistent, must adopt some kind of premillennial and dispensational position, although there are some who

claim to deny infant baptism and yet hold to an amillennial position. (See David Kingdon's book, *Children of Abraham,* although it is not true that Kingdon succeeds in avoiding dispensationalism. I have discussed this in detail in my book, *We and Our Children.*)

But if the church of both the old and the new dispensation is one, then there is also only one covenant which is established with that church. This covenant is established first of all with Christ, and the promises of that covenant are made and given to Christ alone. Then all that are in Christ, whether they be of the old or new dispensation, whether they be Jew or Gentile, are included in that one covenant. It is true that the covenant in the old dispensation was revealed in types and shadows. It is also true that because of these types and shadows the covenant as it was revealed then is sometimes called the old covenant or the covenant of the law. But this does not alter the fact that the promises of God and the covenant which He established with His people were essentially the same then as they are now. Then the promise was that God would surely save His people through Christ; now that promise is the same. Then God swore that He would surely be the God of His people; now that has not changed. There are not two or three or four covenants; there is only one: the everlasting covenant of grace.

2) If there is only one covenant, there is also only one sign of the covenant. This sign of the covenant may undergo some outward and external changes in keeping with the change in dispensations. But since the essence of the covenant remains the same, so does the essential meaning of the sign of the covenant.

This means that circumcision is the same sign, as far as its meaning is concerned, as baptism. That this is the teaching of the Scriptures is evident from the fact that both signs are, by the Scriptures, given the same significance.

Circumcision was an outward sign that signified an internal reality. It signified the fact that salvation was the work of God whereby God cut away the sin and evil of the hearts of His people and gave them new hearts. It signified the inward cleansing and purifying of the heart through the operation of the Spirit of God.

This is taught in many passages in the Scriptures. In Deuteronomy 10:16 we read: "Circumcise therefore the foreskin of your heart, and be no more stiffnecked." In Jeremiah 4:4: "Circumcise yourselves to the Lord and take away the foreskins of your heart, ye men of Judah and inhabitants of Jerusalem: lest my fury come forth like fire, and burn that none can quench it, because of the evil of your doings." And in Ezekiel 36:25, 26 there is a reference to this same truth. It is true that here no specific reference is made to circumcision, but the significance of this passage is that the old dispensational sign of sprinkling, as it foreshadowed the sacrament of baptism, is mentioned here. "Then will I sprinkle clean water upon you, and ye shall be clean: from all your filthiness, and from all your idols, will I cleanse you. A new heart also will I give you, and a new spirit will I put within you: and I will take away the stony heart out of your flesh, and I will give you an heart of flesh."

From all this it is evident that circumcision was an Old Testament sign of inward cleansing from sin and spiritual renewal unto holiness. Now the Scriptures very clearly teach that baptism in the new dispensation has the same significance as circumcision did in the old. It also is an outward sign of inward cleansing and renewal. It too speaks of the taking away of the heart of sin and the creation of a new heart that is filled with the life of Christ.

Several texts can readily be quoted as proof of this. Romans 4:11-13 speaks of the righteousness which is by faith as being signified by circumcision. And while the text does not specifically mention baptism, it does point out that this righteousness which is by faith belongs to all in the new dispensation as well as in the old. "And he received the sign of circumcision, a seal of the righteousness of the faith which he had yet being uncircumcised: that he might be the father of all them that believe, though they be not circumcised; that righteousness might be imputed unto them also: and the father of circumcision to them who are not of the circumcision only, but who also walk in the steps of that faith of our father Abraham, which he had yet being uncircumcised. For the promise, that he should be the heir of the world, was not to Abraham, or to his seed, through the law, but through the righteousness of faith."

That this righteousness of faith is signified in baptism the apostle explains in detail in Romans 6:3-11. We will quote only the first part. "Know ye not that so many of us as were baptized into Jesus Christ were baptized into his death? Therefore we are buried with him by baptism into death: that like as Christ was raised up from the dead by the glory of the Father, even so we also should walk in newness of life. For if we have been planted together in the likeness of his death, we shall be also in the likeness of his resurrection: knowing this, that our old man is crucified with him, that the body of sin might be destroyed, that henceforth we should not serve sin. For he that is dead is freed from sin."

Peter also speaks of this truth in his first epistle, chapter 3:18-22, when he speaks of baptism as not being the putting away of the filth of the body (as if the outward sprinkling cleansed outwardly the body), but as the answer of a good conscience towards God.

John the Baptist spoke also of his baptism as being a sign of inward renewal inasmuch as it was a baptism unto repentance and forgiveness of sins.

Always baptism signified the inward cleansing and renewal of the heart. It pointed to the righteousness which is by faith in Jesus Christ. It thus had the same essential significance as circumcision had in the dispensation of types and shadows.

And if all this is not enough, there is one passage in the Scriptures which literally speaks of the fact that baptism has taken the place of circumcision inasmuch as the outward sign of circumcision was fulfilled in the blood of the cross of Christ. This passage is Colossians 2:11, 12: "In whom also ye are circumcised with the circumcision made without hands, in putting off the body of the sins of the flesh by the circumcision of Christ: buried with him in baptism, wherein also ye are risen with him through the faith of the operation of God, who hath raised him from the dead."

In close connection with all this is the truth that the saints in the old dispensation were saved in the same way as we in the new. In Genesis 15:6 we read: "And he believed in the Lord; and he counted it to him for righteousness." While this passage is referred to more than once in the New Testament, Paul clearly connects it with the sign of circumcision in the whole of Romans 4. After quoting the passage in Genesis 15, Paul goes on to argue that Abraham our father was justified by faith and that circumcision was a sign of this: "And he received the sign of circumcision, a seal of the righteousness of the faith which he had yet being uncircumcised: that he might be the father of all them that believe, though they be not circumcised; that righteousness might be imputed unto them also: and the father of circumcision to them who are not of the circumcision only, but who also walk in the steps of that faith of our father Abraham, which he had being yet uncircumcised" (verses 11, 12). It is clear then that circumcision and baptism are both signs of the same salvation.

It cannot be denied then that baptism has taken the place of circumcision as the sign of the one covenant which God establishes with His people throughout all time. But if this is true, then also the command to circumcise children in the Old Testament is a command which holds for baptism in the New. If children belonged to the covenant in the old dispensation, they belong to that covenant in the new. If they had to bear the sign of that covenant in the old dispensation, they have to bear it also in the new.

3) The third line of proof for baptism of infants is the fact that God, when He established His covenant with Abraham and gave him the sign of circumcision as a sign of that covenant, spoke emphatically of an *everlasting* covenant. We read in Genesis 17:7-14: "And I will establish my covenant between me and thee and thy seed after thee in their generations for an everlasting covenant, to be a God unto thee, and to thy seed after thee. And I will give unto thee, and to thy seed after thee, the land wherein thou art a stranger, all the land of Canaan, for an everlasting possession; and I will be their God. And God said unto Abraham, thou shalt keep my covenant therefore, thou, and thy seed after thee in their generations. This is my covenant, which ye shall keep, between me and you and thy seed after thee; every man child among you shall be circumcised. And ye shall circumcise the flesh of your foreskin; and it shall be a token of the covenant betwixt me and you. . . ." Here God specifically speaks of the fact that this glorious covenant which He established with Abraham, and in which He was Abraham's God, was not a covenant that some day would come to an end. It was an everlasting covenant that would endure throughout all time and on into eternity. Of this everlasting covenant circumcision was given as a sign. Yet it could not continue to be a sign of an *everlasting* covenant unless the sign of baptism came in its place and continues as a sign of that one unchangeable covenant of grace. But once

again, if the covenant in both the old and new dispensations is one covenant, and if there is one sign although that sign may differ in outward form, then also the children of believing parents must be baptized now even as the children of believing parents were once circumcised. This cannot be denied.

4) Finally, we call attention to the fact that although it is true that in the new dispensation there is no mention of the baptism of infants, this is with good reason. On the one hand, there is no mention of it because it is simply assumed that inasmuch as infants were to be circumcised in the old dispensation, and inasmuch as baptism had taken the place of circumcision, there was no need of any special mention. The early church simply took it for granted that this was the case. But on the other hand, we must also remember that the church was, during the time in which the New Testament Scriptures were written, in the process of breaking out of the narrow confines of national Israel and was spreading throughout all the known world. The gospel had become the catholic gospel gathering the catholic church, the people of God from all nations under heaven. Thus, new generations, new branches were being grafted into the old olive tree and brought into the family of God. For this reason the emphasis in the work of the apostles falls upon the preaching of the gospel to adults with the subsequent baptism of adults.

But it is also precisely for this reason that it is so important that the Scriptures again and again speak of "houses" that were baptized. We are well aware of the fact that Baptists claim that this cannot be interpreted to include children; but, after all, there is no reason why it should not include children. And it would be more than passing strange if all these families were childless or old people whose children had moved elsewhere. Paul baptized the household of Lydia in Philippi and the household of Stephanus in Corinth. And this was common practice. In Acts 16:31-34 we read: "And they said (to the Philippian jailor), Believe on the Lord Jesus Christ, and thou shalt be saved and thy house. And they spake unto him the word of the Lord, and to all that were in his house. And he took them the same hour of the night, and washed their stripes; and was baptized, he and all his, straightway. And when he had brought them into his house, he set meat before them, and rejoiced, believing in God with all his house."

This passage in the book of Acts is especially significant. The question quite naturally is: why could Paul promise salvation to the *house* of the jailer upon the faith of the jailer alone? The force of this question is evident when we remember that Paul knew nothing at this point of the jailer's family. They were all still in the prison. The only answer which can be given is that Paul knew that God saves *families.* God would save the family of the jailer, not the jailer alone. And finally this truth is emphatically stated by the apostle Peter in his stirring Pentecostal sermon: "For the promise is unto you, and to your children, and to all that are afar off, even as many as the Lord our God shall call" (Acts 2:39).

All this is illustrative of the fundamental truth that God establishes His covenant in the line of generations with parents and their children. Presently we shall discuss this more in detail; but suffice it now to say that this was true in the old dispensation when the covenant followed the lines of Adam-Seth-Enoch-Noah-Shem-Abraham-Isaac-Jacob-Judah-David-Solomon-Mary. But this is not altered in the least in this dispensation. The gospel spreads over the whole world and brings many new branches into the olive tree of old Israel; but it nevertheless remains a fact that *branches* are brought in, generations are gathered into the church and into God's covenant. Believers and their seed are saved. Children of believing parents as well as the parents themselves are included in God's salvation through Christ. They as well as adults must bear the sign of this covenant.

These matters have also their practical significance. Although we shall treat these matters more extensively a little later, it is important in this connection to notice that several truths follow if one is committed to the theory of adult baptism. The first result is that the salvation of infants, especially those who die in infancy, is denied, or at least ought to be denied in the interests of consistency. Some who deny infant baptism nevertheless teach that all children who die in infancy are saved and brought to heaven in spite of the fact that God does not save children until they gain maturity. But after all, without disputing the question of whether infants who die in infancy go to heaven, it ought to be obvious that there is no shred of evidence for this on the basis of the Baptists' position, nor are there any grounds whatsoever on which to base such a conviction. If our children are not included in the covenant until they become older, if they are not saved until years of maturity, there is no reason why we may suppose that this is altered when these same children die in infancy. Only when we believe, on the basis of God's Word, that God gathers His church from believers and their seed, can we also have a sure ground to base the conviction that our children taken from us early in life are also included in the covenant of grace. This is not to say that this personal and deeply emotional matter for parents who have lost a child must in itself form the basis for this truth. But it is rooted in the Scriptures and as such brings consolation to the hearts of the people of God.

In close connection with this, it is always a mystery how there can be people who maintain the principles of sovereign grace, but who deny the salvation of children. There are many who maintain the truths of sovereign predestination, of irresistible calling, of perseverance of the saints, and especially the truth of sovereign grace in the work of salvation, but who nevertheless deny that God can and does save children from infancy on and before they arrive at years of discretion. Cannot God, the sovereign God of all grace, save children if He saves without the cooperation of the will of man? Cannot God, Who alone works the work of salvation through the Spirit of Christ also apply the blessings of the cross to the hearts of children? This has indeed been the dilemma of Baptists. And exactly because of this, Baptists have as often as not departed from the truth of sovereign grace to walk the treacherous paths of Arminianism. And this is not difficult to understand. If it is true that God saves only those who come to years of maturity and believe in Christ, it is but a small jump to say that God saves these only because they in maturity fulfill the condition of faith. And from this position it is but a small jump to the position that God's grace is dependent upon the will of man.

But sovereign grace also makes possible the salvation of children, in the line of the covenant generations of believers. Children too are made heirs of salvation and citizens of the kingdom of heaven.

Finally, those who deny the need for baptism of children really lose all basis for covenant instruction. It is true, of course, that even those who deny this need for infants to be baptized, do teach their children the ways of the Lord. But if these children are not already saved in their infancy and youth, this instruction is really a considerable waste of time. Until our children are saved (unless one prefers the devious roads of Pelagianism and Arminianism and their denial of total depravity), they are without any saving grace. Until God brings the work of grace in their hearts, they are wholly without any good and inclined to all evil. But then also they cannot hear the words of the truth nor respond to covenant instruction; nor can that instruction of the truth do them any good. They are without ears to hear and without hearts to believe and to understand. We may perhaps teach them in the pious hope that when and if at last they are saved, they will recall some of the things they learned. But this is rather weak ground to serve as a basis for covenant instruction. How much more meaningful and important does not covenant instruction become when it is based on the truth that the seed of God's covenant are being instructed; that those who are taught are already the saved children of God from infancy on; that they do have ears to hear and hearts to understand and believe. Then there is good reason to devote our best efforts to see to it that our children are brought up in the fear of Jehovah which is the beginning of all wisdom; to teach them the way that they should go so that when they are old they will not depart from it.

Chapter 11

BAPTISM AND COVENANT CHILDREN

Our discussion of the covenant with Abraham up to this point has led us to the subject of this present chapter: Baptism and the children of the covenant. To this we now turn our attention.

Among those, primarily of the Reformed faith, who have held to the doctrine of infant baptism, there has been considerable discussion concerning the question why all the children of believing parents ought to be baptized. The Scriptures teach the baptism of infants of believers, but why does God command that the children of believers be baptized without exception? Why must all be baptized when it is obvious that not all of them are saved?

This question is precisely the point which is made by those who deny infant baptism. They argue that children who are not saved are given the mark of the covenant; that these children bear the sign and seal of incorporation into the covenant when in fact they are not among God's elect; and that this very fact argues in favor of believers' baptism. It is therefore, so they argue, a serious mistake to baptize anyone else but those who, when come to years of understanding, profess faith in Christ Jesus.

Before we present some answers to this question, answers which have been given over the years by those who have confessed the Reformed faith, it will have to be admitted that this problem is not really solved by those who wait until a child is grown and has confessed his faith before baptizing. They too will have to admit that they are never successful in baptizing only true children of God. Even though a person may perhaps confess for a time that he believes in Christ, history has proved that many such confessions are not sincere and from the heart but are merely outward confessions. Our Lord Himself teaches that this happens whenever the Word of the gospel is preached. In the so-called Parable of the Sower (Matthew 13:3-9, 18-23) He speaks of the seed that falls on hard-packed soil, on shallow earth, and among thorns. This the Lord later explains as being the effect of the Word on some who are never actually saved. They may seem to receive that seed of the Word of God for a time. They may even be moved by that Word in a superficial and emotional manner so that they appear to confess the truth. But when the heat of persecution comes and the trials and cares of life weigh upon them; or when the thorns and thistles of riches grow in them, they are quickly shown to lack that abiding faith in Christ that perseveres through every trial. They fall away and reveal that they never possessed true faith in Christ even though they confessed it. The apostle John refers to these when he writes: "They went out from us, but they were not of us; for if they had been of us, they would no doubt have continued with us but they went out, that they might be manifest that they were not all of us" (I John 2:19).

Thus the problem of baptizing only true believers is not solved by those who baptize mature children and adults who confess faith in Christ.

Yet among those who hold to infant baptism there are differences of opinion concerning the basis of infant baptism. And to this question we now turn.

There are some who attempt to solve this problem by teaching what is called "presupposed regeneration." This theory was first propounded by Dr. Abraham Kuyper, a Dutch theologian of the turn of the century. This view holds to the idea that it is the calling of parents and the church to baptize all children of believing parents because parents and the church must "presuppose" that all children born of believing parents are actually saved. While we know from the Scriptures and from experience that this is not true, we must nevertheless assume that it is true and that on the basis of this assumption all the children of believers ought to be baptized. Presupposing that these children are all, without exception, children of the covenant, they must all bear the sign and seal of the covenant.

This view is, however, not only contrary to the teaching of the Scriptures, but is also extremely dangerous. It is contrary to the Scriptures because the Scriptures emphatically teach that all the children born of believing parents are not saved. And experience shows this Scriptural teaching to be true.

Already this was true in the nation of Israel. From the earliest days of Israel's existence as a nation there were many wicked in the nation.

False seed, reprobate people constantly appeared and departed from the ways of Jehovah and turned to idols and the evils of the heathen nations. With many God was not well-pleased. In fact, the Scriptures speak of the people of God, the true children of the covenant as being a remnant, a minority, a small number, a hut in a cucumber patch. Usually the majority were wicked and only "seven thousand" did not bow the knee to Baal. God preserved only a handful in comparison with the large numbers who forsook the ways of Jehovah, a remnant according to the election of grace. Yet they were all circumcised.

The same was true in the new dispensation. The Scriptures insist that they are not all Israel that are of Israel (Romans 9:6); that many departed from the truth already in the days of the apostles and that this is always the experience of the church of Christ. Many who are born in covenant lines turn to the world and depart from the church. Although born of believing parents, they are not the elect of God. Although baptized, given covenant instruction, and brought up in the ways of Jehovah, they depart and walk with the world. In fact, the greatest grief of believing parents is exactly to see their own flesh and blood leave that which the parents have learned to love. How many sorrowing fathers and mothers have, in the anguish of their hearts, said, "I would rather carry them to the grave."

We may not "presuppose" what the Scriptures say is not true.

But this view is also dangerous from a practical viewpoint. Baptists have charged those who hold to infant baptism with harboring in the church those who are unregenerate and keeping in the church's fellowship the wicked who are instrumental in destroying the church. And it is certainly true that this charge can be justly levelled against those who hold to presupposed regeneration. The danger is very real that this view leads to a denial of the need for the exercise of the keys of the kingdom of heaven. If a child is baptized and presupposed to be regenerated and if such a child departs from the ways of the Lord, falls into the clutches of the devil and wanders in the paths of sin without confessing his sin, then Christ tells the church to cut such a member off from the body of Christ. But if such a one is "presupposed" to be regenerated, the danger very really exists that he will be tolerated in the church lest a regenerated member be excommunicated. Then, contrary to the command of Christ and at great spiritual danger to the church, such a one is given opportunity to spread his false doctrine or exert his worldly influence upon other members. Christian discipline is lost.

There are others who find another basis for the baptism of all children of believers. They too believe that infants ought to be baptized without exception but, facing this problem of the possibility of baptizing unbelieving and unregenerate children, they find the solution in another direction.

They teach that all the children of believing parents are actually included in God's covenant, baptized as members of that covenant, incorporated into it by the sacrament. As such, these children stand in a very favorable position. They are given a place in the church of Jesus Christ, blessed with the blessings of catechetical instruction, the preaching of the Word, covenant training in the home and Christian school, and a Christian environment in which to grow up. Besides, they have the revelation of God in the Scriptures, the knowledge of the truth which is given to them throughout the early and formative years of their life, and the preaching of the cross of Jesus Christ. They receive even more than this. At the moment of baptism God comes to them and gives them all the riches of the inheritance of the promise of salvation. God says to each child at the moment of baptism: "I will be your God. I will love you and bless you. I will bestow on you all of salvation. I will make you an heir of the blessings of the blood of My own Son: the forgiveness of sins, the adoption of sons, the inheritance of heaven. I will save you from death and hell and take you into My own house to dwell with Me forever." This promise comes through baptism to every single child who is baptized.

Of course, the question immediately arises how this can be true when in fact many children of believing parents grow up and forsake the church. How can they receive the promise of God that they will be saved when actually they never are? How can they receive the mark of baptism as a sign of incorporation into the covenant when they finally live and die outside the covenant?

Those who teach this view have a ready answer to these questions. They teach that it is only *objectively* true that these children receive the promises of God. But these promises are *not necessarily* realized *subjectively* in their hearts. They have these promises, so to speak, in their hand, but lack them as yet in their hearts. They have them in the form of objective promises, but the actual promises are not subjectively their possession.

For such children two things are possible. When these children come to years of understanding they may reject these promises and throw them away, which, if they do this, will make them liable to divine punishment and make it impossible for them to receive these promises in their hearts. Or they can make these promises their own by accepting them in faith and believing in Jesus Christ.

A very simple illustration, used in fact by some defenders of this view, will make this clear. The promise of God which every baptized child receives is like a check. This check is made out to the one baptized, is signed by God, and promises to pay to the one who receives it the amount of salvation. There are a number of things such a child can do when he grows older. He can take that check, frame it and hang it on the wall. But that check will never do him any good. He is comparable to the one in the church who boasts of his baptism, is proud of his place in the church, but never receives the gift of salvation in his heart. It is also possible for such a child at a later age to despise that check and throw it into the waste basket. Then too the check is worthless to him and he never really receives what the check promises. He is a covenant breaker, who despises God's covenant and tramples under foot the blood of the covenant. But it is also possible for such a child, when he comes to the age that he knows what he is doing, to endorse that check and cash it in the bank. Then he will surely receive the full value of the check. This is comparable to the man who makes the promise of God his own by accepting it by faith. He goes to the "bank" of heaven and cashes his check to obtain by faith the riches of the promise.

So, although all the children of the covenant receive the mark of the covenant and its promises, by no means all of them actually become the heirs of the salvation promised. Only those who accept God's promises by faith are saved.

This may appear, at first glance, to be a convenient explanation for a perplexing problem. Yet very serious and weighty objections can be brought against this view.

In the first place, the question must be asked whether or not this promise of God which is given to all the children at the time of baptism is sincerely given by God. Does God mean what He says when He promises salvation to a child who never accepts that promise? Does God actually want to save him? Is it God's intention and desire to save him? A little consideration of this will immediately show that this view is identical with what is called the free and well-meant offer of the gospel. It is a transfer of the offer of the gospel to the doctrine of the covenant. As such, it is subject to the same criticism as the well-meant offer. It puts conflict in God Who, on the one hand, wills to save all to whom the promise comes, but Who, on the other hand, wills, according to the decree of election, to save only some. Further, it presents God as being insincere in His promise. God really deceives. God promises that which He has no intention of giving. It is like my promising my children $10,000 when I know very well in my own heart that I have absolutely no intention of ever giving it to them. I mock my children. To ascribe such conduct to God is tantamount to blasphemy.

But if, on the other hand, God is sincere in His promise to all the children of the covenant, then another difficulty arises: if it is true that God does intend to give this wonderful gift of salvation to all who are baptized, why is it then that all these children are not really saved? Is the promise of God of none effect in these cases? Does God not succeed in accomplishing what He sincerely intends to do? Why is it then that all are not actually brought to salvation and glory?

The answer which is usually given to this question is that the promise as it is made through baptism is a *conditional* promise. God promises to every baptized child that He will save that child *if* that child believes and accepts the promise when he comes to years of understanding.

But several objections can be brought against this idea as well. For one thing, it makes of the covenant a bilateral pact or agreement subject to conditions, stipulations, obligations, and promises on both sides – a view which we have criticized in an earlier chapter. In the second place, the condition of faith must be fulfilled by man. The final decision rests with the child who received the conditional promise. He must himself finally decide whether or not he wishes to make the promise his own. God promises sincerely to give it all to him. But man is the final determining factor. God cannot accomplish what He promises until man agrees to accept it. Faith then becomes man's work and man determines his own final destination while God stands helplessly waiting. And we are once again back into the mire of God-dishonoring Arminianism.

It is objected by those who hold this view that, while indeed faith is the condition to the promise, God Himself fulfills this condition. In this way it is hoped the error of Arminianism can be escaped. But this will never do. It is a ploy that just will not work. The question still is: does God sincerely promise to all the children salvation? If He does, then that salvation must be available to them. I would be a monster of deceit if I would promise each of my children $10,000 if my total assets were nearer to $100. Would God promise a salvation which is not available? The only way to get around this is to teach that indeed Christ died for all, or at least, for all those to whom the promise is made, some of whom will eventually go to hell. But there is more. Can a conditional promise be truly a promise? The question is whether God promises *salvation.* If God promises salvation, then He also promises *faith.* And if He promises faith, faith is His gift. But then it cannot be a condition to that salvation, for then faith is a condition to faith. And one winds up in nonsense. The only solution to this problem is to make faith man's work. God will indeed promise and give salvation, but man must exercise faith. And this denies the sovereignty of grace.

But the Scriptures' teachings are quite different. The Scriptures teach that the promise of God's covenant is particular and unconditional. God's promise also accomplishes what God intends it to do. It is, after all, the promise of the living God. It is the oath which God swears by Himself that He will surely save His people to the very end. It is therefore only to the elect. The fact that all are baptized makes no difference. God's promise comes only to those whom God has chosen from all eternity. It comes promising the great blessings of the cross of Christ, but only to those for whom Christ died. And that promise is unconditional. It comes as God's Word of sovereign grace to His people. It comes without strings attached. It comes as God's great gift of grace and love to those whom He has determined to save.

While this is surely the general teaching of all the Scriptures, there are texts which explicitly state this. One such text is found in Acts

2:39: "For the promise is unto you, and to your children, and to all that are afar off, even as many as the Lord our God shall call." Now, for the first part of this text it may appear as if this promise of God is general to all those to whom Peter is speaking and to all their children. But Peter himself severely limits this by the last clause of the text. He emphatically states that this promise is not to all who hear, but only to those people and their children who are called by God. Thus the sovereign and efficacious calling of God is the divine limitation also of the heirs of the promise.

This same truth is taught by Paul in Romans 9:6-8 where the apostle exactly discusses who are "the children of the promise." He is facing the question of the rejection of Israel. Not all those who received the sign of circumcision were saved; in fact, the majority were lost. This is not, the apostle says, because the Word of God is of none effect. God never said He was going to save all Israel. He never promised such a thing. Further, "They are not all Israel, which are of Israel: neither, because they are the seed of Abraham, are they all children; but in Isaac shall thy seed be called. That is, they which are the children of the flesh, these are not the children of God; but the children of the promise are counted as seed." Thus the apostle argues that not all born in the line of the covenant, even though they receive the mark of circumcision, are the children of the promise. Both Ishmael and Isaac were circumcised. But both were not heirs of the promise. The promises were not made to both. Only "in Isaac shall thy seed be called."

The same truth may be argued from that beautiful text in Galatians 3:16 which we have had occasion to quote earlier. God makes His promise to Christ centrally, and only through Christ does God make His promise to man. But then this promise comes only to those men who belong to Christ according to the decree of election, and for whom Christ died. Not all the children who are born and baptized receive these promises; only those who are in Christ Jesus.

God's promise does not depend upon man or upon what he does. When God established His covenant with David, this very truth was made clear. We read of this in Psalm 89:28-35. God is speaking of His promise to give David a son, typically Solomon, but in reality Christ. He says to David: "My mercy will I keep for him for evermore, and my covenant shall stand fast with him. His seed also will I make to endure for ever, and his throne as the days of heaven. If his children forsake my law, and walk not in my judgments; if they break my statutes, and keep not my commandments; then will I visit their transgression with the rod, and their iniquity with stripes. Nevertheless my lovingkindness will I not utterly take from him, nor suffer my faithfulness to fail. My covenant will I not break, nor alter the thing that is gone out of my lips." How beautiful this is. God speaks of the fact that His law will be broken and His covenant violated by the disobedience of His people. And although He will chastise their iniquity with stripes, yet He will never take away His lovingkindness from His people nor break His covenant. God's covenant is maintained by the sovereign grace and power of God without any conditions whatsoever.

This view of a conditional promise to all baptized children will never stand the test of the Scriptures.

We must now face the question: why are all the children of the covenant to be baptized? We know that they are not all saved. We know that they are not all included in the covenant. Yet it is God's will that they all bear the mark of the covenant. What can be the reason for this?

Notice, our question is not: what is the basis for the baptism of infants? We have answered this question earlier. The question now is: why must *all* children born of believing parents be baptized when we know they are not all elect, but that among them are reprobate children?

To answer this question, we must understand that the Scriptures teach that God always deals with men *organically.* While this word "organically" is perhaps not too familiar a term, the meaning is clear enough and the idea taught throughout all the Scriptures.

Perhaps the best way to understand this term is to speak of it in terms of its difference from the word "individually." Although, e.g., God elects and reprobates *individuals* and although, in a certain sense, God deals also with men as individuals, this does not alter the fact that God's dealings with men are always to be considered organically. That is, and this is the meaning of the term, God always deals with men *in their relationships to their fellow men* in all the different relationships of life. God deals with men as they are a part of the societal units of life. God deals with men in their family relationships, their church relationships, their national and ethnic relationships, etc. But this is true not only as far as the relation between a man and his contemporaries is concerned, but also as far as the relation between a man and his forebears and successors is concerned. God's dealings with men in all these relationships are dealings in the moral and ethical spheres of life, as a man stands above all in relation to God. God looks at a man, not only as an individual, but also as a part of a whole unit of society.

This is a very important doctrine of Holy Writ, one that we ignore only with the gravest of consequences, although it is not often recognized. In fact, it can be said that one of the chief errors of all Pelagianism and Arminianism is precisely their refusal to reckon with this truth. And, if we may interject this for a moment, the denial of this fundamental truth leads to a host of very serious errors in the doctrine and life of churches which have fallen into the error of Arminianism. Arminianism is wholly individualistic. It denies out of hand the fundamental truth that God deals with men and judges them also in the relationships in which they stand to their fellow men.

This is true in the whole of our life. We may briefly illustrate this with a few examples. In World War II, it was quite possible that not all the citizens of Germany agreed with Hitler in his expansionist policies and his determination to subject all of Europe to his rule. If they had had a vote in the matter, they would have refused to go along with him. But they were a part of the nation, and they, as a part of the nation, had to suffer the terrible calamities of the entire nation. Their sons were called into service and perhaps killed on the battlefield. Their homes were bombed and their lives destroyed by the ravages of war. The hardships and sufferings which came upon the people did not leave the objectors to the war unscathed. Because they were Germans, all the grievous horrors of the war were visited upon them. The same is true of a home where the father is a drunkard. Perhaps this man's wife and children are not only opposed to drunkenness and consider it a sin, but do all they can to fight against this great evil. Nevertheless, they are a part of the family unit, and the sin of the father has its consequences in their own lives. Anyone knows how a family suffers even though the wife and children are themselves innocent of this sin.

While these are but illustrations of what we mean, the same fundamental truth holds for God's dealings with men throughout history. God deals, e.g., with the entire human race in Adam. Adam was created by God, as we noticed in Chapter II, as the organic and legal head of the entire human race. As the organic head from whom the whole human race came forth, he was also the federal head. Adam stood in Paradise as the representative of all men. All men incurred the guilt of Adam's transgression and all men are born in depravity because of the corruption of Adam's nature. We enter the world depraved and wholly wicked because we are guilty before God for what Adam did. Someone might say: "How can God make me guilty for what Adam did? I was not even there. I had nothing to say about whether or not Adam should eat of the forbidden tree." All this makes no difference whatsoever; God judges all men to be guilty and punishes them with total corruption of nature because of this.

The Arminian denies this. But it will never do to complain that this is unjust of God. It will never do to raise objections. The fact is that it is true. God deals with men in their relationships with each other; and God is just and right in all He does.

This principle is followed throughout the Scriptures. God assures Israel in the law that He will visit the iniquities of the fathers upon the children unto the third and fourth generation of them that hate Him. When Israel, through unbelief, refused to enter into the promised land, the entire nation was punished and forced to wander forty years in the bleak and barren wilderness where an entire generation died. Were there not those in Israel who wanted to enter the promised land? Of course. Moses, Joshua, and Caleb, to mention a few. But God dealt with the nation as a whole. The result was that the entire nation was kept from Canaan for forty long years.

Nor did this change during the rest of Israel's history. When the nation departed from the ways of Jehovah, God sent upon them every form of pestilence and trouble. Their fields did not produce their increase; heathen nations came against them, and they fell in battle. At last they were taken to a foreign land where they could only hang their harps upon the willows, for they could not sing the songs of Zion in a strange land. There were faithful people of God also in this number; but the sins of the nation brought the entire people into captivity.

When Israel entered Canaan and fought against Ai, the armies of

Israel were defeated in battle and some of the soldiers were slain. The reason for this was the sin of Achan, who had taken of the forbidden treasures of Jericho. It is striking that no one in Israel even knew of this sin; but God punished the whole nation because of it. In fact, when Joshua in anguish inquires of the Lord as to the reason for this crushing defeat, the Lord tells him, "Israel hath sinned, and they have transgressed my covenant which I commanded them: for they have taken of the accursed thing, and have also stolen, and dissembled also, and they have put it even among their own stuff" (Joshua 7:11). In fact, the chapter begins with the words, "But the children of Israel committed a trespass in the accursed thing. . . . And the anger of the Lord was kindled against Israel." How could this be? The only answer was that the sin of one man, unknown to the people, was charged to the whole nation. This same truth is repeatedly mentioned in the beautiful prayer of Daniel recorded in Daniel 9. We find Daniel on his knees in prayer confessing his sins. How strange. He was a godly and upright man who served his God faithfully. Yet throughout this confession of sin he uses the first personal pronoun: "And I prayed unto the Lord my God, and made my confession, and said, O Lord, the great and dreadful God, keeping the covenant and mercy to them that love him, and to them that keep his commandments; we have sinned, and have committed iniquity, and have done wickedly, and have rebelled, even by departing from thy precepts and from thy judgments. . ." (verses 4, 5). Daniel considered the sin of the nation, of which he had not been guilty, as his own.

This principle remains true in the new dispensation. When Jesus, during the week of passion, utters His terrible woes on the house of Israel, He speaks of the sins of the Pharisees as well as the sins of their fathers, all of which were related to one another: "Woe unto you, scribes and Pharisees, hypocrites! because ye build the tombs of the prophets, and garnish the sepulchres of the righteous, and say, If we had been in the days of our fathers, we would not have been partakers with them in the blood of the prophets. Wherefore ye be witnesses unto yourselves, that ye are the children of them which killed the prophets. Fill ye up then the measure of your fathers. Ye serpents, ye generation of vipers, how can ye escape the damnation of hell? Wherefore, behold, I send unto you prophets, and wise men, and scribes: and some of them ye shall kill and crucify, and some of them shall ye scourge in your synagogues, and persecute them from city to city: that upon you may come all the righteous blood shed upon the earth, from the blood of righteous Abel unto the blood of Zacharias son of Barachias, whom ye slew between the temple and the altar" (Matthew 23:29-35). It is evident from the text that the punishment which was presently to come upon the house of Israel was a punishment not only for the sins of those who lived in Jesus' day, but a punishment for all the sins of the whole nation from the days of Cain on.

Stephen says much the same thing in his powerful speech before the Sanhedrin: "Ye stiffnecked and uncircumcised in heart and ears, ye do always resist the Holy Ghost: as your fathers did, so do ye. Which of the prophets have not your fathers persecuted? and they have slain them which shewed before the coming of the Just One; of whom ye have been now the betrayers and murderers" (Acts 7:51, 52).

All of life is filled with this truth. A nation is responsible as a whole for what the nation, through its leaders, does. Any organization is a corporate community that bears corporate responsibility whether there be those who disagree or not. The sins of parents are often magnified in their children. The judgment of God comes upon children and children's children in the way of these sins. A family may leave the church of God and join itself to another church where the truth is not preached. The result is that the children and grandchildren drift farther from the truth than their parents ever thought possible.

So God deals with nations in the preaching of the gospel. Not all in any given nation hear the gospel. Yet the nation as a whole is judged on the basis of what they did with the gospel of Christ. Jesus speaks of Tyre and Sidon as corporate entities rising in judgment against the house of Israel. Always the conclusion is the same. God does not deal with men as individuals only, but also in the organic relations of life.

But this is not only true in the negative sense of God's judgments; this is also true in the positive sense of God's work of salvation. God saves in the line of continued generations. God deals with His people in the organic sense of the word, i.e., in covenant generations, with believers and their seed. It is true that there are both believers and unbelievers in the line of the covenant; the lines of election and reprobation run also through the covenant line, but this does not alter the fact that all who are born within the covenant must be treated in the same way.

This, too, is clearly taught in the Scriptures.

In Psalm 80 this truth lies at the very foundation of the entire plaintive cry of Asaph. "Thou has brought a vine out of Egypt: thou hast cast out the heathen, and planted it. Thou preparedst room before it, and didst cause it to take deep root, and it filled the land. The hills were covered with the shadow of it, and the boughs thereof were like goodly cedars. She sent out her boughs unto the sea, and her branches unto the river. Why hast thou then broken down her hedges, so that all they which pass by the way do pluck at her? The boar out of the wood doth waste it, and the wild beast of the field doth devour it. Return, we beseech thee, O God of hosts: look down from heaven, and behold, and visit this vine; and the vineyard which thy right hand hath planted, and the branch that thou madest strong for thyself" (verses 8-15). None can deny that the vine spoken of here is the whole nation of Israel from the time of her deliverance from Egypt until the time of the calamity which befell the nation during the days of Asaph. This nation, living over hundreds of years with both elect and reprobate in it, is here considered as one vine.

Isaiah uses the figure of a vineyard to describe the nation: "Now will I sing to my wellbeloved a song of my beloved touching his vineyard. My wellbeloved hath a vineyard in a very fruitful hill: and he fenced it, and gathered out the stones thereof, and planted it with the choicest vine, and built a tower in the midst of it, and also made a winepress therein: and he looked that it should bring forth grapes, and it brought forth wild grapes. And now, O inhabitants of Jerusalem, and men of Judah, judge, I pray you, betwixt me and my vineyard. What could have been done more to my vineyard, that I have not done in it? wherefore, when I looked that it should bring forth grapes, brought it forth wild grapes? And now go to; I will tell you what I will do to my vineyard: I will take away the hedge thereof, and it shall be eaten up; and break down the wall thereof, and it shall be trodden down: and I will lay it waste: it shall not be pruned, nor digged: but there shall come up briers and thorns: I will also command the clouds that they rain no rain upon it. For the vineyard of the Lord of hosts is the house of Israel, and the men of Judah his pleasant plant" (Isaiah 5:1-7).

It is impossible to understand a passage of this sort without taking it in the organic sense. The nation as a whole had departed from the ways of Jehovah, but this does not preclude the fact that there were always in that nation the faithful remnant according to the election of grace. God calls His vineyard His wellbeloved; but this does not mean that God loved every Israelite head for head. But the nation, as a nation, was God's beloved. Always within that nation were the reprobate shell, but also the elect kernel. But God deals with the entire nation from the viewpoint of that elect kernel, not the reprobate shell. They are Israel, God's people, His vineyard, His heritage, His wellbeloved. Not because all are the true Israel, but because the nation is considered in its organic unity.

These same figures are to be found in the New Testament. Paul speaks of the fact, e.g., that the whole nation of Israel was baptized in the cloud and in the Red Sea. Does this mean that also the reprobate who perished in the wilderness were baptized? Of course it does. They were born in the line of the covenant and had to have the sign of the covenant in their flesh. "Moreover, brethren, I would not that ye should be ignorant, how that all our fathers were under the cloud, and all passed through the sea; and were all baptized unto Moses in the cloud and in the sea; and did all eat the same spiritual meat; and did all drink the same spiritual drink; for they drank of that spiritual Rock that followed them: and that Rock was Christ. But with many of them God was not well pleased: for they were overthrown in the wilderness" (I Corinthians 10:1-5).

Jesus teaches this same truth when He speaks of His relation to His people as being that of a vine and its branches. "I am the true vine, and my Father is the husbandman. Every branch in me that beareth not fruit he taketh away: and every branch that beareth fruit, he purgeth it, that it may bring forth more fruit. Now ye are clean through the word which I have spoken unto you. Abide in me, and I in you. As the branch cannot bear fruit of itself, except it abide in the vine; no more can ye, except ye abide in me. I am the vine, ye are the branches: he that abideth in me, and I in him, the same bringeth forth much fruit: for without me ye can do nothing. If a man abide not in me, he is cast forth as a branch, and is withered; and men gather them, and cast them into the fire, and they are burned" (John 15:1-6).

It is obvious that Jesus looks at the church here from the organic point of view so that the generations of the covenant are considered as branches. And among these branches come branches that bear no fruit and that must therefore be cut off. They are, in a sense, "in Christ," although only because they are born in the line of the covenant from believing parents. But because they bear no fruit they must be pruned from the vine through Christian discipline. Yet they grow in the vine and are said to be a part of the vine. The whole number of the branches, including the dead branches, is called a vine. But the vine is not viewed from the viewpoint of the dead branches, even though they are there, but are emphatically a vine. So it is true of the church. The church is the gathering of believers and their seed. Within that church are elect and reprobate. But it is God's church, because the church is not spoken of from the viewpoint of the reprobate element, but from the viewpoint of the elect. The presence of reprobate does not alter this in the least.

Paul uses the same figure in Romans 11 when he speaks of the church of the old and new dispensation as one olive tree. The old olive tree is the nation of Israel. But when the nation rejected Christ, these branches were cut out of the tree, and the Gentiles (branches from a wild olive tree) were grafted in. This one olive tree is the one church of Christ in both dispensations.

We speak the same language in connection with certain phenomena of the Scriptures. We may, e.g., work in an orchard. In this orchard are many trees with branches that for one reason or another have to be pruned off. We do not speak of these trees from the viewpoint of the branches that are cut off. We know very well that they are worthless to the tree; that, in fact, the tree will grow better and produce more if these branches that hinder it are cut away. But these branches are not the tree itself. The tree is an apple tree or a cherry tree altogether apart from the fact that it contains worthless branches. So it is in the historical dispensation of God's covenant. Always, in its historical manifestation, there is the elect nucleus and the reprobate outer shell. But it is *God's* covenant; and the people in it, organically considered, are God's covenant people.

The same is true of a field of wheat. The farmer may have ever so many weeds in the field, but the field is emphatically a *wheat* field even if the weeds outnumber the wheat, for the farmer looks at his field from the viewpoint of its ultimate purpose; and that is the crop of wheat. He knows that the weeds will ultimately be destroyed and the wheat harvested. This is true even when he fertilizes the field, irrigates it, and does what is important for the wheat to grow. The same fertilizer and water, and the sunshine from heaven, cause the weeds to grow as well as the wheat. The farmer knows this, but it is his wheat field being cared for with a view to the harvest. So God sends the "rain and sunshine" of His Word and the sacraments upon His church. In that church are reprobate as well as elect, and they must, according to Jesus in the parable of the tares of the field, grow together until the harvest. But it is the *church*, for God looks at that church from the viewpoint of His own purpose. This very figure is found in the Scriptures in such passages as Isaiah 55:8-11 and Hebrews 6:4-8.

The Scriptures often use a slightly different, though basically identical figure when they speak of the wheat and the chaff. (Cf. such passages as Psalm 1:4 and Matthew 3:12.) In a field of wheat or corn stands the individual wheat or corn stalk. When finally the wheat or corn is ripe, only a small fraction of the entire plant is saved as of any use. In a wheat plant, the entire stalk, as well as the shell, is thrown away. In a corn stalk the stalk, the tassel, the husks, even the cob are thrown away. From a six or seven-foot high plant with large ears on it, only a small handful of corn is saved while the rest is discarded. The purpose of the entire plant is to bring forth that small handful of corn. So it is in God's church. The wicked are as the chaff which the wind blows away, while the elect as the wheat are gathered into the granaries. And this figure emphasizes too a truth so often taught in the Scriptures: the reprobate seed are for the purpose of the elect. They serve election as the chaff serves the wheat, according to the purpose of God. They are, in relation to the elect, like the scaffold to a building, which, when the building is completed, is torn down and discarded. But the wheat plant and the corn plant are one plant.

This truth is so important that the Scriptures can hardly be understood without taking it into account. How is it possible to read the prophets, with their alternating blessings and cursings, unless one understands that the prophets were speaking to the nation of Israel, with both seeds in it, organically considered? All the apostles addressed the churches to which they wrote in the same way. They were well aware of the fact that wicked men were present in the churches, but this did not keep them from addressing the churches as "saints in Christ Jesus." In fact these apostles (as in I Corinthians and Galatians) admonish the church to cut off the wicked members. But the church is looked at from its organic viewpoint as the one church of Christ. Jesus also does this in the letters which He commands John to write to the seven churches of Asia Minor. Some of these churches had very wicked members and very grave sins which the Lord castigates. But the church as a whole, organically considered, is addressed. And the admonitions and warnings, the promises and encouragements are addressed to the entire congregation.

Any minister of the gospel also does this same thing. He addresses his congregation as "Beloved in our Lord Jesus Christ." He knows, of course, that there are in the church those who are not true children of God, who have never been regenerated. But he does grave injustice to the congregation if he fails to address them in any other way than as beloved in Christ. He considers his congregation from the point of view of the elect, as God does. To ignore this and to consider the congregation as a mixture or to address them from the viewpoint of the reprobate element among them would be a serious error. It would indeed distort his entire ministry and spoil the gospel of comfort and hope which he brings to God's people. He, as the prophets of old, speaks in the name of God: "Comfort ye, comfort ye my people, saith your God. Speak ye comfortably to Jerusalem, and cry unto her, that her warfare is accomplished, that her iniquity is pardoned" (Isaiah 40:1, 2).

And so all those who are born in the historical dispensation of the covenant are treated exactly alike. They must all receive the outward sign of the covenant in baptism. They must all come under the preaching of the gospel. They must all receive the privileges of belonging to the historical dispensation of the covenant. There is no difference in these outward things. God wills that so it should be.

This is not to deny that the reprobate receive this covenant only in an outward sense of the word, while the elect receive these promises in their hearts. Nor is this to deny the calling of the church to exercise the keys of the kingdom. But the fact remains that as long as the church is here upon earth, there are evil and apostate members in that church throughout all time. It may not and cannot be any different. It is only finally at the end of the world that all are brought to the shores of eternity and final separation is made between the wicked and the righteous.

Paul speaks in the first verses of Romans 9 of the casting away of the nation of Israel. He describes this nation as follows: "Who are Israelites; to whom pertaineth the adoption, and the glory, and the covenants, and the giving of the law, and the service of God, and the promises; whose are the fathers, and of whom as concerning the flesh Christ came, who is over all, God blessed forever. Amen" (verses 4, 5). But, when God cast away the nation of Israel, did He cast away His people? This is surely not true. For "they are not all Israel that are of Israel" (verse 6). And, "God hath not cast away his people which he foreknew. Even so then at this present time also there is a remnant according to the election of grace" (11:2a, 5). But the fact remains that the nation as a whole received the adoption, and the glory, and the covenant, and the giving of the law, and the service of God, and the promises. The reprobate shell shared in these things only outwardly because they were part of the organic unity of the nation.

This is the reason why all the children born in the line of the covenant are baptized. They are organically a part of the church. They belong to the historical development of God's covenant. They all receive the outward sign of the covenant and are brought up under the administration of the covenant.

But it must be clearly understood that God wills it this way. We might be inclined to conclude that this is merely a sad but necessary part of things. We might be inclined to wish it were otherwise, but that in the nature of the case it cannot be so. No, God wills this. God has His purpose in this. When the outward benefits of the administration of the covenant fall upon all who are born within the covenant, God uses those very outward benefits to accomplish His sovereign purpose. And that sovereign purpose is the salvation of His people and the damnation of the wicked. Just as the rain and sunshine fall upon wheat and weeds alike, causing both to grow and manifest themselves as they truly are, so these outward benefits of the covenant cause the elect and reprobate to grow and manifest themselves as they truly are. Their true nature becomes apparent. The sign of baptism, the preaching of the gospel, covenant instruction, all these benefits cause the reprobate seed to grow in hatred and loathing of the covenant so that they manifest themselves as, by nature, weeds. But these same benefits, worked in the hearts of the true seed of the covenant by the gracious operations of the Holy Spirit, cause them to repent of sin, turn to God, love Him with all their hearts, and confess God's name in the midst of the world.

This is why these benefits can never be called "grace" as the proponents of common grace would have it. God accomplishes His purpose sovereignly, and the very benefits which the wicked receive work towards their greater judgment and condemnation. After all, it will be more tolerable in the day of judgment for Sodom and Gomorrah than for Chorazin and Bethsaida (Matthew 11:21, 22) because the former never heard the preaching of Jesus while the latter saw all His wonderful works.

The sacraments operate according to the purpose of God in the same way as the preaching, to which preaching the sacraments are inseparably connected. Just as the preaching has a twofold effect, to save and to harden (See II Corinthians 2:14-17.), so also the sacraments accomplish this twofold sovereign purpose of God.

It must be understood, however, that in the new dispensation, when the church becomes truly a catholic church, these covenant lines are gathered from every nation and tribe and tongue. While some generations are being constantly cut out of the covenant line through apostasy and unfaithfulness, new generations are being brought in. As the gospel comes to a new nation where that gospel has never been preached before, God saves, not only individuals, but new generations who are grafted into the old olive tree: believers and their seed.

The historical line of the covenant can be compared to a mighty river. In the Old Testament, that river ran through the nation of Israel exclusively. But in the new dispensation that covenant line runs through every nation, tribe, and tongue. Throughout the course of its pathway through history, it is always one river, just as the Mississippi River is one river from its source in Minnesota to its mouth in Louisiana at the Gulf. But as that river progresses southward, much of the water in that river never gets to the mouth. It is taken out through evaporation, through pumping out of the river, through water being absorbed in the ground and through water being caught in eddies. At the same time, water is constantly being added to that river through creeks and streams, rain, and other rivers. When the Missouri River reaches the Mississippi, it is absorbed in the Mississippi and is no longer the Missouri. The Mississippi remains, throughout, one river, called by that name. So the covenant runs through all history. Many born within that covenant and swept along for a time are not really a part of it and are drawn out along its course. But new generations are constantly being added – not individuals, but believers and their seed. Always it is the one covenant of God. And it is finally only the elect, the true seed of the covenant who are brought to its final destination, the glory of God's everlasting covenant of grace in heaven.

And so not only must infants be baptized according to the Scriptures, but all the infants of believers must be baptized. This is the teaching of the Scriptures throughout, and this is the truth of baptism as a sign of God's covenant.

Chapter 12

THE COVENANT AND PREDESTINATION

In the preface to this book we made the point that from the beginning of the development of covenant theology at the time of the Protestant Reformation until today covenant theologians were caught in a kind of tension between the truth concerning the covenant and the truth of predestination. This was due, in large measure, to the fact that most covenant theologians considered the covenant as some kind of agreement between God and man, or between God and His people. Because the covenant was defined in terms of an agreement, no unity and harmony between the covenant and sovereign predestination could be found. This is not strange. Just as soon as the covenant is defined in terms of an agreement, man has a role, however small, in the establishment and continuation of the covenant: he must agree to the provisions of the covenant before that covenant can be in force; and he must continue to maintain certain stipulations to make that covenant a continuing reality. Thus a covenant which is an agreement is, of necessity, a conditional covenant. It depends upon certain conditions which man must fulfill.

It is true, as every one knows, that those who wished to remain Reformed in their conception of the covenant insisted that God fulfills all the conditions by His work of grace in the hearts of His people. But this insistence, as good as it may be, does not avoid the danger of giving some role to man in both the establishment of the covenant and in its continuation. And this in turn easily leads to various Arminian errors which hold man responsible in some measure for his salvation.

The result of this tension was that genuinely Reformed theologians such as Turretin, e.g., did not give to the covenant the prominent place in their theology that it ought to have. In the interests of maintaining the sovereignty of grace, the truth of the covenant was somewhat neglected and did not form an integral part of the whole system of truth. On the other hand, those who emphasized strongly the truth concerning the covenant (were in the deepest sense of the word covenant theologians and proceeded in their treatment of theology from the viewpoint of the covenant) could not consistently maintain nor harmonize the truth of sovereign predestination with their thought. The result was that they either failed to emphasize properly this truth or held this truth in tension with the truth of the covenant.

Added to this difficulty was the whole problem of the place of infants in the covenant. With this also covenant theologians struggled. It stands to reason that if the covenant is an agreement, no infant can have a place in that covenant because he cannot as yet enter into an agreement. This in turn raised the question of the baptism of infants, for baptism is a sign and seal of the covenant. Reformed theologians, therefore, found it difficult to maintain the baptism of infants and to define the place which they occupied in the covenant.

It is our contention that the Scriptures do not teach a covenant which is, in its nature, an agreement; but rather that the Scriptures emphasize the fact that the covenant is a *bond* of friendship and fellowship between God and His people in Christ in which God is the God of His people and His people are His sons and daughters. Proceeding from this central truth of the Scriptures, it is not difficult to see that the truth of sovereign predestination harmonizes beautifully with the truth of the covenant. God chooses from all eternity those who are His people. With them He sovereignly and graciously establishes His covenant by taking them into His own fellowship and becoming their friends. Within this view the question of the place of infants is also answered: infants as well as adults are comprehended in the covenant of grace.

The Scriptures very clearly teach this truth of sovereign predestination in relation to the covenant. We have a detailed description of this in the history of Jacob and Esau, the children of Isaac and Rebekah. This history is recorded for us in Genesis 25-28, and we urge our readers to read this history carefully before continuing with this chapter.

Although no single truth of the Scriptures has been attacked so consistently and bitterly as the truth of predestination, it has formed a part of the confession of the church almost from the beginning of her history. Already as early as the fifth century, Augustine developed and defended this truth over against the heresy of Pelagianism. In this he was followed by Luther, Calvin, and all the Reformers, and by those who have remained faithful to the Protestant Reformation.

This truth is not a mere corollary to the faith of the church, a rather unimportant and insignificant doctrine. The church has always maintained that sovereign predestination lies at the very heart of the Christian faith. And this is also the teaching of the Scriptures: "Nevertheless the foundation of God standeth sure, having this seal, The Lord knoweth them that are his" (II Timothy 2:19).

Yet in spite of this the times in which the church as a whole has consistently stood for this truth are few and far between. While there have always been those who maintained it, the church itself has been less than faithful. This is not only true of those churches who have unabashedly repudiated the principles of the Reformation; this is also true of those churches who have claimed to be heirs of the Reformation and have called themselves Calvinists. With deception they have smuggled into the church the heresies which undermine this doctrine and destroy a truth precious to the saints.

Although Augustine developed it and fought for it, his views were lost in the work righteousness of Roman Catholicism. Although Gottschalk passionately believed and defended it, he rotted in prison for his faith. Although all the Reformers taught it, the Arminians of the fifteenth and sixteenth centuries almost robbed the churches of it. Although the Synod of Dordt was a mighty victory in defense of it, not many years passed before these same Reformed churches began to listen to the siren calls of Arminianism once again. Arminius himself would undoubtedly have been surprised (and very pleased) if he could have known how successful his heresy would be in capturing the fancy of the church. And today Arminius has been almost completely victorious, for the truth is almost nowhere heard in all its purity.

Looking now at the question of predestination from the viewpoint of our past discussions, the question arises: if it is true that God saves His people in the line of continued generations, how is it to be explained that not all the children of believers are saved? That this is a fact, no one will deny. Already in the old dispensation this became evident. Adam and Eve brought forth not only Abel, but also Cain the murderer. Noah had three sons, but the covenant lines were continued, at least during the old dispensation, in only one: Shem. Abraham was the father of Isaac, the child of the promise, but he was no less the father of Ishmael. And Isaac himself and his wife Rebekah had twins: Jacob and Esau; but only Jacob was saved. Throughout the entire old dispensation this remained true. By no means all the children born in the historical lines of the covenant were saved. In fact, usually the larger number by far were not. Throughout Israel's history usually only a remnant were saved, so much so that Isaiah plaintively speaks of the church as a hut in a garden of cucumbers, a besieged city, a very small remnant; and Elijah was told by God that there were only 7,000 who had not bowed the knee to Baal.

The new dispensation is no different. Many children, born of believing parents, brought up in the ways of the covenant, nevertheless depart from the covenant and forsake the truth. They receive the sign of baptism, are instructed in God's Word, are under the preaching of the gospel, become thoroughly acquainted with the Scriptures; but they nevertheless despise all they have learned and turn their backs on the faith. They join the ranks of the enemies of the gospel and enter into a confederation with the wicked world.

What is the explanation for this? Is it due to the fact that, although God would save them, they despise the offers of grace? Is this to be explained by the fact that, although God earnestly sought to save them and even made strong overtures of grace to them, they resisted God's purpose? Was God unsuccessful in what He intended and desired to do? Nothing could be farther from the truth. God always accomplishes His purpose. And that purpose is to be found in the truth of sovereign predestination.

The relation between predestination and the covenant is most clearly set forth in the history of Esau and Jacob, sons of Isaac and Rebekah.

In this history it is almost as if God Himself did everything to emphasize the sovereignty of His own eternal choice. There were as few differences between Jacob and Esau as is possible between brothers. They were, for one thing, twins, conceived and born together. More than this, Esau was born before Jacob and was, by virtue of his birth, the heir of the birthright blessing. He, from a human and natural point of view, should have been the son of the promise. They both received the same upbringing, the same covenant education, the same environment of a God-fearing home. It is even true that from a natural point of view Esau was a much more likely candidate for the promise than Jacob. Esau was strong and robust, a man of the field, the favorite of his father, altogether a pleasant man to know. Jacob was shy and retiring, something of a mama's boy, with a streak of treachery and deceit in his make-up which he carried with him all his life. From every point of view, Esau was the logical choice for the honor of being the heir of the covenant promise.

Yet this was exactly not the case. Jacob was the man of God's choice while Esau was cut out of the covenant lines.

It was evidently about twenty years after Isaac and Rebekah were married that they sadly concluded that Rebekah was barren; the Lord withheld from her the joys of motherhood. This was a deep disappointment to these covenant parents and a reason for deep spiritual struggles. They knew that the Lord had purposed to continue His covenant line through them, that line which would culminate in Christ. Isaac, therefore, prayed to God that He would be pleased to give them children.

The Lord heard this prayer of His faithful servant, and Rebekah soon conceived. But something strange happened before she gave birth. She carried within her twins and they struggled (evidently in a noticeable way) within her womb. She interpreted this as some kind of sign sent from God and went to her God to inquire as to the meaning. The Lord told her: "Two nations are in thy womb, and two manner of people shall be separated from thy bowels; and the one people shall be stronger than the other people; and the elder shall serve the younger" (Genesis 25:23).

At the appointed time she gave birth to twins. But again, in the birth of these twins, the Lord sent a sign. Although Esau was born first, Jacob took hold of his brother's heel as he was born, evidently in an effort to escape first from the womb (Genesis 25:26).

These two signs pointed to a pattern which would determine the entire life of these twins. In order to understand this, we must understand what, in the Old Testament, was the significance of being the firstborn. Three distinct advantages belonged to the firstborn: 1) he was the heir to a double portion of all his father's possessions, so that he received twice as much as any other brother; 2) he received the covenant blessing which signified that he stood in the line which would some day bring forth Christ; 3) he was, by right of birth, the ruler over his brethren.

As a general rule, this birthright was reserved for the firstborn son. On certain occasions the Lord willed otherwise and pointed out to covenant parents that not the firstborn but another was to receive the birthright. This was later the case in the family of Jacob. In this family the birthright was divided, but the eldest son received no part of it at all. Reuben was denied the birthright because of his sin of incest (Genesis 49:3, 4). Levi and Simeon, the next two oldest boys, were denied the birthright because they had on their hands the blood of the men of Shechem (Genesis 49:5-7). The covenant blessing fell upon Judah, and from him Christ was born (Genesis 49:10). The double portion was given to Joseph, for he received two tribes in the land of Canaan [Ephraim and Manasseh] (Genesis 48:13-22).

The same was later true in the family of David. Not his oldest son received the birthright blessing, but Solomon, the son of Bathsheba who had formerly been the wife of Uriah the Hittite (I Kings 1:1-40).

God Himself departed sometimes from the normal pattern to show His people that He alone made sovereign choice of the firstborn, and that this choice was not dependent upon the circumstances of birth or upon any goodness found in the children themselves.

It is striking that because the whole idea of the birthright pointed ahead to Christ, He is called in the Scriptures the true Firstborn. He is the Firstborn from the viewpoint of the eternal purpose of God's counsel: "(God) hath delivered us from the power of darkness, and hath translated us into the kingdom of his dear Son: In whom we have redemption through his blood, even the forgiveness of sins: Who is the image of the invisible God, the firstborn of every creature: for by him were all things created, that are in heaven, and that are in earth, visible and invisible, whether they be thrones, or dominions, or principalities, or powers: all things were created by him, and for him: and he is before all things, and by him all things consist. And he is the head of the body, the church: who is the beginning, the firstborn from the dead; that in all things he might have the pre-eminence. For it pleased the Father that in him should all fullness dwell" (Colossians 1:13-19).

Christ as the Firstborn receives the covenant blessings of all salvation. He receives the position of being Lord over all His brethren, for He is exalted at the Father's right hand in heaven. And as the Firstborn of all His people, he bestows upon them the riches of the Father's possessions which are entrusted to Him. He is the fulfillment of all the firstborn in the time of types and shadows.

It was this birthright which was the occasion for the struggle in all the life of Jacob and Esau. Esau was the firstborn and had the natural right to the birthright. Isaac, because his faith was sometimes weak and because he personally liked Esau considerably better than Jacob (Genesis 25:28), was determined also that Esau should have this birthright blessing.

But Rebekah understood better. When she went to inquire of the Lord at the time the twins were struggling in her womb, she understood very well that the Lord meant (when He explained the sign) that not Esau but Jacob was to be the heir of the birthright blessing. And she determined that he should have it.

The faith of these saints of old was not as strong as it should have been. We are very much like them. They did not wait for the Lord to give this birthright blessing to Jacob in His own way and at His own time; instead, all their busy life was absorbed in plotting how they could wrest the birthright from Esau. Jacob tried once by buying it for a bowl of lentil soup (Genesis 25:29-34). But he learned that these blessings could not be purchased with money. Later, when it seemed that Isaac was intent on blessing Esau in spite of what God had said, Rebekah and Jacob formed a plan to deceive Isaac and gain the birthright by a clever strategem. Only when Jacob was finally blessed through this trickery did Isaac also confess that this was the way it was supposed to be. When he realized that he could no longer bless Esau, he concluded with words, wrung from his soul, "Yea, and he shall be blessed" (Genesis 27:33).

But even this did not secure for Jacob the birthright blessing entirely. He was forced to flee from his mother's home and live in the exile of Padan-aram for twenty years. Only when God Himself blessed him did he finally become the heir.

But the question is, why did God choose Jacob above Esau as the heir of the birthright blessing? Was it because Jacob had performed good works and Esau had not? This question is intensified when we remember that, although Esau surely showed his wickedness by despising the birthright, Jacob was equally wicked when he tried to gain it by trickery and deceit. But we must remember that, in spite of what happened during the early lives of these two boys, the decision had been made by God before either was born.

The Scriptures point us to the fact that God, in carrying out His eternal purpose, chose Jacob and not Esau. And, if you should ask, but why did God choose Jacob and not Esau, the answer is not to be found in the fact that one made himself worthy while the other did not, but rather in the simple statement of the Scriptures: God loved Jacob and hated Esau. Now was this love for Jacob and hatred for Esau based upon what each had done in the way of meriting such an attitude of God? The Scriptures tell us that the only answer is to be found in the inscrutable and sovereign purpose of God which He determined in His eternal counsel. It is the mystery of sovereign predestination.

Malachi, many years later, speaks of this astounding fact when in the first three verses of his prophecy he says, "The burden of the word of the Lord to Israel by Malachi. I have loved you, saith the Lord. Yet ye say, Wherein hast thou loved us? Was not (and this is the Lord speaking again and answering Israel's question) Esau Jacob's brother? saith the Lord: yet I loved Jacob, and I hated Esau, and laid his mountain and his heritage waste for the dragons of the wilderness." God explains His love for Israel, not in terms of what they deserved, but in terms of His sovereign purpose at the very beginning of Israel's history when He made sovereign distinction between Jacob and Esau.

Many years after Malachi, Paul refers back to the history of Jacob and Esau and quotes these words of the prophet Malachi in that astounding and profound ninth chapter of the book of Romans. Paul is speaking here of the reason for Israel's rejection as a nation. Why is it, Paul is asking, that the nation of Israel has been rejected? Has the word of God been of no effect? Is it perhaps because the purpose of God has been frustrated by Israel's wickedness in crucifying Christ, so that God could not do what He intended? Is it because Israel, by its sin, defeated what God Himself desired? This could hardly be the case. In fact, Paul says, it is all a manifestation of the sovereign purpose of God. And this purpose is the purpose of sovereign predestination. But, the apostle wants us to notice, even though the nation of Israel as a nation is rejected, and that according to sovereign reprobation, nevertheless, a remnant is saved according to sovereign election; while at the same time this sovereign election extends also to those chosen from among the Gentiles.

It never was God's purpose to save all the children born of believing parents. This was because, "they which are the children of the flesh, these are not the children of God: but the children of the promise are counted for the seed" (verse 8). And the children of the promise are determined, not on the basis of works, but by the decree of election, as was the case in the family of Isaac and Rebekah: "And not only this; but when Rebecca also had conceived by one, even by our father Isaac; (For the children being not yet born, neither having done any good or evil, that the purpose of God according to election might stand, not of works, but of him that calleth;) It was said unto her, The elder shall serve the younger. As it is written, Jacob have I loved, but Esau have I hated" (verses 10-13).

It is precisely at this point that Paul anticipates an objection on the part of his readers (an objection, by the way, which has been repeatedly raised by the enemies of sovereign predestination): "What shall we say then? Is there unrighteousness with God? God forbid" (verse 14). And that this objection is not valid, Paul says, is proved by what God said to Moses: "I will have mercy on whom I will have mercy, and I will have compassion on whom I will have compassion" (verse 15). God, not man, determines those who are to be the objects of His mercy. The conclusion is: "So then it is not of him that willeth, nor of him that runneth, but of God that sheweth mercy" (verse 16).

Let it clearly be understood that this sovereign determination to show mercy to whom He will also implies the sovereign choice to hate Esau, to refuse to show mercy unto whom He will; in fact, to harden those whom God chooses to harden. Pharaoh, Paul says, is a case in point: "For the Scripture saith unto Pharaoh, Even for this same purpose have I raised thee up, that I might shew my power in thee, and that my name might be declared throughout all the earth" (verse 17). So God chooses whom He will bless and God chooses whom He will harden: "Therefore hath he mercy on whom he will have mercy, and whom he will he hardeneth" (verse 18).

Here too the wicked have objections ready at hand, objections which charge God with unrighteousness. And Paul faces these objections head on: "Thou wilt say then unto me, Why doth he yet find fault? For who hath resisted his will? Nay but, O man, who art thou that repliest against God? Shall the thing formed say to him that formed it, Why hast thou made me thus? Hath not the potter power over the clay, of the same lump to make one vessel unto honour, and another unto dishonour?" (verses 19-21).

Always the choice belongs sovereignly to God. And this choice is His decree of sovereign predestination.

In order to understand the decree of predestination, we must remember that predestination is a decree in God's counsel. The Scriptures often speak of this counsel of God. We need to point only to a few texts to show how true this is. Asaph sings in Psalm 73:24: "Thou shalt guide me with thy counsel, and afterward take me to glory." Isaiah speaks the Word of God that came to him which says, "Remember the former things of old: for I am God, and there is none else: I am God, and there is none like me, declaring the end from the beginning, and from ancient times the things that are not yet done, saying, My counsel shall stand, and I will do all my good pleasure" (Isaiah 46:9, 10). Peter ascribes the crucifixion of Christ to the counsel of God when he says in his great Pentecostal sermon: "Him, being delivered by the determinate counsel and foreknowledge of God, ye have taken, and by wicked hands have crucified and slain" (Acts 2:25). Paul assures the elders of Ephesus that he was faithful in his preaching because he did "not shun to declare unto you all the counsel of God" (Acts 20:27). In writing to the Church of Ephesus, Paul does not hesitate to tell the saints that the deepest cause of their salvation is God's counsel: "In whom also we have obtained an inheritance, being predestinated according to the purpose of him who worketh all things after the counsel of his own will" (Ephesians 1:11). And the writer to the Hebrews connects the counsel of God with the promise of the covenant when he writes: "Wherein God, willing more abundantly to shew unto the heirs of the promise the immutability of his counsel, confirmed it by an oath: that by two immutable things, in which it was impossible for God to lie, we might have a strong consolation who have fled for refuge to lay hold upon the hope set before us" (Hebrews 6:17, 18).

There are several truths which the Scriptures reveal to us concerning the counsel of God which have a direct bearing on the decree of predestination. In the first place, God's counsel is His own living will. It is not a dead blueprint which is tucked away in the pigeonhole of some desk in heaven to be consulted on occasion. God is the living God, and His counsel, the Scriptures tell us, is His will. It is the living will of the living God.

For this reason, God's counsel is eternal. God Himself is eternal, and His will is also eternal. Thus, because His counsel is His will, His counsel is also eternal.

There are two truths implied in this. On the one hand, God always possessed His counsel. He was never without it. There was no moment, so to speak, when God was without His counsel. On the other hand, the eternity of God's counsel also means that it is not a part of or like our temporal history. It is not affected by the passage of time nor subject to change as is all that belongs to time.

Thus the eternity of God's counsel also implies its immutability. God's counsel is unchangeable. This stands to reason. If the counsel were a part of time and influenced by time, it would change. Time is change. Time as an ever-flowing stream bears all its sons away. They fly forgotten as a dream dies at the opening day. But God never changes. "For I am the Lord, I change not; therefore ye sons of Jacob are not consumed" (Malachi 3:6). God's counsel is not altered to suit the changing circumstances of history. It is not a flexible plan which can be adapted to what happens here upon earth. God does not incorporate additional decrees into His counsel because He discovers that things do not work out the way He had originally anticipated. God does not react to what happens in the world and to what man does.

Nor do even our prayers alter that counsel. There is a rather popular expression: "Prayer changes things." If this is to be interpreted to mean that our prayers alter God's sovereign will, then it is utterly false. One sometimes gets the impression that people think this is true. Prayer chains are organized, groups meet together to pray all night for something they earnestly desire; and it is hoped that the result will be that heaven is so bombarded with prayers that God is influenced by this perpetual praying to do other than He had originally intended. Prayer may and ought to change us so that, through prayer, we learn to bow in humble submission to God's will; but God's eternal purpose stands unchanged in the heavens.

Now all these things which are true of the counsel of God apply equally as well to the decree of predestination. God's determination to save His people in Christ, as well as His determination to reveal His justice through the just condemnation of the wicked is an eternal decree. It is not subject to change. In the passage quoted above from Romans 9 Paul emphatically asserts that before Jacob and Esau had done either good or bad, that the purpose of God according to election might stand, God said to Rebekah, "The elder shall serve the younger." Not only is God's sovereign decree not dependent in any respect upon the good or evil which men do, but it remains God's unchangeable decree which He determined and which is never subject to alteration. "There are many devices in a man's heart; nevertheless, the counsel of the Lord, that shall stand" (Proverbs 19:21).

Thus, also that counsel of God is sovereignly free. This means simply that God determined His counsel according to His own good pleasure. God chose to do all His counsel as it seemed good to Him. He neither needed nor took any advice from any one. He made His counsel, not after deliberation with others, but as it pleased Him. "For who hath known the mind of the Lord? or who hath been his counsellor? Or who hath first given to him, and it shall be recompensed unto him again? For of him, and through him, and to him, are all things; to whom be glory for ever. Amen" (Romans 11:34-36).

This too must be applied to the truth of predestination. Arminianism has always taught that the decree of election and reprobation was not sovereignly free, but was dependent upon what man did. God only elects people who are worthy of election because they believe in Christ and accept Him as their Savior. And (insofar as Arminians still teach reprobation, for most of them do not), God reprobates those who reject the gospel and thus make themselves worthy of being condemned. The Scriptures teach, however, that God is free in His sovereign and selective choice. He is free in His choice of election, and He is free in His sovereign determination of reprobation. All is according to God's sovereign good pleasure, for He has mercy on whom He will have mercy; and He hardens whom He will (Romans 9:18).

God's counsel is therefore also efficacious. That is, God's counsel is surely carried out in time. There is nothing that can prevent that from happening. It is surely true that this is implied in all we said, but it needs emphasis. Nothing can frustrate God's eternal purpose.

All shall infallibly come to pass. God's counsel is, after all, His own sovereign and unchangeable will. God wills and what He wills is also effected.

So also is this true of predestination. Election and reprobation are the one decree of God. Those who are elected shall surely be saved and brought to glory, and the counsel itself is the final cause of the salvation of God's people. The full number of the elect shall be rescued from sin and death. The elect body of Christ shall be gathered before the throne. No power on earth or in hell can prevent this. But the same is true of reprobation. They shall surely be cast away from God's presence as vessels of wrath to reveal God's justice. "My counsel shall stand; I shall do all my good pleasure" (Isaiah 46:10).

Finally, God's counsel is all-comprehensive. All that takes place in history is determined by the counsel of God. There is nothing that escapes this counsel or is not determined by it. The events not only on earth but also the events in heaven are determined by God. Not only this but also what transpires in hell is under the controlling direction of the Almighty Who has determined it all. Jesus speaks of the fact that even the hairs of our head are numbered and not one can fall to the ground without the will of our heavenly Father. Everything is but the historical realization of what God has eternally determined to do.

This too stands connected with predestination. The Scriptures are very clear on the point that everything which God determines to do is finally because all things must serve the salvation of the people of God. After all, "We know that all things (emphatically, *all things*) work together for good to them that love God, to them who are the called according to his purpose" (Romans 8:28).

We discuss this truth in some detail for various reasons. For one thing, this one truth of the Scriptures is perhaps the most violently attacked doctrine of all God's Word. It is attacked by vicious and slanderous charges made against it. It is denied by many who profess to be students of the Scriptures and who ought to know better. It is ignored and even deliberately avoided by men of "Reformed" convictions who claim to stand in the tradition of the Protestant Reformation – while they ignore the fact that every reformer, without exception, maintained it.

No doubt, in large part, the answer to this strange fact can be found in man's perpetual desire to ascribe some part of the work of salvation to himself. Arminianism and Pelagianism have always been plagues in the church. Ever and again attempts have been made to preserve some glory for man. Always trying to salvage some last remnant of his sinful pride, man has tried constantly to take from God that which rightly belongs to Him alone and to give it to himself. Predestination stands in the way of all this. If God sovereignly elects and reprobates, then the whole work of salvation belongs to God alone. There is no room left for man and his work. All that remains is to humble one's self before the face of almighty God.

So, after all, the question at issue is the question of whether or not we want a sovereign God. A sovereign God is the God of the Scriptures. He is the Lord of heaven and earth. He created all things and gives to every creature its existence from moment to moment. We cannot even breathe, but that the breath we have is a gift sovereignly bestowed. God does what it pleases Him to do with His own creatures who owe their life to Him. He does all things for the honor and glory of His own name. To no one must He give account. All He does is His sovereign prerogative.

The alternative is a god (an idol) who abandons his throne and turns his power over to man. He wants to save all men, but is helpless to save any. He makes salvation possible somehow, but stands helplessly by while man makes up his mind. He does not know who will be saved and who will not. It all depends upon the fickle and changeable choice of little man. This may be the kind of god you want; but to bow before him is to do the same as Israel and the heathen who bowed before idols of wood and stone which their own hands had fashioned.

There are certain other points which we must make before we leave this subject.

Election is the divine decree of God according to which He chooses His people in Christ Jesus to be the objects of His love and the heirs of everlasting life. He determines, according to His own good pleasure, who are His people and who shall be saved. This decree of election is not only a personal decree, according to which God chooses individual people; it is also a decree which elects one church, the organism of Christ's body of which He is the Head. There is no election apart from Christ. In fact, just as there is no church, no elect body apart from

Christ, there is no Christ apart from the election of the church. Christ and His church are one in the decree of election. Not only this, but God determined the whole way in which that church shall be saved. By means of election, God fixes in His immutable counsel the whole pathway of life with all its detailed circumstances as the means to prepare the elect for the place He has determined for them in His own everlasting kingdom. And from this decree, therefore, flow all the blessings of salvation. The rich inheritance which Peter calls an "inheritance incorruptible, and undefiled, and that fadeth not away" (I Peter 1:4), including all the rich and glorious blessings of salvation, is a mighty stream of grace that flows forth from the fountain of eternal election. Without election there are no blessings; because of this decree, all these blessings are the treasure of the saints.

To this decree reprobation belongs.

There have always been those who claim to be willing to accept the doctrine of election, but who insist that they want no part of reprobation. This is impossible. Election implies reprobation. To choose some means to reject others. To make some elect means that there are others who are reprobate. It cannot be any different.

This truth is taught also in the Scriptures. It is not only taught in that mighty ninth chapter of Romans, but elsewhere as well. In I Peter 2:4-8 Peter discusses the fact that the church can be compared to a temple in which all the elect are stones, with Christ as the chief Cornerstone. But there are those who stumble at the stone and fall into destruction: "But unto them which be disobedient, the stone which the builders disallowed, the same is made the head of the corner, and a stone of stumbling, and a rock of offence, even to them which stumble at the word, being disobedient: whereunto also they were appointed." This is clear language. Those who stumble at the stone through disobedience were appointed to this disobedience.

The same is clearly taught by our Lord in various places in the gospel according to John. When Jesus explains the unbelief of the wicked Jews, He finds the reason for this unbelief in God's decree of reprobation: "But ye believe not, because ye are not of my sheep, as I said unto you" (John 10:26). We must not turn this around as some would do and read the text as if it said: "Ye are not my sheep because ye believe not." This would simply mean that by unbelief the Jews made themselves unworthy of being the sheep of the Great Shepherd. But Jesus is emphatic. The deepest reason and explanation of the unbelief of the Jews is to be found in the fact that they are not His sheep. This same truth is set forth in John 12:37-41: "But though he had done so many mighty miracles before them, yet they believed not on him; that the saying of Esaias the prophet might be fulfilled, which he spake, Lord, who hath believed our report? and to whom hath the arm of the Lord been revealed? Therefore they could not believe, because that Esaias said again, He hath blinded their eyes and hardened their hearts; that they should not see with their eyes, nor understand with their heart, and be converted, and I should heal them. These things said Esaias, when he saw his glory, and spake of him." The wicked Jews *could not* believe. And the reason was what God had spoken through Isaiah, that God Himself would blind their eyes and harden their hearts.

The decree of reprobation is not easy to discuss. It deals with profound mysteries and we must not attempt to go beyond what the Scriptures teach. But it is clear that the Scriptures teach that reprobation is also the sovereign work of God. God is no less sovereign in this work than in any other of His works.

Yet at the same time it must be understood that reprobation is not accomplished in the same manner as election. We have already said, and this is the teaching of the Scriptures, that election is the fountain and cause of salvation. But we must not make the mistake of drawing a parallel between election and reprobation in this respect. Reprobation is not the cause of sin. This would make God the Author of sin, and this we may not do, at the peril of blasphemy.

On the other hand, however, it is not true either that sin and unbelief are the cause of reprobation. This is Arminianism which makes reprobation dependent upon the free will of man. A man does not become reprobate because he sins and persists in rejecting the gospel. He is eternally reprobate according to the decree of God.

We must and can maintain that God sovereignly reprobates; but that He accomplishes the decree of reprobation *in the way of* sin. The sin which a man commits is his own. He goes to hell, not because he is reprobate, but because he is a sinner. He sins willingly and deliberately. He sins because he chooses to sin, because he loves sin and seeks it. And even when at last he receives the just reward for all his sins, he must admit that he receives what is justly coming to him; that God has justly judged him and gives him what he deserves. God's decree of reprobation stands behind it all, but this does not alter the fact that God's decree does not force him to be a sinner nor compel him to sin against his will.

All this involves the whole question of the relation between God's sovereign decree and the sin of man. And the Scriptures in a multitude of places insist both that God is sovereign over sin, and that man remains responsible for his own deeds. The clearest expression of both these truths is found in the crucifixion of our Lord, of which Scripture says: "For of a truth against thy holy child Jesus, whom thou hast anointed, both Herod, and Pontius Pilate, with the Gentiles, and the people of Israel, were gathered together, for to do whatsoever thy hand and thy counsel determined before to be done" (Acts 4:27, 28). And with this we must be content.

Yet election and reprobation are one decree. And they are one decree because reprobation serves election. The reprobate are for the purpose of the elect. Their damnation serves the salvation of the people of God. They are the chaff which serve the wheat, but are burned with fire when their purpose is served and the wheat is gathered into the granary. They are the scaffolding to erect the temple of the church which, when the temple is completed, is torn down and destroyed. They are on this earth for the sake of those whom God loves. They must find a place in the inscrutable wisdom of God to serve redemption.

This truth, too, is taught in various places in the Scriptures, but perhaps nowhere as clearly as in Isaiah 45:1-4. God is speaking here of Cyrus, king of Persia, and it is interesting to notice that this prophecy was written many years before Cyrus was the means in God's hand to return Judah from captivity. "Thus saith the Lord to his anointed, to Cyrus, whose right hand I have holden, to subdue nations before him; and I will loose the loins of kings, to open before him the two leaved gates; and the gates shall not be shut; I will go before thee, and make the crooked places straight: I will break in pieces the gates of brass, and cut in sunder the bars of iron: and I will give thee the treasures of darkness, and the hidden riches of secret places, that thou mayest know that I, the Lord, which call thee by thy name, am the God of Israel.

For Jacob my servant's sake, and Israel mine elect, I have even called thee by thy name: I have surnamed thee, though thou hast not known me."

And surely this is implied in Romans 8:28 and I Corinthians 3:21-23 where Scripture expressly states that *all things* are for the elect's sake. How marvelously this was revealed in the cross when God used the wicked deeds of Herod, Pilate, and the Jews to accomplish salvation for the elect through the blood of atonement!

Although many objections have repeatedly been raised against this doctrine, it is interesting to note that these objections were raised already at the time of the apostle (See Romans 9.) and always arise out of man's reason. He who would humbly bow before the Scriptures can conclude only that the Scriptures teach these truths.

We must conclude with a few remarks.

This is the truth which stands so intimately connected with the truth of God's covenant. You will recall that we began our discussion by asking the question: why is it that not all the children born within covenant lines are saved? The answer to that question is that the lines of election and reprobation cut through covenant lines. God sovereignly determines who are the true seed of the covenant and who are not. This was emphatically the case with Jacob and Esau and it remains the truth for all time.

But it must be remembered that not only are there reprobate children born within the covenant line, but also that God has His elect in every nation and tribe and tongue. This is why the gospel must be preached to all creatures according to the command of Christ. It is sometimes said that the truth of predestination makes missionary work impossible. This is nonsense and utterly untrue. In fact, it is just because of this truth that missionary work can and must be done by the church. Arminianism is the view that makes missionary work ultimately impossible. It leaves the whole matter of salvation to man's will and choice. God wants to save all; but the simple fact of the matter is that throughout the history of the world, there have been countless millions who never had a "chance" to be saved, for they never heard the gospel. God did not make it possible for them to be saved even though He wanted to save them. What kind of nonsense is this? But the world can be compared with a large pile of trash in which are to be found many iron filings. The gospel, as it is preached by the church and as it goes forth under God's direction and control, is like a magnet which draws out of that pile of trash the iron filings of the elect and incorporates them into the church.

In other words, while there are generations of people who, though born in the covenant, are cut out by sovereign determination, there are others who are brought in through the preaching of the gospel. And then, through mission work, not just simply individuals are saved, but generations; for also on the mission field God gathers believers and their seed. This is why Paul tells the Philippian jailer: "Believe on the Lord Jesus Christ, and thou shalt be saved, and *thy house*." And in this way God gathers a universal church and brings them into His covenant.

It is sometimes said that the truth of sovereign predestination must not be preached. It is said that the hidden things belong to the Lord our God while the revealed things belong to us and our children. And this is interpreted to mean that predestination belongs to the hidden things of God. But this is a sad mutilation of the Scriptures. Why, if predestination belongs to the hidden things, is it written large on every page of the Scriptures? It is true that who are elect and who are not is not known to us. Luther was right when he said that in heaven we shall find many there whom we did not expect to find, and we shall find that many are not there whom we expected to meet beyond the grave. And we must not presume to judge. But the truth itself must be emphatically preached. For it is this truth which explains to us God's great and glorious works as He realizes the counsel of His will.

And it is exactly in the preaching of this truth that the believer finds his comfort. The truth of election is not a cold and lifeless doctrine, a theological "fine point" which one can take or leave at his pleasure. It is the living, warm, vibrant, pulsating confession of the church of Christ. It is the truth which forms the final basis of all their comfort and hope in the midst of the world. They are set about by all kinds of enemies, the devil, the world, and their own evil flesh, which constantly threaten them and seek their destruction. They know that they are wretched sinners, not deserving of the least of God's blessings. They know that they lack entirely any ability to save themselves or to protect themselves from the threatening hordes that could easily overwhelm them. Upon what basis then can they find comfort that will give them peace and hope in this life and for all time and eternity? It is upon the rock, the immutable rock of sovereign election. God has chosen them from all eternity. They are engraved on the palms of His hands and are ever before Him. All things work for their good, for they are called according to God's purpose. Nothing can separate them from the love of God in Christ Jesus. God will perfect that good work which He has begun in their hearts.

And if we should ask: why has God chosen me? There are so many others. I am no better than thousands who perish. Why me? The answer is God's sovereign good pleasure. And the doxology of praise that wells up within the heart of the humbled believer is: "Blessed be the God and Father of our Lord Jesus Christ, who hath blessed us with all spiritual blessings in heavenly places in Christ: according as he hath chosen us in him before the foundation of the world" (Ephesians 1:3, 4).

Chapter 13

THE COVENANT WITH ISRAEL – THE BONDAGE IN EGYPT

The basis for this discussion of the development of the covenant of grace in the old dispensation is found in the promise which God made to our first parents Adam and Eve immediately after the fall: "I will put enmity between thee and the woman, and between thy seed and her seed; it shall bruise thy head, and thou shalt bruise his heel" (Genesis 3:15).

This promise contains in principle all the truth of all the promises of God. Everything which God has determined to give to His church in Jesus Christ is contained in this one promise. It includes all of salvation in this life and in the life to come as that salvation is merited for the church in the cross of Jesus Christ.

Nevertheless, this was not all immediately clear to Adam and Eve, and so the history of the church in the old dispensation is a history of the unfolding of that promise so that the church could see more and more of the riches which God had prepared for His people in His grace. Each step of the way, as the church was led through its history, the Lord continued to make more light to shine on the promise, showing more clearly and in greater detail what this promise really meant.

There are two suppositions to this. In the first place, the history of the old dispensation was *revelatory*; i.e., the history itself revealed God's purpose with respect to the promise. As we have the infallible record of that revelation in the Scriptures, we speak of that history as "sacred history," because through it God spoke of His promise. In the second place, the revelation of God's promise in the Old Testament was all in the form of types and shadows. God spoke, not in the reality, which was to come with the new dispensation, but through pictures. We may compare the people in the Old Testament with children who learn through a picture book. God gave them this book filled with many beautiful and wonderful pictures: the flood, the rainbow, the Aaronitic priesthood, the tabernacle and temple, the altar of burnt offering, etc. At these pictures the church looked and gained some idea of the beauties of God's promise. But these things were all pictures, and however beautiful pictures may be, they are not the reality. It is one thing to see pictures of the Grand Canyon of the Colorado River; it is quite another thing to stand on its rim, smell the pine trees, see the colors, hear the distant rumble of the river far below and sense the awesome size of this magnificent work of God. The saints in the Old Testament "all died in faith, not having received the promises, but having seen them afar off, and were persuaded of them" (Hebrews 11:13). The patriarchs lived in the land of Canaan as pilgrims and strangers, but in that land they desired "a better country, that is, an heavenly" (Hebrews 11:16).

One more remark is in order before we begin our discussion of the nation of Israel. The events which we treat are only the major events in old dispensational history. Many other truths are recorded which we have not discussed. This must not be construed to mean that these other truths have no importance in the history of the promise of God. Each event recorded for us in Holy Writ shows some aspect of the truth of God's promise. For example, we have not even mentioned such important historical events as Abraham's sacrifice of Isaac, Jacob's flight to Padan-aram and his return to Canaan, his wrestling with the Angel of Jehovah at the Jabbok, and such like things. These events, too, have their place in the unfolding of the promises of God. But to discuss all the details, as interesting and important as they are, would require a commentary on the entire Old Testament. This is outside our purpose. We can only draw the general lines, and the rest must be left to individual study. But it must be remembered, as someone once said, "Wherever the artery of the Scriptures is cut, it flows with the blood of the Lamb."

To turn now to the history of Israel itself, you will recall that Jacob was the father of twelve sons, who became the twelve patriarchs of Israel and whose names were given to the twelve tribes. Joseph, a son of Rachel, was hated by his brothers because he was favored by his father. In a fit of jealous rage, these brothers sold Joseph as a slave into Egypt. In Egypt Joseph, after many trials, was raised to the highest position in the government under Pharaoh the king. In this position he was instrumental in preparing Egypt for the seven years of famine that came upon the land. But this famine was not only confined to Egypt; it extended also to Canaan where the family of Jacob lived. They had no food to eat.

All these things were a means to bring the entire family of Jacob to Egypt. This was what the Lord had already told Abraham would happen: "Know of a surety that thy seed shall be a stranger in a land that is not theirs, and shall serve them; and they shall afflict them four hundred years" (Genesis 15:13).

It then became evident that the Lord had a higher purpose in Joseph's sojourn in Egypt. The sovereign God overruled the jealousy of Joseph's brothers and caused their sin to work for the salvation of "the heirs of the promises." Joseph himself speaks of this when he tells his brothers after Jacob was dead, "But as for you, ye thought evil against me: but God meant it unto good, to bring to pass, as it is this day, to save much people alive" (Genesis 50:20).

All went well in Egypt while Joseph occupied this favored position in Pharaoh's court. Jacob died and was buried in the land of Canaan, but not before he had given the birthright blessing, the covenant blessing, to Judah: "Judah, thou art he whom thy brethren shall praise: thy hand shall be in the neck of thine enemies; thy father's children shall bow down before thee. . . . The sceptre shall not depart from Judah, nor a lawgiver from between his feet, until Shiloh come; and unto him shall the gathering of the people be" (Genesis 49:8, 10).

In fact, several of the kings that followed Pharaoh also treated the Hebrews with kindness and favor because they remembered all the good that Joseph had done for the land.

But there arose a king at last that no longer remembered these things; and he was deeply troubled by this strange people who inhabited the land of Goshen. They were a foreign lot; they were shepherds who were despised by the Egyptians; they were rapidly growing into a mighty people. A solution to this problem had to be found.

The solution that presented itself to Pharaoh was obviously to integrate these Israelites into the nation of Egypt. Through intermarriage the races could become mixed. The religions of the Egyptians and the Hebrews could be interwoven; their cultures intertwined; their lives united in such a way that the Hebrews would become a part of the nation of Egypt and add to its power.

But there was one serious obstacle to this plan: Israel, as a whole, would have nothing of all this. The Hebrews were peculiar in this way. They would permit no intermarriage. In fact, if one of their women married an Egyptian, he was ostracized from the nation unless he, through circumcision, the sign of the covenant, became a part of Israel. They would tolerate no suggestions to merge their culture and their religion with that of the Egyptians. The Hebrews worshipped Jehovah. They had a tradition handed down to them from their fathers which was the revelation of the promises of their God. They were commanded by God to remain a distinct people separate from all the peoples of the earth. Their strength and purity of faith lay in their isolation. So every attempt to integrate them with the Egyptian people failed.

This vexed Pharaoh, and in fact filled him with fear. He saw the nation of Israel rapidly increasing in size, and he considered the possibility of their joining with one of Egypt's enemies to drive the Egyptians out of the land.

Something had to be done. And if the Hebrews resisted all efforts towards integration, the only solution was to destroy them. This Pharaoh now proceeded to do by making them his slaves to work for him. When this plan failed also and the number of Israelites continued to increase, he tried various other means to kill all the male children that were born to the Hebrews. But Israel maintained its distinctiveness and resisted every effort to destroy them.

We will quote some relevant passages in this connection, for this harsh slavery forms an important part of our discussion.

"And the children of Israel were fruitful, and increased abundantly, and multiplied, and waxed exceeding mighty; and the land was filled with them. Now there arose up a new king over Egypt, which knew not Joseph. And he said unto his people, Behold, the people of the children of Israel are more and mightier than we: come on, let us deal wisely with them; lest they multiply, and it come to pass, that, when there falleth out any war, they join also unto our enemies, and fight against us, and so get them up out of the land. Therefore they did set over them taskmasters to afflict them with their burdens. And they built for Pharaoh treasure cities, Pithom and Raamses. But the more they afflicted them, the more they multiplied and grew. And they were grieved because of the children of Israel. And the Egyptians made the children of Israel to serve with rigour; and they made their lives bitter with hard bondage, in mortar, and in brick, and in all manner of service in the field: all their service, wherein they made them serve was with rigour. And the king of Egypt spake to the Hebrew midwives, of which the name of the one was Shiphrah, and the name of the other Puah: and he said, When ye do the office of a midwife to the Hebrew women, and see them upon the stools; if it be a son, then ye shall kill him; but if it be a daughter, then she shall live. But the midwives feared God, and did not as the king of Egypt commanded them, but saved the men children alive. . . . And Pharaoh charged all his people, saying, Every son that is born ye shall cast into the river, and every daughter ye shall save alive" (Exodus 1:7-17, 22).

This bondage grew worse as the years progressed. "And it came to pass in the process of time, that the king of Egypt died: and the children of Israel sighed by reason of the bondage, and they cried, and their cry came up unto God by reason of the bondage" (Exodus 2:23).

Even when the Lord was beginning to make preparations for the deliverance of His people, this bondage grew worse. Other kings followed the same policy: "And the king of Egypt said unto them, Wherefore do ye, Moses and Aaron, let the people from their works? Get you unto your burdens. And Pharaoh said, Behold, the people of the land now are many, and ye make them rest from their burdens. And Pharaoh commanded the same day the taskmasters of the people, and their officers, saying, Ye shall no more give the people straw to make brick, as heretofore: let them go and gather straw for themselves" (Exodus 5:4-7). But the number of bricks which they made had to remain the same.

All this severe bondage was necessary for the Lord's purpose. For it soon became evident that the Lord had a higher purpose in Israel's sojourn in the land of Egypt – a purpose that had considerable to do with the promises of God. "And God heard their groaning, and God remembered his covenant with Abraham, with Isaac, and with Jacob. And God looked upon the children of Israel, and God had respect unto them" (Exodus 2:24, 25). More light had to shine on the promise of God so that the true nature of that promise was made clearer. Through Israel's bondage, through the dark and gloomy and hopeless background of this bondage, Jehovah caused the light of His promise to shine in the glorious deliverance of His people.

During this time of suffering, Moses was born into the home of Amram and Jochebed, two pious saints of the tribe of Levi. His life was threatened so that the parents hid him in a small box made of bulrushes, which they placed in some of the backwaters of the Nile River. There Moses was found by Pharaoh's daughter, who adopted him as her own son. Forty years Moses spent in Pharaoh's court and forty more years in the wilderness watching the sheep of Jethro after he fled Egypt. But all this was preparation for Moses' work, for he had been appointed to be the leader of Israel and to deliver the people of God out of the house of bondage.

At the end of this eighty years God appeared to Moses in the wilderness: "And God spake unto Moses, and said unto him, I am the Lord: and I appeared unto Abraham, unto Isaac, and unto Jacob, by the name of God Almighty, but by my name JEHOVAH was I not known to them. And I have also established my covenant with them, to give them the land of Canaan, the land of their pilgrimage, wherein they were strangers. And I have also heard the groanings of the children of Israel, whom the Egyptians keep in bondage; and I have remembered my covenant. Wherefore say unto the children of Israel, I am the Lord, and I will bring you out from under the burdens of the Egyptians, and I will rid you out of their bondage, and I will redeem you with a stretched out arm, and with great judgments: and I will take you to me for a people, and I will be to you a God: and ye shall know that I am the Lord your God, which bringeth you out from under the burdens of the Egyptians. And I will bring you in unto the land, concerning the which I did swear to give it to Abraham, to Isaac, and to Jacob; and I will give it you for an heritage: I am the Lord" (Exodus 6:2-8). There are many aspects to this history with which we cannot deal. We cannot discuss the years that Moses spent in Pharaoh's court, years that climaxed in Moses' choice of faith when he "refused to be called the son of Pharaoh's daughter; choosing rather to suffer affliction with the people of God, than to enjoy the pleasures of sin for a season; esteeming the reproach of Christ greater riches than the treasures in Egypt: for he had respect unto the recompense of the reward" (Hebrews 11:24-26). We cannot make detailed mention of his flight from

Egypt when "by faith he forsook Egypt, not fearing the wrath of the king: for he endured, as seeing him who is invisible" (Hebrews 11:27). We cannot speak of the forty years he spent in the wilderness caring for the sheep of his father-in-law, Jethro, a period of time in which he was prepared spiritually for his calling. As interesting as it may be, we have not the space to discuss his calling by the Lord Who appeared to him in a flaming bush that was not consumed; of the command which came to him to return to Egypt and place the demand before Pharaoh to let Israel go. Even the ten plagues which God sent upon Egypt we must pass over lest we be carried too far away from the main point of this history.

The main thought in this entire narrative is to be found in the actual deliverance of Israel from the slavery of Egypt. The question which we have repeatedly faced and which we now face is: what new truth is God revealing with respect to His covenant in this miraculous deliverance of His people? What greater light is made to shine on that promise of God to establish His covenant with His people? The answer to this question we find in the truth that Egypt was a picture of the bondage of sin and deliverance from Egypt was a picture of salvation in Christ. This was new light which God revealed, something which had not previously been made clear. God was saying something new, something in addition to what He had already revealed, something He had not yet said. God was speaking concerning the reality of sin. He was introducing His people to ever greater wonders of this salvation that He had prepared for them. He was telling them that salvation was deliverance from sin – from sin which bound them in a terrible slavery.

Before we enter into this point in more detail, there is especially one point which needs some attention.

The first has to do with Pharaoh's refusal to let Israel leave the land of Egypt.

Previously we discussed, in connection with the history of Jacob and Esau, the sovereign work of God in the decree of predestination, a decree which includes both election and reprobation. In that connection, we made an emphatic point that God is also the sovereign God over sin.

In the case of Pharaoh, we have a very emphatic and clear illustration of this truth. It is true, of course, that Pharaoh refused to let the people of Israel go. He hardened his heart, adamantly refused to obey the Word of God, set himself against God's command, persisted in his evil determination to keep the Israelites as his slaves, and received the terrible punishments of God as a result of this sin.

But we are reminded throughout the narrative that God was sovereign over this sin of Pharaoh; that God hardened Pharaoh's heart; and that God was sovereignly executing His purpose in all this. The Scriptures are very clear on this point. Already before Moses went to Egypt, when he stood before that miraculous burning bush, the Lord stated that Pharaoh would refuse to let Israel leave the land: "And I am sure that the king of Egypt will not let you go, no, not by a mighty hand. And I will stretch out my hand, and smite Egypt with all my wonders which I will do in the midst thereof: and after that he will let you go" (Exodus 3:19, 20). Even more explicitly the Lord says to Moses a little later: "When thou goest to return unto Egypt, see that thou do all those wonders before Pharaoh, which I have put in thine hand: but I will harden his heart, that he shall not let the people go" (Exodus 4:21). Again the Lord repeats the same words when Moses is told to announce the first plague: "And I will harden Pharaoh's heart, and multiply my signs and wonders in the land of Egypt. But Pharaoh shall not hearken unto you, that I may lay my hand upon Egypt, and bring forth my armies, and my people the children of Israel, out of the land of Egypt with great judgments. And the Egyptians shall know that I am the Lord, when I stretch forth mine hand upon Egypt, and bring out the children of Israel from among them. . . . And he hardened Pharaoh's heart, that he hearkened not unto them; as the Lord had said" (Exodus 7:3-5, 13).

The meaning of these words is unmistakable. Although it is true that we also read repeatedly that Pharaoh hardened his heart, this does not alter in the least the fact that behind Pharaoh's sinful refusal stood the sovereign decree of God being sovereignly executed. For this reason we cannot accept the word of a well-known commentator, who in commenting on Romans 9:18 says: " 'Whom he wills he hardens' cannot mean that God hardens some of the wretched and lost in consequence of an absolute eternal decree. . . . The only hardening that is effected by God and which the Scriptures are acquainted with is judicial; the only objects of this hardening are men who have first hardened themselves against all God's mercy and have done that to such an extent that they are beyond the reach of mercy. . . .

"Ten times Exodus reports that Pharaoh hardened himself; then, only in consequence of this self-hardening, we read ten times that God hardened this self-hardened man. . . . The door of mercy is not shut at once on the self-hardened so that they crash into the locked door with a bang. *We* might rush to close it thus. God's mercy closes it gradually and is ready to open it wide again at the least show of repentance in answer to his mercy; and not until all the warnings of the gradually closing door are utterly in vain does the door sink regretfully into its lock" (R.D.H. Lenski, *Commentary on Romans, in loco*).

This exegesis is a misrepresentation of the text which speaks emphatically of the Lord hardening Pharaoh's heart *before* the command ever came to him through Moses. This is sheer evasion and the sophistry of synergism. The fact is that God hardened Pharaoh's heart. And this is exactly corroborated by the text in Romans 9: "For the scripture saith unto Pharaoh, Even for this same purpose have I raised thee up, that I might show my power in thee, and that my name might be declared throughout all the earth. Therefore hath he mercy on whom he will have mercy, and whom he will he hardeneth" (verses 17, 18). It is difficult to imagine how much plainer words can be. Very clearly God acted sovereignly throughout. And the purpose was, as the Lord told Moses, and as Paul points out, that the Lord might use Pharaoh to reveal His power. This was exactly what happened in the terrible judgments that came upon Pharaoh and the mighty deliverance by which God brought His people out of the bondage of Egypt.

But to return to the main idea in all this as far as God's covenant promises are concerned, the bondage of Egypt was typical of the bondage of sin in which we are born and from which God delivers us.

It is a sad fact that the word "sin" has all but passed from the theological vocabulary of the church. Today people are urged to have a positive self-image, to look at themselves with pride. They are told that a preoccupation with sin leads to a guilt-complex which can be harmful for their psychological health. They are urged to develop good thoughts about themselves and good feelings towards themselves. Or, if sin is at all discussed, it is described in terms of mere bad habits which one acquires because of bad influences in the environment, bad upbringing, or bad examples from one's peers.

This is the fruit of Arminianism which has corrupted so much of modern thinking. Arminianism plays down the importance of sin and wants to make room for the good in man, particularly his ability to contribute in some way to his salvation. Arminianism brings forth the wretched fruits of pride.

And this is appealing to man. To preach and teach that sin makes man thoroughly corrupted, ugly and repulsive, wholly depraved and incapable of doing any good, humbles man. He does not like this. He prefers to have ministers and teachers tell him that he is basically good; he likes to have others pat him on the back; he enjoys being told that he is not so bad as some would make him out to be.

But the Scriptures are very emphatic about the all-encompassing and totally-corrupting power of sin. In fact the Scriptures make it quite clear that there is not even any knowledge of salvation without first the knowledge of sin. The consciousness of sin always comes first. The awareness of our total depravity always precedes the awareness of salvation in Christ. Only when we understand and confess our utter hopelessness and helplessness can we also see the wonder of the cross. To say, "God be merciful to me, a sinner" must precede our confession: "I am righteous in Christ before God." Only when we first confess, "O wretched man that I am; who shall deliver me from the body of this death?" can we also say, "I thank God through Jesus Christ my Lord" (Romans 7:24).

Of this grim reality Egypt was a picture. In the land of Egypt, Israel was held in the cruel yoke of a heathen power. The nation was subjected to the bondage of its Egyptian masters. The Israelites were slaves of this foreign power, always owned by their masters who controlled their entire lives. They were literally and completely in the hands of those who held the whip over them. Working for their oppressors, they were constantly subjected to the cruel treatment of heartless masters. They were without any hope in themselves of deliverance.

It was God's will that it should be so. God had led their fathers into Egypt to demonstrate vividly this very truth. Egypt was the "house of bondage," the bondage of sin. God made this clear when He gave Israel His law which was introduced with the words, "I am the Lord thy God, which have brought thee out of the land of Egypt, out of the house of bondage" (Exodus 20:2, Deuteronomy 5:6).

How terrible and complete is the power of sin in our lives. It is a slavery far more awful than any physical slavery can ever be. An earthly master can hold only our bodies in his hand; sin holds our hearts, our minds, and wills, in its heavy chains. Sin we are bound to serve even while sin drags us deeper into suffering and at last into hell. From it there is no escape. It is a prison without doors, shackles without keys, a pit that opens only to hell. We cannot run away from it because we cannot run away from ourselves. No, worse, we do not want to run away from it, for we love this horrible monster which controls our lives. While it ruins us, kills us with its power, rules over us to destroy us, makes our existence unbearably wretched, and drags us to destruction, we grimly choose for it, clutch it to our hearts, cherish it as our dearest possession, and would not part with it for any price.

Sin is first of all a total corruption of our entire nature. When Adam sinned in Paradise, he was punished for this sin by God. This punishment consisted in spiritual death. Adam became guilty before God, and this guilt brought upon him the just sentence of a righteous God. The execution of this sentence is the total corruption of Adam's nature.

But all men are guilty in Adam. All men are responsible for Adam's sin. All men are guilty of eating of the forbidden tree. And because of this universal guilt, the same punishment which came upon Adam comes upon the whole human race. How clearly this is taught in the Scriptures. When David looks for the deepest reason for his sin of adultery and murder, he finds it in his corrupt nature that he received from his parents at the moment of his birth: "Behold, I was shapen in iniquity; and in sin did my mother conceive me" (Psalm 51:5). When Jesus tells the parable of the Pharisee and the publican, He speaks of the publican as crying out, "God be merciful to me a sinner" (Luke 18:13). The publican does not say, "Be merciful to me, for I have sinned." This is not the point. The point is that the publican sinned because he was a sinner, because his nature was a corrupt nature which made him a sinful man. This was the cause of his anguish and grief.

This is always the way it is with the people of God. Their sins trouble them deeply, and they hate their sins with an undying hatred. But the fact is that their sins are but the outward evidence of a corrupt nature within them. They cannot do anything else but sin. They cannot overcome their sins. They cannot escape from sin's power (as the proud Arminian alleges) because they are corrupt in their being. Deliverance must begin with their nature.

It is precisely here that those who hold to the Scriptures part ways with the Arminian. The Arminian finds sin only in the *act*; the Scriptures teach that it is a matter of the *nature.* It is not only that we sin sometimes, but that sin is the foul stream that proceeds from a nature dead in trespasses and sins.

The Scriptures teach this very clearly. The Word of God does not paint a very nice picture of us, surely not the rosy picture drawn by modern radio preachers. "The ox knoweth his owner, and the ass his master's crib: but Israel doth not know, my people doth not consider. A sinful nation, a people laden with iniquity, a seed of evildoers, children that are corrupters: they have forsaken the Lord, they have provoked the Holy One of Israel unto anger, they are gone away backward" (Isaiah 1:3, 4). Then more terrible yet: "From the sole of the foot even unto the head there is no soundness in it; but wounds, and bruises, and putrifying sores: they have not been closed, neither bound up, neither mollified with ointment" (1:6). A bit later this same prophet says, "But we are all as an unclean thing, and all our righteousnesses as filthy rags; and we all do fade as a leaf; and our iniquities, like the wind, have taken us away" (Isaiah 65:6). The apostle Paul, in quoting from the Psalms, says, "As it is written, There is none righteous, no, not one: there is none that understandeth, there is none that seeketh after God. They are all gone out of the way, they are together become unprofitable; there is none that doeth good, no, not one. Their throat is an open sepulchre; with their tongues they have used deceit; the poison of asps is under their lips: whose mouth is full of cursing and bitterness: their feet are swift to shed blood: destruction and misery are in their ways: and the way of peace have they not known: there is no fear of God before their eyes" (Romans 3:10-18). Job abhors himself and repents in dust and ashes (Job 42:6). Paul speaks frankly of the fact that we are "dead in trespasses and sins" (Ephesians 2:1).

The Scriptures teach that man is incapable of doing any good. All his works are evil continually. No matter what he does, it is wrong. Does he observe in some outward fashion the law of God so that perhaps he does not go around shooting at his neighbor? He really only does this for his own good, not for the love of God. And God says this is sin. Does he build hospitals, institutions of learning? It is also corrupt, for God demands truth within, and man does these things for his own honor and fame, that his name may live after him. Does he give his surplus food to the poor and attempt to feed the hungry in the world? It is wicked, for he forgets God in his pride. Does he advance with giant strides on the frontiers of science and subject the forces of creation to his use with powerful inventions? Yet he does this to establish a kingdom which stands in opposition to God. Does he seek peace on earth? God hates his efforts, for he wants peace without the blood of the cross. Does he develop mighty systems of philosophy? Even Augustine called all these works of the heathen "splendid vices."

Yet his deeds are only the outward expressions of a wicked and vile nature. He is conceived in iniquity. His heart is a foul fountain spewing out dirty waters of sin. His will is bound in the slavery of the cruel bondage of sin so that he cannot even will to do the good. His mind is darkness so that it is filled with the lie. He cannot do good because he is wicked throughout. All he wants in the world is sin. All he enjoys is enmity against God. He will not do good for anything; he cannot do good. And this is not the picture of a lowly man, a wretch and scoundrel on the lowest rung of the social ladder, a skid-row resident. This is the picture of every man wherever you find him in all this world.

This teaching is not popular. It is not man's own testimony of himself. He is always bragging about his own goodness. It is not what men like to say as they point you to all men's mighty deeds and works of love and charity. But it is God's verdict. And we must listen.

Preach this from the pulpit and no one will want to listen. Maintain this witness of God in the world and you will be laughed out of court. But what God says is what finally counts.

It is not first of all what man *does,* but what man *is.* What kind of a man is it that needs saving? Is he, after all, capable of some good? Then he can surely contribute also to his salvation. He can desire to be saved. He can seek after God. He can accept Christ. He can take the initiative in his own rescue.

But with this Arminainism we have to part company, an Arminianism which teaches that *how* a man is saved depends entirely upon *what kind of a person* man is. If he is less than a totally depraved sinner, he is saved, in some measure, by what he does. But if a man cannot even want to do good, he cannot do anything to save himself either. If he is trapped in the slavery of sin, a slavery so complete that even his will is bound to evil, then he is saved by a power other than his own. God must come with irresistible power to destroy all man's resistance. God must break down the doors of sin, loosen the fetters of sin, force His own way into man's heart, and throw sin out. He must work without man *wanting* to be saved or without man able to assist in any way. Only when once man is saved does he long for his salvation. He is not hungry for the Bread of life until God makes him hungry. He has no taste for the Waters of life until God creates this thirst in his soul. Man is a sinful fool. He is sinking in the quagmire of sin and he loves it. He is dancing along the road to hell and he sings as he goes. Only God can rescue him by sovereign grace.

One must see this all as reality for himself. He must see that he is nothing. He must confess what the Scriptures say that he may be brought very low. He must cry out for salvation from the bottom of a pit out of which he cannot climb.

Or to put it a little differently, when God saves His people, He does this in such a way that they know their sin before they know their salvation. Sin is so great that man cannot even see his sin without grace. He is a sinner and will not acknowledge it. He is so completely in sin's clutches that he cannot see himself as he is nor confess his unworthiness. To know that we are sinners and to confess this sin is also the fruit of God's work of grace. Only when God begins to save us can we see and confess that we are totally depraved. God leads His people in this way so that their first experience is always that of their great sin. Only then can they enjoy salvation. Mercy is revealed over against hopelessness. The light of salvation shines against the black background of total depravity. Love and grace that are impossibly great are shown to us when we know our own unworthiness. The way to the cross is the way of tears of sorrow and repentance. For only when we know our own great sin can we see the total need we have for salvation worked by God through the cross of our Lord Jesus Christ.

When I survey the wondrous cross
  On which the Prince of glory died;
My richest gain I count but loss
  And pour contempt on all my pride.

Or, to quote another well-known hymn:

Beneath the cross of Jesus my eyes at times can see
  The very dying form of One Who suffered there for me.
And from my smitten heart with tears two wonders I confess:
  The wonders of His sovereign love,
  And my own worthlessness.

All this was typically revealed in the bondage of Egypt. And it was revealed to Israel (and to us) that they and we might know that salvation is from God alone. To be brought into God's everlasting covenant of friendship and fellowship is by grace.

And when we come to know the great horror of our sins, then we can also know the great grace shown to us that we, unworthy sinners, are brought into the fellowship of the living God.

Chapter 14

THE COVENANT WITH ISRAEL – DELIVERANCE FROM EGYPT

Many attempts have been made to picture in story form the life of the Christian in the world. Perhaps the best known is John Bunyan's *Pilgrim's Progress.* Anyone who has read this Christian classic could not fail to be impressed with the many truths of the Christian's life which this author portrays in the journey of "Christian" to the gates of the Celestial City.

Yet we have in the Old Testament Scriptures a much more vivid and accurate description of the life of the child of God than any novelist can give us. In this description more than any other, we stand face to face with ourselves, in all our struggles and failures, with all our sins and daily need of forgiveness, with all our temptations and weaknesses, with all the abundant manifestations of the mercy of God toward us.

I refer to the history of the nation of Israel from the time they departed from the land of Egypt to the day they entered safely into the promised land of Canaan.

It may seem to some that this analogy is not correct, that it is hardly true that the life of the child of God is pictured here. But consider: 1) that the nation of Israel in the old dispensation was in fact the church of that time and a picture of the whole church of Jesus Christ (Acts 2:38); 2) that the land of Egypt was an Old Testament picture of the bondage of sin, while the land of Canaan, the land flowing with milk and honey, was a picture of heaven (Hebrews 3:11-19, 4:1-11, 11:9, 10, 13-16); 3) that the wilderness in which Israel wandered for so many years was a picture of the spiritual barrenness of life in this present world of sin and death, in which, as the Psalmist expresses it, "We wander in a desert land, where all the streams are dry;" 4) that Israel's repeated rebellions throughout this history become, in the New Testament, occasions to issue to the church strong warnings against unbelief and worldliness (I Corinthians 10:6-11, Hebrews 3); 5) that Israel's entrance into Canaan was a wonderful display of God's mercy, a mercy which God showed to them no more than He now shows to us when we arrive safely, in spite of our sins, in heaven.

Although we do not intend to enter into the details of all this fascinating and important history, some phases of it which speak especially of God's covenant we must treat.

Israel's deliverance from Egypt was a mighty work of God. By ten terrible plagues Egypt was destroyed. During that awful midnight when the Angel of death stalked the land of Egypt and killed all the firstborn of men and cattle, Israel was delivered. Yet they were spared the ravages of the Angel of death only because they were quietly celebrating the Passover Feast, protected by the blood of the lamb which they smeared on their doorposts.

It was the blood of the passover lamb that made division and separation between Israel and Egypt. The blood marked Israel as God's people, while it also signified that Egypt, as God's enemies, were to be destroyed. Precisely for this reason the blood became the power of Israel's deliverance.

It is not at all difficult to see the significance of this, for the blood of the lamb was but a picture of the blood of Calvary. And surely the blood of Calvary is the distinguishing mark between the church and the world throughout all time. Christ died for His people only, not for all men. And the mark of His own precious blood is placed upon His people to distinguish them from the world by its cleansing power.

The cross is therefore the power of salvation. Just as the blood of the lamb in Egypt signified the power by which Israel was separated and delivered from the Egyptians, so also is the blood of the true Lamb of God the power of the deliverance of the church. All their salvation is in the cross. The strength of the entire journey of the Christian pilgrim is to be found only in the atonement of Calvary. All of the journey, from its beginning through its long days to its final destination, is a journey which the believer can walk only because he is strengthened throughout by the blood of his Christ. Not the will of man sets man upon the road of salvation; not accepting Christ begins the journey to glory. The cross is the sole power of salvation. It is God reaching down through the cross by the Spirit of Christ that begins us on the road to heaven. We are born in sin, spiritually in the land of Egypt, the house of bondage. We are delivered through the blood of atonement. We are set on the path to the heavenly Canaan through the power of Christ's finished work.

Instead of leading Israel to Canaan by the most direct and shortest route, God led Israel through the way that led to the Red Sea, and thence to Mount Sinai, where Israel received the law.

You, who know something of Old Testament history, know also of the mighty deliverance of Israel through the Red Sea upon dry ground and the destruction of Pharaoh and his armies by the surging return of the waters. Paul speaks of this as being a sign of baptism. In I Corinthians 10:1, 2 he says, "Moreover, brethren, I would not that ye should be ignorant, how that all our fathers were under the cloud, and all passed through the sea; and were all baptized unto Moses in the cloud and in the sea."

While Paul's purpose here is to show that the sign of the covenant was administered to all who were born within the historical lines of the covenant (a point which we discussed earlier in this book), and that not all who received this sign of the covenant were in fact saved (I Corinthians 10:1-10), we want now to concentrate our attention upon the typical significance of this event.

Baptism in the Red Sea spoke the same language to Israel as the blood of the passover lamb. It pictured the blood of Christ which destroys the power of sin and delivers the church from this sin and guilt. This part of the pilgrim's sojourn was important for an understanding of Israel's place in the covenant. On the one side of the flood of the Red Sea stood the bondage of Egypt typically representing the bondage of sin. On the other side was the land of Canaan, the earthly picture of heaven. What made separation for the people of God was the water of the Red Sea which destroyed that power that formerly held them in bondage and which delivered them from their oppressors. And this water was typical, according to I Corinthians 10, of the water of baptism which is the New Testament symbol of the cleansing power of the blood of Christ which delivers us from sin and brings us to glory.

But deliverance from Egypt through the waters of the Red Sea led the nation to Sinai. Israel came to the mountain of the law.

We have no intention of entering into a long discussion of the law that came through the hand of Moses to Israel; nor of its significance for Israel, as important as that may be. We want only to make a few remarks about the relation between the law and the covenant of grace. We do this because there is considerable misunderstanding concerning the place of the law in Israel's life and in the life of the church. On the one hand, it is becoming increasingly common in our day to insist, within the context of post-millennialism, that the whole law of God is still in force in the new dispensation. Under the rather appealing name of "Theonomy" it is maintained that the observance of the whole law in this dispensation is the foundation for a society which shall emerge in our modern world in which Christianity shall be, at least for a time, triumphant.

On the other hand, it has been customary in the history of covenant theology to make a distinction between the law and the gospel. Those who have held to this position hold to the view that the law as given from Sinai was, in fact, a reiteration of the covenant of works, which was given by God to emphasize the utter failure of that old covenant established with Adam, and so to make room for the introduction of the covenant of grace. We have criticized earlier the conception commonly held of the covenant of works and have shown that this view is contrary to the Scriptures.

What then is the law? And what is its purpose?

Normally, the body of legislation given by God through Moses is divided into three parts: the civil law, the ceremonial law, and the moral law. While in a certain sense this distinction holds, we must never forget that the law is basically one body of legislation, and that its inner and organic union must be maintained. We may picture the entire body of Mosaic legislation as three concentric circles, the inner circle being the moral law which was embodied in the ten commandments, the next circle the ceremonial law, and the outside circle the civil law. But these three circles were organically related to each other. The moral law stood at the heart of the entire law of God and permeated all the other precepts of the law. It did this with its central command to love the Lord God with all one's heart and mind and soul and strength. No keeping of any part of the law, whether moral, ceremonial, or civil, was of any value without the keeping of that central precept. Further, the civil and ceremonial law were, on the one hand, the concrete embodiment of *how* Israel was, in a specific and concrete way, to love God; and on the other hand, the civil and ceremonial law marked Israel as God's own people, distinct from all the peoples of the earth, the one people in whose midst God chose to dwell in covenant fellowship.

Bearing these things in mind, we must remember that God never gave the law with the intent of teaching Israel a way of salvation. It is true that repeatedly the law said, "Do this and thou shalt live." But the implication of this command and its promise was not to prescribe a way of salvation that Israel might know the road to heaven. Rather, it was this command which connected the entire law, in the context which we described above, with the original creation ordinance which set before man his obligations as a creature, created by God, called to serve the purpose for which he had been created. God never nullifies the demands of His law. Whether the creature obeys or not makes not one particle of difference. God is God, righteous and just in all His ways. He always insists and must insist that man keep His law. He must, because He is God, maintain the just demands which He sets forth in His holy will for the creature. God did not give the law as signposts marking heaven's highway.

Paul describes the whole purpose of the law in Galatians 3:24: "Wherefore the law was our schoolmaster to bring us unto Christ, that we might be justified by faith." The law came to Israel with the demand that Israel keep it. This law put Israel in a schoolroom and became a very stern schoolmaster over them. It came to Israel as if they were a classroom of very disobedient children, as indeed they were. And the lessons the law thundered all the day long were: "Keep the law to do them." This law followed Israel in her whole life. It entered into their homes to tell them how to eat and drink, to live together as a family; how to build their homes and preserve them. It followed them into their fields and told them how to plow, how to sow seed, how to reap the harvest, what to do with the harvest. It dogged their footsteps in all their walk insisting on how they must dress, what they must do to preserve proper relationships with their fellow Israelites. It looked over their shoulders while they were teaching their children, while they were conversing and dealing with their fellow men, when they entered into their inner closets, when they went to the tabernacle or temple to worship their God. And always the law demanded perfect obedience and holiness in all of life.

But Israel could never keep that law. They could not even begin to keep it in its smallest parts. And when they failed, the law thundered its curses, beat them with its heavy blows and shouted its damnations at them. The law killed those who did not obey.

Why? Why did God send the law to do this? The answer is, of course, that the just demands of the law must always be met, for God will not lower the demands of His law just because man has made himself unable to keep them. If I run up a bill of one thousand dollars at the grocery store, I am obligated to pay that bill whether I have the money or not. But, more importantly, the law was also gospel. We must never lose sight of this. The law is the gospel, and the gospel is the law. It is not as if the law and the gospel sing two different songs in two different keys. They are one beautiful harmony of the one song of Moses and the Lamb. They do not war against one another at every turn; they walk hand in hand as the single truth of our Lord Jesus Christ.

The law, Paul says, was a schoolmaster to lead to Christ. The law with its harsh demands, with its shouted cursings, drove believing Israel to Christ. This was the lesson that Israel had to learn under the stern discipline of the law. They had to learn to flee to Christ, for only in the arms of Christ, beneath the shadow of the cross could they find escape from the heavy curses of the law. Thus, through the preaching of the law, God so worked His grace in the hearts of His elect that they, out of sheer necessity, in the consciousness of their own inability to keep the law, fled for a refuge to Christ.

This is because God had ordained that Christ was the fulfillment of the entire law. Christ alone could keep the moral law. He was the One Who alone was able to love the Lord His God with all His heart and mind and soul and strength. And Christ kept that law, not only as He went about preaching and teaching and working mighty miracles, but He also kept that law in the depths of hell when on the tree of the cross He bore the full weight of the wrath of God. When He suffered and died, He bore all the sins and guilt of all His people. He assumed responsibility for the perfect keeping of the law and for all the transgressions of it which made His people worthy only of hell. When the curses of the law came upon Him as the substitute for His people, all these curses drove Him into the depths of hell where the billows of

God's wrath overwhelmed Him. But even then, in the depths of hell, He loved the Lord His God with all His heart and mind and soul and strength. In the fury of the storms of hell, he still said, "I come to do Thy will, O God. I love Thee still, oh My God."

But while in this way fulfilling the whole moral law, He also fulfilled the entire ceremonial law. It all pointed ahead to and spoke eloquently of Christ to believing Israel. The sacrifices of bulls and goats, the feast days, the solemn assemblies, the ceremonies of purification, the whole organized and rightly prescribed worship of God in the tabernacle and temple spoke of Him Who had come as the fulfillment of it all. The blood of bulls and goats could not take away sin; but in them all believing Israel saw the hope of the promise, the coming of Christ. And thus they too were all fulfilled in the coming of Christ.

So it was also true of the so-called civil body of legislation. It must be remembered that this law too marked Israel as the people of God and set her apart from all the other nations who were, in the old dispensation, outside God's church. They were, through all these laws, shown how, in every part of their lives, as a theocracy, they were to love their God. But, as Paul makes clear, this was necessary in the infancy of the church before that time when it reached spiritual maturity (Galatians 3:22-4:17). Just as a small child in the home needs laws to govern his life because in his immaturity he cannot discern properly between right and wrong, so the church, in her infancy and childhood, needed all these laws. But just as a child, when come to maturity, is no longer under tutors and governors (Galatians 4:1, 2), so the church, when come to maturity through the Spirit of Christ in her heart (Galatians 4:6), now stands in the liberty wherewith Christ has made her free. These laws, too, pass away with adulthood. Only the general principles remain, principles which express the will of God, but which no longer tie the church down in the bondage of untold "do's" and "don't's." To try as some do to impose Old Testament legislation on the New Testament church is to deny that Christ has fulfilled the whole law and to bring the church back to bondage.

Christ fulfilled the law *for* His church on the cross; but He also, by His Spirit, fulfills the law *in* the church when He writes the law upon our hearts and enables us by grace to keep that law. By His power within us, the power of Him Who died for us and earned everlasting salvation by His perfect atonement, He enables us to keep that law to love the Lord our God and to apply all the truths of the law in all our calling in the midst of life.

This principle of Christian liberty is fundamentally important. There are even some hints of how that law applies in the New Testament. Paul, with obvious reference to the Old Testament law of yoking together an ox and an ass in plowing, applies it to our relation to unbelievers and admonishes us not to be unequally yoked together with them (II Corinthians 6:14-18). In explaining how the law concerning not muzzling the ox while he treads out the corn, Paul applies it to the responsibility of churches to support their pastors (I Corinthians 9:1-13). But the point is that the fulfillment of the law is a positive reality in the hearts of God's people. If they truly love the Lord their God, they will, with wisdom given from on high, be able to apply that principle of love to every area of life. And then they walk in liberty, the liberty wherewith Christ has made them free.

And so the law is not against the promises of God. The law is, after all, gospel, and the gospel is the law. And this is as it ought to be, for the Scriptures are one, one revelation of God in Jesus Christ.

This was the purpose of Sinai. God establishes His covenant through Christ by the fulfillment of the law in Christ and in us by the power of Christ. The author of the epistle to the Hebrews expresses it this way, quoting from the Old Testament: "For by one offering he hath perfected for ever them that are sanctified. Whereof the Holy Ghost also is a witness to us: for after that he had said before, This is the covenant that I will make with them after those days, saith the Lord, I will put my law into their hearts, and in their minds will I write them; and their sins and iniquities will I remember no more" (Hebrews 10:14-17).

Yet we must remember that the purpose which the law served is still, even in our dispensation, the same as in the old; only it has become richer and more blessed. On the one hand, it is still the means whereby we know our sins and our need of Christ. Paul speaks of this in Romans 7:7: "What shall we say then? Is the law sin? God forbid. Nay, I had not known sin, but by the law: for I had not known lust, except the law had said, Thou shalt not covet." Or, to put it a little differently, God is pleased to lead us through life in such a way that we have the fullest and highest experience of the wonder of His grace. In order that He may do this, He leads us first of all to the full knowledge of our sins, for it is only through the knowledge of our sins that we come to know the wonder of divine grace and mercy in the cross. The law still drives us to Christ, for hearing the perfect and just demands of the law, we know that we cannot keep that law of ourselves, that we deserve only its curse. It is only in Christ that we have full and free salvation. The awe in which we stand as we contemplate the light which shines from heaven upon us is an awe that arises out of the despair of the blackness of our night of sin and death. Only when we pass through the valley of the dark reality of sin can we come to that mountain top of faith where the sun of God's mercy shines brightly.

This is the continual experience of the child of God. There are many who in our day have a very superficial religion, who speak of the fact that a Christian must have a good self-image; that he must possess a power of positive thinking to remain mentally healthy; that to abhor and humble himself leads to guilt complexes; that he is not as bad as some old "fire and brimstone" preachers say he is. Or perhaps conversion is pictured as a once-in-a-lifetime experience. You can hear it all the time over the radio, at religious revivals, or in speeches relating one's conversion experience. They talk long and pitifully of what terrible sinners they once were. They were always drunk. They cursed and swore. They were always beating their wives. They lived in debauchery. But suddenly they were converted and now they do these things no more. They have the full consciousness of salvation, and to hear them talk, they live almost without sin. There is no longer a struggle, a battle, a daily humbling of one's self before God. All is light and goodness and bliss.

I am not denying that grace makes radical changes in the lives of those who are converted. Nor am I minimizing in any respect the power of Christ within the hearts of God's people to make saints of sinners. But what I am saying, and it needs saying over and over again, is that the experience of sin is a daily experience of the child of God. The necessity of conversion is a daily necessity. Every day anew the child of God must learn to cry out as Paul did, "Oh, wretched man that I am." Every day anew he is led by God to the law to see how wicked he is in himself. And every day anew he must flee to the cross to find forgiveness and the healing power of Calvary's blood. The same journey must be made every day. The same way of tears and sorrow and a stricken heart must be walked each day anew, for this is the only way to Calvary. Every day anew, standing beneath Calvary, he must see that he is delivered from the curse of the law, which is rightfully his, through the blood of the eternal Lamb. Only when he can say, "O wretched man that I am," can he also say, "Thanks be to God through Jesus Christ our Lord" (Romans 7:24, 25).

His life remains a battle, a struggle, a constant sorrow for sin, a constant fleeing to the cross, a constant clinging to Christ as his only hope. And it is only when at last he is safe in heaven that he shall be delivered from the body of this death, to praise God forever and ever for the wonder of grace.

Chapter 15

THE MEDIATOR OF THE COVENANT

In the typical dispensation of the Old Testament, Moses appears as the mediator of the covenant. There are in the Old Testament Scriptures several passages which point this out. In the controversy which Moses had in the wilderness with Miriam and Aaron, God made this very clear. We read in Numbers 12:3-8: "(Now the man Moses was very meek, above all the men which were upon the face of the earth.) And the Lord spake suddenly unto Moses, and unto Aaron, and unto Miriam, Come out ye three unto the tabernacle of the congregation. And they three came out. And the Lord came down in the pillar of the cloud, and stood in the door of the tabernacle, and called Aaron and Miriam: and they both came forth. And he said, Hear now my words: If there be a prophet among you, I the Lord will make myself known unto him in a vision and will speak unto him in a dream. My servant Moses is not so, who is faithful in all mine house. With him will I speak mouth to mouth, even apparently, and not in dark speeches; and the similitude of the Lord shall he behold: wherefore then were ye not afraid to speak against my servant Moses?" In Exodus 32 and 33 this is especially emphasized when Israel sinned in worshipping the golden calf at Sinai. It was through the intercession of Moses, according to these chapters, that the fierce anger of the Lord was turned away from His people. Moses, as it were, came between the people and God and through his intercession averted the destruction of the nation.

The same truth is taught in the New Testament. In Galatians 3:19 reference is made directly to Moses as the mediator of the law: "Wherefore then serveth the law? It was added because of transgressions, till the seed should come to whom the promise was made; and it was ordained by angels in the hand of a mediator." This same truth is taught in Hebrews 3:1-6 where it is specifically stated that in this capacity Moses was a type of Christ: "Wherefore, holy brethren, partakers of the heavenly calling, consider the Apostle and High Priest of our profession, Christ Jesus; who was faithful to him that appointed him, as also Moses was faithful in all his house. For this man was counted worthy of more glory than Moses, inasmuch as he who hath builded the house hath more honour than the house. For every house is builded by some man; but he that built all things is God. And Moses verily was faithful in all his house, as a servant, for a testimony of those things which were to be spoken after; but Christ as a son over his own house; whose house are we, if we hold fast the confidence and the rejoicing of the hope firm unto the end."

It is to the truth of Christ as the Mediator of the covenant that we turn in this chapter.

It might be well, before we enter into this subject in detail, to remind ourselves of the fact that the covenant is not to be considered as a pact or agreement between two parties, but that it is rather a living bond of friendship and fellowship between God and His people. It is important to remember this, for we can form no clear and correct conception of Christ as the Mediator of the covenant unless we understand this fundamental truth. This is not difficult to demonstrate. Throughout the history of the Reformed and Presbyterian churches, much confusion has characterized the discussion of this truth; and this confusion has been present, in large measure, because, in keeping with the idea of the covenant as a pact or agreement, the covenant between God and Christ has also been explained in terms of an agreement between the Father and the Son, i.e., between the First Person of the holy trinity and the Second Person. The two enter into an agreement between themselves in which each assumes various obligations and responsibilities, by means of which the agreement is brought into reality.

While we cannot go into detail on the lengthy controversy which centered in this idea, it ought to be evident that the chief error of such a view is that in moving the whole covenant of grace into God's own trinitarian life, it has no place for the Holy Spirit, Who is, in the nature of the case, excluded from the arrangement. This, clearly, we cannot do if we believe that God is one in essence. We must proceed from a different perspective in our understanding of this matter, an understanding that, as we made clear in an earlier chapter, God lives a covenant life in Himself, altogether apart from the covenant of grace. The covenant of grace is the revelation of God's own covenant life through Jesus Christ the Mediator and Head of the covenant. As such it belongs to the whole work of salvation in Christ and is its essential character.

In order to concentrate our attention on what the Scriptures teach concerning this important truth, we shall not refer to Moses other than in passing, although the reader is urged to consult the history of Moses' life as recorded for us in Exodus, Leviticus, Numbers, and Deuteronomy. Throughout he stands as the Old Testament type of Christ in that peculiar capacity of mediator.

Before we enter into this matter in detail, in passing we ought to note that while we have spoken of mediator up to this point, the Scriptures speak of Christ as both Mediator and Head of the covenant of grace. These two terms are closely related to each other. Christ is the Mediator of the covenant because through Him God realizes the covenant which He establishes with His people. But Christ is Mediator because He is Head. Because He is eternally appointed by God to be the Head of the covenant, He is also Mediator through Whom this covenant is brought to realization with the elect who are given to Christ from all eternity.

To turn then to the idea of Christ as the Head of the covenant, we must ask the question first of all: to Whom do we refer when we speak of Christ as the Head and Mediator of the covenant? This might appear at first glance as a self-evident question which needs no explanation or elucidation. Yet it is precisely at this point that much confusion enters into the discussion.

Negatively, the reference to Christ as the Head of the covenant is not as such to the Second Person of the holy trinity. As the Second Person of the holy trinity, Christ is equal with God. He is essentially God – in the technical sense of that word. He is, as one of the ancient creeds expressed it, very God of very God. He is with the Father and the Holy Spirit the one true God subsisting in unity of essence.

As God, along with the Father and the Holy Spirit, He is the Author of all the works of God. This means that He is, with the First and Third Persons, the Author of God's everlasting counsel. Further, He is, with the Father and the Spirit, the Author of the realization of that counsel; i.e., He is the Creator of all things, the Author of everlasting redemption, the One Who sovereignly works salvation in the hearts of the elect. All the works of God without exception are the works of the triune God.

Even here already we must be careful. To ascribe, e.g., the work of creation to the First Person, the work of redemption to the Second Person, and the work of sanctification to the Third Person is basically tritheism and a denial of the holy trinity. All God's works are the works of God triune.

When, however, the Scriptures speak of Christ, they speak of Him as the eternal Son of God, the Second Person of the trinity, *in our flesh.* We must be careful that we make the distinction, therefore, between the Second Person of the trinity as such, the Son as He is with the Father and the Holy Spirit, the one only true God, and the Son as He entered into our flesh and assumed our nature.

As the eternal Son, He is equal with God; as Christ, in our nature, He is subordinate to God. As Son, He is the Author of the eternal counsel which God has determined in Himself from all eternity; as Christ He is a part of that counsel, a decree within that counsel. As Son He is the Author of all the works of God as the triune God executes His counsel in time; as Christ He is One of those works – the chief and central work, but nevertheless, a work. As Son, He wills the eternal will of the triune God; as Christ He comes to do the Father's will, delighting in that will, making His will subordinate to the will of His heavenly Father. Christ could alone apply to Himself the Psalm which reads: "Sacrifice and offering thou didst not desire; mine ears hast thou opened: burnt offering and sin offering hast thou not required. Then said I, Lo, I come: in the volume of the book it is written of me. I delight to do thy will, O my God: yea, thy law is within my heart" (Psalm 40:6-8). (See Hebrews 10:5-7, John 4:34, etc.) Christ made His will subordinate to the will of His Father when He prayed in the deepest anguish of the Garden of Gethsemane: "Not my will, but thine be done."

This is indeed the great mystery of God become flesh. But it must be remembered that all the works of God are the works of the triune God, not simply of one Person. And as all the works of God are the works of the triune God, so also they are works which the triune God performs through Christ, the Son of God in our flesh, and by the Holy Spirit as the Spirit of Christ. The triune God is the Father of our Lord

Jesus Christ. He is the Father of our Lord Jesus Christ in our Lord's incarnation, for: "The Holy Ghost shall come upon thee, and the power of the Highest shall overshadow thee; and that holy thing which shall be born of thee shall be called the Son of God" (Luke 1:35). He is the Father to Whom Christ prayed in the years of His earthly ministry. Christ did not pray to the first Person of the trinity, but to His Father, the triune God. Upon Christ was poured the fullness of the wrath of almighty God when He suffered upon the cross for our sins. Into the hand of the triune God, His Father, Christ commended His spirit. From the corruption of the grave the triune God raised Christ in power and great glory, gave Him a name above every name and exalted Him to the highest pinnacle of authority in heaven.

Thus Christ is wholly subordinate to the triune God in His human nature. He is the Servant of Jehovah, Who comes to do God's will. He is the One Who, according to Philippians 2, never considered Himself equal with God, but counted Himself of no reputation and took upon Himself the form of a servant. He is the One Who came to do His Father's will because He was obedient in His Father's house. Of Him Paul writes concerning that subordination even in His exaltation in heaven: "Then cometh the end, when he shall have delivered up the kingdom to God, even the Father; when he shall have put down all rule and all authority and power. For he must reign, till he hath put all enemies under his feet. The last enemy that shall be destroyed is death. For he hath put all things under his feet. But when he saith all things are put under him, it is manifest that he is excepted, which did put all things under him. And when all things shall be subdued unto him, *then shall the Son also himself be subject unto him that put all things under him,* that God may be all in all" (I Corinthians 15:24-28).

It is this crucial distinction which must be maintained if we are to understand how Christ is the Head and Mediator of the covenant; for because all this is true, Christ is the One through Whom the everlasting covenant of grace is realized.

In order to understand this, we must proceed from the idea of revelation. God is in Himself a covenant God. He lives a perfect covenant life within Himself as the triune God, one in essence and three in persons. But God chooses to reveal this covenant life which He lives in Himself through Jesus Christ. He does this in such a way that He takes His people into that very covenant life which He lives in Himself. This is the great and marvelous wonder of our salvation. When God reveals that covenant life which He lives in Himself through Jesus Christ and through His people, He does not simply tell His people about this life so that they are informed of some aspects of it. Rather, He causes them to share in that very covenant life itself.

Perhaps to understand how this is related to Christ as the Head of the covenant we can proceed from the typical nature of the covenant in the old dispensation. There was a figure of this in Old Testament times. In the time of the dispensation of types and shadows God dwelt with His people in covenant fellowship in the tabernacle and temple. In those buildings God dwelt, as it were, under one roof with His people in much the same way as, e.g., a husband and wife live together in the covenant fellowship of marriage in the same house. God dwelt in the Most Holy Place between the wings of the cherubim on the mercy seat of the ark of the covenant. His people dwelt in the outer court.

But it was the Old Testament, when the blood of atonement was not yet shed. The result was that the people could not, as it were, come very close to God. They were separated from God by the veil which divided the Holy Place from the Holy of Holies, by the Aaronitic priesthood, by the sacrifices which had continually to be made upon the altar of burnt offering. It was something like a husband and wife living together in one house, but separated from one another by several rooms and locked doors. To be able to live together in the same house would surely be nice for them, but not really the ideal of the marriage state. It was the time of the incompleteness of the reality.

But in the new dispensation all this changes. And it changes because Christ is Himself the true temple of God. Christ makes this clear at the time when He cleansed the temple at the very beginning of His earthly ministry. He was asked by the unbelieving Jews for a sign which would prove that He had authority to cleanse the temple. He answered this question by saying: "Destroy this temple, and in three days I will build it up" (John 2:19). The gospel narrative which records this event informs us that Jesus spoke of the temple of His body. It is very striking that the Jews never forgot these words of the Lord; it was as if these words filled them with an unidentifiable terror, for at the time Christ was tried by the Sanhedrin, they returned to these words in their false testimony and, perverting Christ's words, reminded themselves of the fact that Christ had said He would destroy the temple. And, while Christ hung on the cross, part of their mockery was to call Him a temple-destroyer.

The fact is, however, that Christ referred specifically to His resurrection. In His body in which He suffered and died, rose again from the dead, and ascended into glory, He becomes the true temple of God. His own body is that temple, as is evident from the Lord's words. This is true because, on the one hand, Christ is, also in His human nature, very God. Paul writes to the Colossians: "In him dwelleth all the fulness of the Godhead bodily" (Colossians 2:9). God triune, with the whole of His divine essence, dwells in Christ. But, on the other hand, the church for which Christ died is also the body of Christ. So it is called in many places in Holy Writ. We read, e.g., in I Corinthians 12:27: "Now ye are the body of Christ, and members in particular." The church is really and surely Christ's body, bone of His bone and flesh of His flesh (Ephesians 5:30). And the result is that God triune and the church come together in Christ Jesus in mystical union as close as it is possible to come. God and His people dwell together in covenant fellowship in Christ as the Head of the covenant.

That Christ is the Head of the covenant implies a twofold relation between Christ and His people.

Christ is first of all the legal Head of His people. This truth is taught very clearly in Romans 5:15-21, where the relationship between Christ and His people is compared to the relation between Adam and the human race. Adam's relation to the human race, as we discussed in an earlier chapter, was a legal relation so that Adam's sin of eating of the forbidden tree was imputed to the whole human race. The whole human race is guilty before God for this one sin so that death comes upon all men for that all have sinned. We are all responsible for Adam's sin and worthy of death because of it. But in the same sense of the word, by legal arrangement, the righteousness which Christ earned on the cross is legally imputed to all who belong to Christ. All the elect are so in Christ that what Christ did on the cross is legally the responsibility of all those for whom Christ died. Righteousness is imputed because Christ stood in the place of His people as legal Head. "For as in Adam all die, even so in Christ shall all be made alive" (I Corinthians

15:22). Thus as the legal Head of His people, Christ is the Head of the covenant.

But Christ is also the organic Head of His people. This was also true in the relation between Adam and the human race. The whole human race comes forth from Adam, and the corrupt nature which was Adam's punishment for his sin becomes the corrupt nature of all men. But in the same way, Christ is also the organic Head of His people. This is clearly taught in the Scriptures in many passages. In Ephesians 4:15, the apostle writes: "But speaking the truth in love, may grow up into him in all things, which is the head, even Christ." In the same epistle, chapter 5:23, we read: "For the husband is the head of the wife, even as Christ is the head of the church: and he is the saviour of the body." Colossians also expresses this truth more than once. In chapter 1:18 the Scriptures tell us: "And he is the head of the body, the church: who is the beginning, the firstborn from the dead; that in all things he might have the preeminence." And in 2:19 we read: "And not holding the Head, from which all the body by joints and bands having nourishment ministered, and knit together, increaseth with the increase of God." Christ and His people become organically one by faith so that Christ and His people are one body, one living organism, one unity. All that Christ merited for His people by His perfect work becomes in fact the full possession of the people of God. And united to Him by faith as a part of His body, the church and God dwell together in perfect covenant fellowship.

It is because of this twofold relationship that Christ is also called the Mediator and Surety of the covenant. There are four passages where this truth is found, all in the epistle to the Hebrews. In 8:6 we read: "But now hath he obtained a more excellent ministry, by how much also he is the mediator of a better covenant, which was established upon better promises." In 9:15 this same truth is expressed: "And for this cause he is the mediator of the new testament, that by means of death, for the redemption of the transgressions that were under the first testament, they which are called might receive the promise of eternal inheritance." In 12:24 the same term is used: "And to Jesus the mediator of the new covenant, and to the blood of sprinkling, that speaketh better things than that of Abel." And in 7:22 the word "Surety" is used: "By so much was Jesus made a surety of a better testament."

It is clear from these passages that we must not think of a mediator in the sense in which the term is used in our everyday parlance. In human relationships, the term refers to one who comes between two quarreling parties to attempt to bring about reconciliation by means of some sort of mutually acceptable agreement. So management and labor call in a mediator if they have been confronted by differences impossible to reconcile. Husband and wife, estranged from each other, call in a mediator in the hopes of being reconciled. This idea too, when applied to the covenant of grace, is rooted in the idea of the covenant as an agreement between God and man.

But this is not the idea of the Scriptures. We must remember that Christ is very God in our flesh. He is God's Mediator, sent by God as prepared from all eternity. He is anointed to perform, on behalf of the triune God, the work of redemption and reconciliation. He does all the Father's will in bringing us to God. Mediation comes from God's side alone. He does it all, through Christ. He accomplishes complete reconciliation so that the covenant can be realized in all its perfection. "God was in Christ, reconciling the world unto himself, not imputing their trespasses unto them" (II Corinthians 5:19). God is His Own Mediator in Christ. God does all that is necessary for the covenant to be established, through Jesus Christ.

Christ is therefore also the Surety of the covenant. In Hebrews 7:22 where this term is found, the idea is that because of the oath by which Christ is made High Priest, He is the Pledge and Guarantee of God's gracious covenant; i.e., He is the divine Pledge that God will never forsake His covenant, will do all that is necessary to realize it, and will surely bring that covenant to its full perfection in glory.

There is one element which must be considered in this connection. And that is the truth of the Holy Spirit as the Spirit of Christ.

Here, too, the Scriptures make the same distinction between the Holy Spirit as the Third Person of the trinity and the Holy Spirit as the Spirit of Christ which they made between the eternal Son of God and our Lord Jesus Christ. In fact the Scriptures use some very strong language to make this distinction. In John 7:37-39 we read: "In the last day, that great day of the feast, Jesus stood and cried, saying, If any man thirst, let him come unto me, and drink. He that believeth on me, as the scripture hath said, out of his belly shall flow rivers of living water. (But this spake he of the Spirit, which they that believe on him should receive: for the Holy Ghost was not yet given; because that Jesus was not yet glorified.)" It is interesting to note, and this is precisely the point of the passage, that the little word "given" which appears in our KJV of the Bible is included in italics. This means that the word does not really appear in the Greek original, but was added by the translators who apparently thought that the sense required it. Nevertheless, this is a mistake. The word does not actually belong in the text, and the verse ought to read: "But this spake he of the Spirit, which they that believe on him should receive: for the Holy Ghost was not yet." The idea is emphatically that there was no Holy Spirit as yet; and the reason is that Jesus was not yet glorified. There could be no Holy Spirit as yet, for the exaltation of Christ had not yet taken place.

Now very obviously, the idea is not that the Third Person of the trinity did not yet exist prior to our Lord's ascension. This would be a denial of the trinity, of the co-eternity of the Holy Spirit with the Father and Son, and would contradict the Old Testament Scriptures. We read already in connection with creation that the "Spirit of God moved upon the face of the waters" (Genesis 1:2). But the reference is very emphatically to the Holy Spirit as the Spirit of Christ. In this sense He did not exist prior to our Lord's exaltation. Peter speaks of this very fact in his great Pentecost sermon: "Therefore being by the right hand of God exalted, and having received of the Father (the triune God) the promise of the Holy Ghost, he hath shed forth this, which ye now see and hear" (Acts 2:33). At His exaltation, Christ received the Spirit Whom the Father had promised to Him, and which He in turn poured out upon the church.

It is, of course, by means of the Spirit that all the blessings of salvation which Christ has earned on the cross are given to the church. But we must pay special attention to the fact that it is by means of the Spirit that the covenant of grace is actually realized.

On the evening before our Lord suffered and died, when He celebrated the last supper with His disciples, he spoke at length of the Spirit in that gloriously comforting discourse recorded for us in John chapters 14 through 16, a discourse concluded with Christ's High Priestly prayer. Christ spoke these words to His disciples because He had announced to them emphatically and without any possibility of doubt that He was going away from them. This announcement, as was to be expected, filled them with a great sorrow, for they had fastened all their hopes upon an earthly kingdom in which Christ would smash the power of the Romans, establish the old throne of David, and rule with His disciples over a glorious kingdom of the Jews. That Christ was leaving them filled them with dismay and this announcement was to them the end of all their hopes.

But the Lord assured them in this discourse that He must go away. And the necessity of His departure was exactly because only in going away could He return to them again in a way far richer than His physical presence in Palestine. His return to them would be by the Spirit. No fewer than four times does the Lord refer to this. In John 14:16-18 we read: "And I will pray the Father, and he shall give you another Comforter, that he may abide with you forever: even the Spirit of truth; whom the world cannot receive because it seeth him not, neither knoweth him: but ye know him, for he dwelleth with you, and shall be in you. I will not leave you comfortless: I will come to you." In 14:26 we read: "But the Comforter, which is the Holy Ghost, whom the Father will send in my name, he shall teach you all things, and bring all things to your remembrance, whatsoever I have said unto you." In 15:26 Jesus says: "But when the Comforter is come, whom I will send unto you from the Father, even the Spirit of truth, which proceedeth from the Father, he shall testify of me." And finally in 16:13 we read: "Howbeit when he, the Spirit of truth, is come, he will guide you into all truth: for he shall not speak of himself; but whatsoever he shall hear, that shall he speak: and he will shew you things to come."

These texts, while having many important implications for the work of the Spirit in the church during the ages of the new dispensation, nevertheless assure the disciples that when the Comforter, the Holy Spirit, is given, Christ Himself will return to His church. And the idea is that through the Spirit Christ comes to dwell in the hearts of His people in such a way that they are indeed made one with Him to become one body by faith with Christ. When Paul speaks in I Corinthians 12 of the implications of the truth that the church is Christ's body of which He is the Head, we are told that this takes place through the giving of many gifts by the Spirit of Christ Who is given to the church. So it is by means of the Spirit of our Lord Jesus Christ that this mystical union with Christ is accomplished, and in such a way that in Christ's body God and His people are one in covenant fellowship.

All of this emphasizes the fact that the work of the realization of the covenant is the work of God alone, through Christ and by the Spirit of Christ given to the church. God reveals His own glorious covenant life in and through Jesus Christ that His own glory may be revealed, and that through the revelation of this glory, He may be glorified and praised. This praise and glory belong to Him from His covenant people whom He has brought sovereignly and graciously into His covenant.

It is exactly because of this that the whole idea of the covenant as an agreement, with its necessary conditionality, is abhorrent to the whole concept of the covenant and stands in opposition to it. The very idea of conditionality militates against all that the Scriptures teach concerning this truth. The covenant is God's work throughout. It is established by God in Christ; it is realized sovereignly in our hearts by the Spirit of Christ; it is maintained by sovereign grace as God works His eternal purpose.

All this does not mean that God's covenant people do not have a part in that covenant. And to this we shall presently return in another connection. But let it be clearly understood now that that part of the covenant which is our obligation is centrally to praise and magnify the name of our God Who has done so wondrously for us.

Chapter 16

THE COVENANT WITH ISRAEL – ENTRANCE INTO CANAAN

The land of Canaan into which Israel entered at the end of forty years wandering in the wilderness is called in the Scriptures the land of rest. According to the author of the epistle to the Hebrews (See especially chapters 4 and 5.), this land was a typical picture of the sabbath which is given to the people of God; and this sabbath is a foretaste of the eternal rest which remains for the people of God, and is, therefore, a picture of the rest of the full realization of God's covenant with His people.

There are several points of the history recorded for us in the Scriptures concerning Israel's wandering in the wilderness and the final entrance of the people into the land of Canaan which we briefly call to the attention of our readers to serve as a background for our discussion of this important point.

In the first place, because of Israel's unbelief while wandering in the wilderness, especially manifested in the refusal of the nation to enter the land of promise (Numbers 13, 14), all those who had come out of Egypt who were over twenty years old, with the exception of Joshua and Caleb, perished in the wilderness. The Scriptures apply this in more than one place to the unbelief of those in the New Testament who refuse to enter into God's rest by faith and who consequently perish. In Hebrews 3 and 4 this is the great theme of the apostle, summed up in the words of 4:1: "Let us therefore fear, lest, a promise being left us of entering into his rest, any of you should seem to come short of it." (See also I Corinthians 10:5-12.) We will not speak of this in detail in this connection, for we will return to this point a bit later in the chapter.

In the second place, the children of Israel were, after these years of wandering, brought at last into the promised land. This land was the real goal of their life. An inheritance in this land had been promised them already in the days of Abraham (Genesis 15:18-21). It was towards this land that they set their eyes when they went into Egypt, when they lived there for a time, and when finally they were brought forth by the strong arm of God (Genesis 50:24, 25; Exodus 12:25).

In the third place, in the conquest and subsequent inheritance of the land, Joshua was their leader and captain. As Hebrews makes clear, Joshua was a unique picture of Christ in that both bore the same name and both performed the same work, Joshua typically and Christ in reality. The name Joshua means "Jehovah Salvation" in the Hebrew language. In the Greek of the New Testament, the name Jesus has this same meaning (Matthew 1:21; Hebrews 4:8). In this latter passage, the KJV reads "Jesus," while the RV reads "Joshua." The latter is correct as is evident from the context. The point is that even as Joshua led Israel into the typical rest of Canaan as a typical captain of Israel's armies, so Jesus is the Captain of our salvation Who leads His people into the true and heavenly rest of God's covenant.

In the fourth place, in fighting the battles which overthrew the heathen in the land of Canaan, Israel was victorious only because the Lord fought for Israel and gave them the victory. Jericho's walls fell, not by the might of Israel's army, for Israel simply marched around them and did nothing towards the conquest of the city (Hebrews 11:30). They fell because the Lord miraculously made them fall and gave them the city without a battle. Israel could not capture Ai because the Lord was not with Israel inasmuch as Achan had stolen from Jericho's accursed spoils (Joshua 7:8-15). In the battle with the five kings of the South, the victory was Israel's because the Lord rained hailstones upon Israel's enemies, made the sun and moon stand still at the prayer of Joshua, and filled the heathen with a paralyzing fright (Joshua 10:11-14). Psalm 44 begins with the words: "We have heard with our ears, O God, our fathers have told us, what work thou didst in their days, in the times of old. How thou didst drive out the heathen with thy hand, and plantedst them; how thou didst afflict the people, and cast them out. For they got not the land in possession by their own sword, neither did their own arm save them: but thy right hand, and thine arm, and the light of thy countenance, because thou hadst a favour unto them" (verses 1-3).

In the fifth place, when Israel finally settled in the land, the land was divided by lot. Each tribe and each family within each tribe received its inheritance through the lot which was cast. All this was indicative of the fact that God Himself appointed to each one in the nation his own inheritance. What each Israelite received was emphatically given him by God, and given as an inheritance, i.e., as a gift graciously bestowed. This inheritance was in the land of rest, the picture of heaven. As such it spoke in powerful, though typical language, of the rest of God's everlasting covenant of grace. And of this we have a foretaste in the sabbath which we celebrate in the new dispensation.

The sabbath day as a day of rest is basically a creation ordinance. God created this rotation and cycle of days at the very beginning. We read: "And on the seventh day God ended his work which he had made; and he rested on the seventh day from all his work which he had made. And God blessed the seventh day, and sanctified it: because that in it he had rested from all his work which God created and made" (Genesis 2:2, 3).

Without going into detail, the point is clear. The true rest of the sabbath is a rest which God Himself enjoys in His own covenant life. He, as the triune God, lives an eternal life of perfect rest. This is not because the Lord is idle, for idleness is not rest; nor is the idea of the sabbath day one of idleness. God rested because He enjoyed perfectly the works of His hands in the creation which He had made. Thus God's rest is a covenant idea. In majestic serenity and infinite peace with Himself, God rests in the perfect knowledge of the perfection of all His works.

But it was God's purpose to take man into this rest. From the very beginning already, this was grace, unmerited favor. It was God's purpose to give to man the perfect experience of the rest which God enjoyed in Himself. That is, God determined to take man into His own covenant life so that man, dwelling with God, might enjoy the blessedness which God possesses in Himself. This was the height of man's joy in the garden of Paradise.

Nevertheless, when man fell, he went far away from that blessedness of God's fellowship and joined hands with the devil in an unholy alliance of rebellion against God. The result was that he lost the possibility of that rest and the enjoyment of God's fellowship. He was now filled with the unrest of sin, the unrest of the terrible hand of God's curse upon him that drove him from God's presence and filled his days and nights with fear and despair.

But the purpose of God was not defeated, for God had appointed another rest for His people in Christ of which even the creation sabbath was but a picture. The creation sabbath had passed away forever. It shall never come back. There is now only the rest of the heavenly sabbath that is reserved for the elect through the work of Jesus Christ.

But before that day of the heaven-rest dawned, there was the figure of Canaan in the old dispensation. It was first of all spoken of in the law of God: "Remember the sabbath day, to keep it holy. Six days shalt thou labor, and do all thy work; but the seventh day is the sabbath of the Lord thy God: in it thou shalt not do any work, thou, nor thy son, nor thy daughter, thy manservant, nor thy maidservant, nor thy cattle, nor thy stranger that is within thy gates: for in six days the Lord made heaven and earth, the sea, and all that in them is, and rested the seventh day: wherefore the Lord blessed the sabbath day, and hallowed it" (Exodus 20:8-11).

A very important idea was connected to this typical sabbath. Israel was commanded in the law to work six days before they could enjoy the seventh day as a day of rest. That is, they had to work in the service of God; they had to work in such a way that they loved the Lord their God with all their being; they had to work with utter perfection. And only when they did this, could they also enjoy the rest of a sabbath, a sabbath which they earned with their faithful labor. Six days of faithful work would bring to them the reward of one day of blessed rest.

All this was closely bound up with the land of Canaan which was a symbol to Israel of their true rest, for Canaan was the land flowing with milk and honey, the earthly symbol of heaven. It was the land in which Israel was destined to dwell in fellowship with God. This is why the very center of all Israel's life in Canaan was to be found in the tabernacle and temple, the dwelling place of God in the midst of His people.

This is also why their life in Canaan was a constant cycle of sabbaths. Sabbaths they had to celebrate every seventh day, every seventh year, and every fiftieth year, which was the multiple of seven times seven and was their well-known year of jubilee. But even here in Canaan, they would enjoy the favor and fellowship of God only as long as they remained faithful. If they lived in obedience to God, kept His commandments, worked out of the principle of love, the land would continue to yield her increase, they would enjoy protection from all their enemies, and they would daily receive the blessedness of God's rest and fellowship in all their life. If, on the contrary, they were disobedient, if they turned from the worship of God to idols, if they trampled God's law under their feet, Canaan would become a barren wilderness, the enemy would come into their land as a flood, and they would have to endure every pestilence and plague until they were finally driven out of the land into captivity (Deuteronomy 28).

Both the Scriptures and the history of the nation of Israel point us to the fact that the typical sabbath was an impossible one to keep. The fact of the matter is that Israel could not keep the law, work in love for God, and earn the sabbath at the end of faithful labor. They could not because they, as well as all men, were depraved. The law demanded of them a spiritual impossibility. Their history was the proof of this. Gradually they turned more and more from God and threw themselves into the arms of the idols of the heathen. The result was that Canaan ceased to be a land flowing with milk and honey, a picture of heaven, and a land of the rest of the true sabbath. Finally they were driven out of the land and scattered among heathen nations for seventy years "to fulfil the word of the Lord by the mouth of Jeremiah, until the land had enjoyed her sabbaths: for as long as she lay desolate she kept sabbath, to fulfil threescore and ten years" (II Chronicles 36:21).

In other words, it was and is forever impossible for man to earn by his own works the sabbath rest of God's covenant. But it was never God's intention to realize the true sabbath through the keeping of the law. This was not the reason why the law was given. The whole law was never intended as a means to bring salvation. We have discussed this before and need only direct you to Paul's pointed words in Galatians 3:24 where the law is described as "our schoolmaster to bring us unto Christ, that we might be justified by faith." Already in the Old Testament, those of God's people who did truly enter into rest did so not because they earned the right to this by their faithful labor, but because by faith they saw the land as a type of heaven, and clinging to the promise by faith, they entered into the true rest. This is the clear teaching of Hebrews 4 and 5 where the unbelief of those who perished is contrasted with the faith of those who typically entered in.

Thus the sabbath was fulfilled in Christ. We have said that a picture of this was to be found in Joshua's conquest of Canaan, but the true Joshua, Jesus, Jehovah Salvation, is the only One Who can bring the true sabbath to God's people. This fulfillment of the sabbath began with the resurrection of Jesus from the dead. Christ fulfilled the law for His people by doing that which they could not – loving the Lord His God with all His being, while at the same time He bore the mighty load of the sin and guilt of His people which was placed on Him. He loved His God with total and perfect love, even in the bottom of hell, where He laid His own body on the altar of God's wrath as a sacrifice for sin when the hammer blows of that wrath crushed Him.

But because of His perfect work, God raised Him from the dead. He rose triumphant over sin and death to enter into the perfect rest of God – into God's perfect covenant fellowship, far from the abandonment which He experienced on Calvary.

It is not without a great deal of significance that Christ arose on the first day of the week, for by it God signified to His people that Christ had earned the rest of the sabbath for them. No longer does the requirement, the impossible demand, come to us to labor faithfully six days before we can rest. Now that rest is ours on the first day. It comes to us not because we have earned it, but out of the fountain of pure grace, for Christ earned it for us. It is not now demanded that we first live six perfect days of work to earn the rest; we first receive the rest at the beginning of the week, and that rest gives us, through grace, the strength to go through the following six days in a life of humble obedience to God.

The Adventists are very wrong in their idea of the sabbath and really lead people back to a work-righteousness which is a denial of sovereign grace.

This rest, then, which the people of God receive on the sabbath is the foretaste of the perfect rest of heaven. It is the beginning of that rest. For in heaven the tabernacle of God shall be revealed to men perfectly and forever. There all our sins shall be completely taken from us and we shall enter into the perfect enjoyment of God's covenant fellowship, for God Himself shall take us into His loving arms through Jesus Christ to comfort us forever. "There remaineth therefore a rest to the people of God" (Hebrews 4:9). And even while we are in this life Jesus calls His people to Himself with the tender words: "Come unto me, all ye that labour and are heavy laden, and I will give you rest" (Matthew 11:28).

All this means that we are pilgrims and strangers while we are yet on this earth. We have not yet arrived in the heavenly Canaan. We are, as it were, still walking in the wilderness of this world. But we are on our journey heavenward. And while we pass through this barren wilderness, God graciously gives to us here and there an oasis of spiritual refreshment. It is the oasis of the sabbath which we celebrate on the first day of the week.

It is as if when we near the end of another week's sojourn in this dry and thirsty land, we stagger with spent strength into the oasis of another sabbath. But in this oasis we are surrounded with what awaits us in heaven. Here we are given the cool waters of life that flow from the throne of God which waters are the Spirit of Christ (John 7:37-39). Here we are fed with the true Bread of Life which is Christ Himself through the Word of the gospel. Here we are sheltered in the cool shade of God's everlasting wings from the burning heat of the sun. Here our flagging spirits are revived, our failing strength is quickened, our souls are fed, and we are given strength to pursue our journey for another week. And presently we shall reach the end of the journey, our eternal destination, our Father's house. And in our Father's house the sabbath shall be perfect, complete, and eternal.

Chapter 17

OUR PART IN THE COVENANT

In the last chapter we talked about the land of Canaan as the typical land of rest; of the land of Canaan, therefore, as the land of the typical covenant. We stressed strongly that the rest of God's covenant is given by grace alone and is never earned. In fact, that has been our emphasis from the very beginning. The whole of God's covenant, in its establishment, its realization, its maintenance, its final perfection, is the gift of grace. Never in any sense is it earned.

The question might well arise whether this implies that we have no part in the covenant at all. Do not the Scriptures teach that we have a role to play in that covenant? Does not Hebrews 4 and 5 particularly emphasize this when it warns us that the Israelites who perished in the wilderness failed to enter the land of rest because of unbelief and warns us that the same thing could happen to us if we believe not?

All this brings sharply to our attention the truth of what the Scriptures teach as our part of the covenant, and to this we now turn our attention.

It is important that we put this in its proper perspective. As we have noticed before, there are those who maintain that the character of the covenant is an agreement or pact which is reached between God and man in which God and man function as parties to the covenant and which include various stipulations, obligations, and provisions on the part of both, the keeping of which is essential for the establishment and maintenance of the covenant. God agrees on His part to bless man with the blessings of salvation provided that man accepts by faith the provisions of the covenant, agrees to walk in obedience to the covenant, and maintain his part in faithfulness. Thus the covenant becomes a *conditional* covenant and the fulfillment of these conditions is essential for the covenant both to be realized and maintained.

The word "condition" has become a central word in this controversy. Those who maintain that the covenant is an agreement insist also that the covenant is *bilateral,* i.e., two-sided and that the two-sidedness of the covenant is especially clear from the conditionality of the covenant. So the three ideas go hand in hand: the covenant as an agreement, a bilateral covenant, and a conditional covenant. They cannot be separated from one another. And, so it is said by the defenders of this view, this idea is important because any other idea makes man nothing else but a stock and a block in the covenant; he is an automaton, a creature robbed of his rationality and morality, a mere stooge who is carried to heaven sound asleep in the reclining seat of an airplane.

If one studies the history of the covenant both in English and in continental thought, one will discover that the idea of a conditional covenant was often, though not always, maintained. However, those who were Reformed in their approach to this doctrine, i.e., those who proceeded from the truths of the five points of Calvinism, especially the truth of sovereign and double predestination, when speaking of a conditional covenant, used the word "condition" in an altogether different sense from which it is commonly used in our day. They meant by "condition" "way" or "means" by which God realizes His covenant sovereignly. They wished to emphasize by the use of this term the fact that faith is the God-given and God-ordained way or means by which the covenant is realized and maintained. God establishes and maintains His own covenant and does so by imparting faith to His people according to the decree of predestination so that faith becomes the means of the realization of that covenant. Used in this way, we can hardly have any objection to the term.

The problem is, however, that this term has taken on quite a different meaning in today's discussion of the covenant. It has acquired the meaning of "prerequisite" or "necessary requirement." And this fits in well with the idea of a bilateral agreement between God and man. The idea then is that no covenant can be established except man fulfill the prior requirement of faith, and that covenant will not be continued and maintained except man fulfill the necessary requirement of continuous obedience. Should man fail in this obedience, the covenant is cancelled and is no longer in effect.

It is said by those who hold this view, but still wish to sound Reformed, that the prerequisite or necessary requirement is fulfilled by God. But this is a subterfuge and red herring, which shifts attention away from the crucial issue. The fact of the matter is that if faith is a prerequisite or requirement to the establishment of the covenant, it is a condition which man can fulfill *before* he is ever in the covenant. He is, therefore, capable of accepting by faith those necessary conditions which he approves and agrees to before that covenant can in fact be established.

This is nothing else but an introduction into the whole idea of the covenant of the old heresy of Arminianism which makes salvation dependent upon the will of man. We have discussed this at length earlier and need not repeat what was already said.

The Scriptures proceed from an entirely different principle. God is in Himself a covenant God. This perfect covenant fellowship which He lives in Himself He chooses sovereignly to reveal by taking His elect people into His own covenant life through Jesus Christ, the Mediator of the covenant. He does this sovereignly and graciously, according to the decree of eternal predestination. The covenant is a bond of friendship and fellowship, wholly unilateral in character, unconditional in both its establishment and realization, wholly dependent upon God that God may be glorified and praised for the riches of His grace in Christ Jesus. There are, therefore, no parties in that covenant.

But all this does not mean that there are not *parts* in the covenant: not parties, but parts, – if we may use an expression which is found in the "Form for the Administration of Baptism" which has been used for centuries in the Reformed churches of the Netherlands and America. The people of God who are graciously taken into that covenant are given a part in it.

It must be remembered in this connection that the part of God's covenant people within the covenant is always the fruit of God's part. God's part is first, decisive, sovereignly the cause of our part. We have our part only because we can, because of God's part, walk in that covenant as a covenant people. In fact, our part in the covenant is even a privilege. By grace we *can* and *will* do our part. By grace we *may* do our part. And only because of this, is it also true that we *must* do our part. The Scriptures emphasize this repeatedly. In Philippians 2:12, the apostle urges upon the church to "work out your own salvation with fear and trembling." But he immediately adds: "For it is God which worketh in you both to will and to do of his good pleasure" (verse 13). The admonition confronts us to work out our salvation *because* God works in us. And this work of God in us is an all-encompassing and completely enabling work because it accomplishes both the willing and the doing. The same is true of II Corinthians 6 where, at the end of the chapter, the apostle uses strong covenant language: "For ye are the temple of the living God; as God hath said, I will dwell in them, and walk in them; and I will be their God, and they shall be my people. Wherefore come out from among them, and be ye separate, saith the Lord, and touch not the unclean thing; and I will receive you, and will be a Father unto you, and ye shall be my sons and daughters, saith the Lord Almighty" (verses 16-18). These are the promises of the covenant. What do these promises mean for God's covenant people? In 7:1 the apostle explains this: "Having therefore these promises, dearly beloved, let us cleanse ourselves from all filthiness of the flesh and spirit, perfecting holiness in the fear of God."

God never saves His people so that they are unconscious of this great salvation. He does not pull His people into heaven as a child pulls a mechanical quacking duck across the floor. How could God ever do this? It is His purpose to take His people into His own covenant fellowship so that they may enjoy that fellowship and praise God Who has graciously given this to them. The result is that God gives His people a part in that covenant. It is a part which they are enabled to perform because they are already in the covenant as His covenant people.

We must be clear on this point. From God's point of view, He works all things sovereignly so that all salvation is given graciously as a gift. Nothing is left to us which makes His salvation dependent upon what we do. We can do nothing, for we are sinners, dead in trespasses and sins. We would always be violators of the covenant if left to ourselves. But God works in us both to will and to do of His good pleasure so that all glory may be His alone.

But from our point of view, God deals with us as rational, moral creatures. Thus the way in which the covenant is maintained is the way of faith and obedience. We are called to believe in Christ. This calling comes to us in all its force. It comes to us as a solemn demand of the covenant. It comes to us in such a way that unbelief results in great sorrow and death. So Hebrews 4 and 5 emphasize the matter. But it is clear from all the Scriptures that the very demand of faith and obedience is itself the power of God by which He works in us that same faith and obedience so that we do actually believe and obey, and in this way enjoy the blessedness of the covenant.

This does not mean that we do not often sin, for we have only a small beginning of that new obedience and the life of faith within us is but a principle. We carry with us our sinful nature from which we will not escape until we die. As members of God's covenant, these sins which we commit are serious and dreadful. In fact, by them we transgress the covenant in which we stand, violate it in our foolishness, and would, with our sin, destroy the covenant were that possible. The result is that we receive from the hand of our covenant God many admonitions, warnings, threatenings, entreaties; we sometimes need to be chastised and rebuked; we often find ourselves in impossible situations which we have brought on ourselves by our sins; and when we walk in this way, we forfeit all right to God's favor and grace and He withdraws from us the conscious experience of His love. But He does this all out of the fountain of His great grace, and His love never changes. Just as a God-fearing parent teaches his child, making use of warnings, threats, chastisements, and promises, but always in love to teach his child the way of obedience, so does God also deal with us.

This truth is very clearly set forth in a passage which we have quoted before, but which we do well to read again. In Psalm 89:30-34 we read, "If his children forsake my law, and walk not in my judgments; if they break my statutes, and keep not my commandments; then will I visit their transgression with the rod, and their iniquity with stripes. Nevertheless my lovingkindness will I not utterly take from him, nor suffer my faithfulness to fail. My covenant will I not break, nor alter the thing that is gone out of my lips."

So our part in the covenant is very real and very important.

What precisely is that part?

In general, as we have already said, that part consists of faith and obedience. Our part is to believe in Christ, to lay hold of Him by a true and living faith, to appropriate Him and all His benefits, to live in Him and out of Him; for He is the Mediator of that covenant and it is only through Him that we enter into fellowship with God.

But our part is also to walk in obedience before Him in all our calling in life. That obedience is, of course, faithfulness to all the

Scriptures, faithfulness to the truth of the Scriptures, and faithfulness to the precepts of the gospel. We can sum it all up in this, that our calling is to walk as God's covenant people in the world, manifesting in all that we do that we are members of His covenant, that we represent the cause of His covenant, and that we look forward to the day when we shall be taken into that covenant perfectly when the tabernacle of God is with men.

We are to do this in every sphere of life in the place in which God has put us. We are to establish Christian homes in which husband and wife reflect that glorious covenant relationship between Christ and His church (Ephesians 5:22-33); we are to bring forth the children of God's covenant and teach them the ways of Jehovah (Deuteronomy 6:4-9, Psalm 78:1-8); we are to train our children in covenant schools in which the fear of the Lord is the beginning of all wisdom; we are to live holily and righteously in every part of life to the praise of the God of our salvation.

But let it always be remembered that the demands and obligations of the covenant are also the privileges which we have by grace. Christ's yoke is easy and His burden is light (Matthew 11:29-31), because we are given by grace the great privilege of being God's covenant people. God is not ashamed to be called our God (Hebrews 11:16); and we cannot be ashamed to be known in the world as God's covenant people. We are not burdened with heavy loads; we are given a great blessing. And this must never be forgotten. Indeed, we *must* walk in the ways of the covenant, for this is the requirement of all the Scriptures. But God graciously makes this "must" the "can" and the "will." We must, but by grace we can and will.

Surely everyone at all sensitive to His calling knows how often we fail and how necessary it is to flee to the cross for forgiveness and pardon. But the humble child of God knows that there is mercy in Calvary and tender love in the blood of Christ. He returns refreshed and renewed, grateful that God is faithful in all his unfaithfulness, in awe of such great love that never forsakes him, and with a heart filled with praise to Him Who keeps covenant and will never let us go.

Chapter 18

THE COVENANT AND THE KINGDOM

Although the general subject of the kingdom is occasioned by the history of the establishment of the kingdom of Israel during the days of David and Solomon, we shall in this chapter discuss the idea of the kingdom in its relationship to the covenant of grace.

Many incorrect ideas of the kingdom are found in the theology of the churches of our day. They range from the very liberal and modern idea of a purely earthly kingdom in which all the problems of history will be ultimately resolved, a view which has given birth to the social gospel, to the more conservative views of the kingdom found in various kinds of post-and pre-millennialism. It is not our intention to investigate all these various ideas and subject them to the scrutiny of the Scriptures, since this would take us too far afield in our discussion of the covenant.

Nevertheless, it is clear that in the Old Testament a very close connection existed between the covenant of grace and the kingdom of Israel in the monarchy which was especially established in the reigns of David and Solomon; and this at least suggests that in the new dispensation, the age of fulfillment, such a relationship, though now on the higher spiritual level, also is present. When, e.g., God established His covenant with David, as recorded for us in II Samuel 7 and Psalm 89, this covenant was revealed to David in terms of a Son whom God would give David and Who would establish the throne of David's kingdom forever.

We ought, therefore, to turn first of all to the history of the establishment of the monarchy in Israel, for in this lay the typical revelation of God concerning the relation between the kingdom and the covenant.

It was during the days of Samuel the judge that Israel came to him with the request to anoint a king to rule over them, so that they could be like the other nations. The years of the judges had been chaotic years and life in the nation of Israel had gradually deteriorated. It was in desperation that at last Israel turned to Samuel with the request for a king. This request of the nation was not in itself wrong. In fact, already in the days of Moses, God had spoken to Israel of the time when they would have a king of their own (Deuteronomy 17:14-20). The error lay rather in the *kind* of king which they wanted. They were not at all concerned about having a king to rule over them who would rule in the name of God. The were interested in a king "as the other nations had." They wanted one who was strong and a mighty warrior; who could lead them in battle and prove a valiant soldier. They wanted a king of whom they could proudly boast. Whether or not he feared the Lord was incidental. And they were sure that if they received such a king as they demanded that all their problems and troubles would be over and they would once again be restored to a strong and powerful nation.

But God showed them they were wrong by giving them a king of the kind they wanted. And when they received such a king, Saul, they found to their profound dismay that this was, after all, not a solution to their problem. After Saul had reigned forty years, things were worse in the land than they had ever been, for Saul was a wicked man and the blessing of the Lord was not upon either him or the nation.

In the place of Saul, God gave Israel a king of His choice. David was taken from the sheepfold of his father Jesse in the humble village of Bethlehem and made king over God's heritage. This was something quite different. David was God's choice, a man after God's own heart. And under his rule the nation prospered.

There are certain elements of David's rule which stand directly related to our subject, and these elements all have to do with the fact that the kingdom of Israel under David and his son Solomon was typical of the kingdom of heaven.

In the first place, the king himself was typical. And the type was of Christ. Though Christ was the Son of David with the royal blood of David's line flowing in His veins, He was also the fulfillment of His father David in David's typical place in the dispensation of types and shadows.

In the second place, the kingdom itself which was established under David's rule was typical. The kingdom was established in the land of Canaan, which land was a picture of heaven. It was a kingdom of a typical people, for Israel, while a part of the church of all ages, was also a type of the church gathered throughout history. The kingdom was surrounded by the trappings of the Mosaic economy – the typical sacrifices offered in the typical tabernacle and temple by a typical priesthood, all of which pointed ahead to Christ and His work. The church and the kingdom were inseparably connected, for the kingdom was in the strictest sense of the word a theocracy.

In the third place, although the kingdom was in typical form, nevertheless it presented some very striking truths concerning the kingdom which would some day be established. These truths centered in the person of David himself. For one thing, David, in much of his life, pointed ahead to the suffering of Christ on the cross. This is evident from the Psalms of David in which he describes the many troubles through which the Lord led him and which were typical of the suffering of Jesus while on earth. There are many of these Psalms, and a reading of them makes clear that Christ Himself was speaking through David in them. (See I Peter 1:11.) David sings of Jesus' own suffering at the hands of sinful men, while at the same time referring to the experiences of his own life. So much is this true that Christ Himself takes the very words of the Psalms on His lips as He did, e.g., on the cross (Psalm 22:1).

For another thing, David was, as king, the captain of the Lord's armies. This began already at the moment David was anointed king. He lived in the palace of Saul but was one of the most valiant warriors in Saul's army. It was he who dared go forth to join battle with the giant Goliath when all the host of Israel shrank in fear from Goliath's curses. And in doing so he showed himself ready to fight the battles of the Lord in faith even against overwhelming odds. It was not without purpose that the daughters of Israel sang after this event: "Saul hath slain his thousands, but David his ten thousands." As the leader of the host of Israel he marched at the front of the armies and led Israel from victory to victory until all the enemies of the nation were destroyed and the borders of the promised land extended to the boundaries which God had promised to Abraham. (See Genesis 15:18-21, II Samuel 5:6-10, 8:1-18, 10:6-19, etc.) All these battles, however, were battles of faith fought in the strength of the Lord (II Samuel 8:6b).

But all this was typical. David fought typical battles with typical weapons against typical enemies of the surrounding nations to win typical victories. In the dispensation of realities, Christ is the Captain of our salvation. He it is Who fights for His people. The enemies are no longer the Amorites and Philistines; they are the enemies of sin, death, Satan, hell. The battles are not fought with typical armies armed with typical weapons of warfare; they are battles fought principally by Christ on the cross, and, through the power of Christ in the hearts of His people, by the saints in the battle of faith. The weapons are the spiritual weapons which alone will prevail against spiritual enemies. They that fight with the sword shall perish with the sword. The saints fight with the armor of God: the girdle of truth, the breastplate of righteousness, the sandals of the preparation of the gospel of peace, the shield of faith, the helmet of salvation, the sword of the Spirit which is the Word of God (Ephesians 6:10-17). The battle is not the defeat of an army of Moabites (or even Russian and Chinese communists), but the defeat of Satan, the world, and the sin of our own flesh. The end is not the extension of the boundaries of Canaan (or of the United States), but the coming of the new heavens and the new earth. That which was typical was given for our instruction upon whom the end of the ages is come (I Corinthians 10:11). And this victory comes by faith, for faith is the victory that overcomes the world (I John 5:4).

In the fourth place, the kingdom of David was given over to Solomon his son. Under Solomon the picture of the kingdom of heaven took on added beauty. We have a stirring description of this, e.g., in Psalm 72, for Solomon ruled over a kingdom of peace and righteousness. It was he that established a kingdom of glorious riches and incomparable splendor. Vividly described in the first chapters of I Kings (4-10) and II Chronicles (2-9), Solomon's kingdom was like none other. But it too was only a picture. It too pointed ahead to another kingdom – the kingdom of heaven. Only, once again, the wealth of the kingdom of heaven is not the wealth of gold and peacocks, of ivory and apes, of rubies and cedar trees, but the spiritual blessings of salvation, treasures incorruptible and undefiled and which never fade away, of which material prosperity in Canaan was but a picture.

Finally, this kingdom of Solomon had, at its center, the glorious temple in which Jehovah dwelt in covenant fellowship with His people.

This temple was the center of the kingdom, for it was the dwelling place of Him Who really ruled over Israel.

But all this was typical. Already the reigns of David and Solomon showed that the true kingdom could not be established through them. Although David was a man after God's own heart, terrible sins characterized his life and reign. And during the time of Solomon the seeds of decline were sown. Under the influence of his many heathen wives, Solomon turned to the worship of idols: "For it came to pass, when Solomon was old, that his wives turned away his heart after other gods: and his heart was not perfect with the Lord his God, as was the heart of David his father. For Solomon went after Ashtoreth the goddess of the Zidonians, and after Milcom, the abomination of the Ammonites. And Solomon did evil in the sight of the Lord, and went not fully after the Lord, as did David his father. . ." (I Kings 11:4ff.).

The punishment for this sin was severe. "Wherefore the Lord said unto Solomon, Forasmuch as this is done of thee, and thou hast not kept my covenant and my statutes, which I have commanded thee, I will surely rend the kingdom from thee, and will give it to thy servant. Notwithstanding in thy days I will not do it for David thy father's sake: but I will rend it out of the hand of thy son. Howbeit I will not rend away all the kingdom; but I will give one tribe to thy son for David my servant's sake, and for Jerusalem's sake which I have chosen" (I Kings 11:11, 12).

This prediction of punishment was fulfilled in the days of Rehoboam when ten tribes under the leadership of Jeroboam the son of Nebat seceded from the kingdom to establish the northern kingdom of the ten tribes. This was the first dimming of the glory of Solomon's kingdom. And the history of the nation was, from that point and with only a bit of relief from time to time, a sad history of spiritual disintegration. The ten tribes, under the leadership of Jeroboam fell into image worship and then idolatry. They departed farther and farther from the worship of Jehovah until they finally became ripe for judgment and were led into captivity by the Assyrians, never to return.

But the kingdom of Judah fared little better. Their history also was one of sad decline. It is true that, unlike the northern kingdom, Judah had her good kings (Jehoshaphat, Hezekiah, Josiah, e.g.), but there were many evil kings also who outdid the kings of Israel in wickedness.

While the kingdom of Judah was spared a bit longer than the northern kingdom, nevertheless, they too were soon brought into captivity by the Babylonians. With the passing of these two kingdoms the old shadows passed away. A remnant of Judah did return from captivity under the leadership of Zerubbabel and Ezra, but even then the kingdom was not restored, and Judah remained under the foreign rule of heathen world powers. Even at the time of Christ, Judah was crushed beneath the heel of mighty Rome. It seemed as if the sceptre had indeed departed from Judah.

But God remembered the covenant which He swore to Abraham, Isaac, and Jacob. While Judah was brought into captivity as punishment for its terrible crimes, nevertheless God was moving aside the typical kingdom which was to have its fulfillment in the coming of Christ. It was of this that the prophets spoke again and again. Standing on the mountain tops of prophecy, they looked ahead to the establishment of the kingdom of heaven which would take place when the promised seed would be born.

Hence, the coming of the kingdom is closely associated with the entire life of Jesus Christ. Already at the time when Gabriel announced Christ's birth to Mary, the angel spoke of this birth of Christ in connection with the kingdom: "And the angel said unto her, Fear not, Mary: for thou hast found favour with God. And, behold, thou shalt conceive in thy womb, and bring forth a son, and shalt call his name Jesus. He shall be great, and shall be called the Son of the Highest: and the Lord God shall give unto him the throne of his father David: and he shall reign over the house of Jacob forever; and of his kingdom there shall be no end" (Luke 1:30-33).

John the Baptist was the prophet of the kingdom in the highest sense of the word. He had been born from the aged Zacharias and Elisabeth to prepare the way for Christ. His ministry clearly showed that he was deeply conscious of his calling to prepare the way for Him Who was to establish the kingdom of heaven. According to Matthew's gospel record, he preached: "Repent ye, for the kingdom of heaven is at hand" (Matthew 3:3-12).

When Jesus spoke to the multitude about John's ministry, He used some very unusual words: "Verily I say unto you, among them that are born of women there hath not risen a greater than John the Baptist;

notwithstanding he that is least in the kingdom of heaven is greater than he. And from the days of John the Baptist until now the kingdom of heaven suffereth violence, and the violent take it by force. For all the prophets and the law prophesied until John" (Matthew 11:11-13).

John was the greatest of all the Old Testament saints; and more particularly, of all the prophets who prophesied in the time of shadows. Yet, in comparison with the new dispensation, when the kingdom of heaven is come, he was the least of all. For the very least in the kingdom of heaven is greater than he. This remarkable fact is true because John still lived in the time of types and shadows, in the age when the kingdom had not actually come. He was the bridge between the two, the transition between the old age and the new, for he was the prophet of the dawn. But the reality of the kingdom of heaven is so much greater than the types and shadows that the greatest of them all is still less than the least of those who really live in the kingdom.

It is also for this reason that the kingdom during John's day suffered violence and the violent took it by force. Imagine if you can that all the saints of the old dispensation never really saw the reality of the kingdom. All they received from God was a picture book in which were drawn for them many pictures of that kingdom. And, while the pictures were very beautiful, they were only pictures. But when John came (and this was why he was greater than them all), he showed the people the door to the kingdom. He did this by pointing out the Christ Who is the door. "Behold the Lamb of God, which taketh away the sin of the world" (John 1:29). And, "Then said Jesus unto them again, verily, verily, I say unto you, I am the door of the sheep" (John 10:7). It was, to continue the figure, as if John pushed this door to the kingdom open just a bit. The result was that the people of God saw a swift glimpse of the kingdom of heaven as it really was, in contrast to the dreary types. Now they stormed that door of the kingdom with violence. They would not be turned away. The kingdom is so exceedingly beautiful that they would not be refused entrance. The violent take it by force.

But all this means that the kingdom was actually established by Christ Himself. His entire ministry was concerned with the kingdom. There was not anything else about which He preached. The glorious sermon on the mount, e.g., was a discourse on the fundamental principles of the kingdom. All the parables He told were to explain the spiritual realities of the kingdom. All the miracles which He performed were so many signs of the power and blessedness of the kingdom.

In the highest sense of the word, the kingdom was realized when Christ shed His blood on the cross. For the kingdom of heaven is a kingdom of righteousness. And that righteousness comes to those who are the citizens of the kingdom through the blood of atonement. On Calvary, the foundation of that kingdom was laid. In the suffering of the faithful Servant of Jehovah the blessings of that kingdom were merited. Without the cross there is no kingdom. Therefore, Christ's resurrection and ascension is the means by which Christ becomes the King of the kingdom of heaven. He ascended into glory and God gave to Him the highest position at God's right hand. All power and authority were given to Him. He was entrusted with the rule over all God's works. To Him was committed the full realization of that kingdom. The kingdom of David and Solomon is fulfilled in its highest reality in the kingdom of Christ.

The kingdom came to God's people at Pentecost. Then the Spirit was poured out on the church and the kingdom was established within the hearts of God's people. What a change was made by this Spirit. We need only consider the tremendous change in the disciples themselves. Prior to Pentecost they understood almost nothing of the kingdom. They were constantly thinking in terms of an earthly kingdom which led them to be busy always in bickering among themselves who would be the greatest. Even at the time of the ascension of Christ, they were still looking for an earthly kingdom. Yet suddenly the Spirit came and they understood it all. Peter could (and did) preach on Pentecost morning a remarkable sermon in which he showed how clearly he understood all that God had done through Christ. Suddenly the cross was clear to him, and he saw the perfect plan of God in fulfilling prophecy through the resurrection and ascension of Christ. He quoted the Scriptures accurately as they applied to the fulfillment of types and shadows. The only difference was the Spirit Who revealed all to them.

And so the kingdom of heaven has come.

What, according to the Scriptures, is that kingdom?

There is a certain similarity in form between the kingdom of heaven and an earthly kingdom. This is not to say that the two must be identified, for the truth is far from this. But evidently God intended that in an earthly kingdom there would be some kind of earthly shadow of what the kingdom of heaven is. This was especially and emphatically true of the kingdom of Israel which was established in the monarchy of David and Solomon. In fact, only in this kingdom of Israel do we have a real picture of the kingdom of heaven. The kingdom of heaven is not a democracy, either representative or parliamentary. It is not even a monarchical democracy. It is not an oligarchy such as we find occasionally today. It is not a dictatorship in the commonly accepted meaning of the word. It is in the strictest sense a monarchy.

Within a monarchy is one king. In the kingdom of heaven God is that King, though He rules through Jesus Christ by Whom that kingdom is established. And just as in an earthly kingdom there are citizens or subjects, so is it true of the kingdom of heaven. And these citizens are the elect people of God who are redeemed through the blood of the cross. Just as in an earthly kingdom there is a certain realm over which the king is supreme ruler, so the kingdom of heaven has such a realm, although that realm is emphatically the hearts of the saints. The rule of the King is set up within the hearts of the people of God. "And when he was demanded of the Pharisees, when the kingdom of God should come, he answered them and said, The kingdom of God cometh not with observation; neither shall they say, Lo here! or, lo there! for, behold, the kingdom of God is within you" (Luke 17:20, 21). Only at the end of the age when the kingdoms of this world become the kingdom of our God and of His Christ shall the realm of the kingdom of heaven be extended to include the entire redeemed and glorified creation.

There are certain treasures that an earthly kingdom also possesses. Its success is measured by its wealth. It includes crown jewels, natural resources, reserves of gold and silver, abundance of land, strength of armies, etc. These treasures of a kingdom are the possession and glory of the king and of his subjects. The kingdom of heaven also has its treasures, but they are, in keeping with the character of the kingdom, spiritual treasures which endure forever. They are the treasures of the blessings of God's everlasting covenant of grace, the riches of salvation in Jesus Christ.

A king has certain obligations in his kingdom: to rule for the well-being of his subjects, to seek the good of the citizens, and to delight in their happiness. The measure of the success of a king is the happiness of the people in the realm. This, too, is true of the kingdom of heaven. While surely the final purpose of the kingdom of heaven is the glory of God, it is also true that our sovereign King makes all His subjects supremely happy forever as He delivers them from sin and death and takes them into His own everlasting fellowship.

But the kingdom is emphatically spiritual in all its parts. In this way it is fundamentally different from every kingdom of this world. How often is this not emphasized in the Scriptures! When Christ was tried before Pilate, this Roman ruler was particularly concerned about the charge that the Jews made against the Lord that He was a King. But even while Jesus acknowledged that He was indeed a King, He assured Pilate, "My kingdom is not of this world: if my kingdom were of this world, then would my servants fight, that I should not be delivered to the Jews: but now is my kingdom not from hence" (John 18:36). It is often said that the Sermon on the Mount is the Constitution of the Kingdom of Heaven. While there may be an element of truth in this, any one who reads carefully Matthew 5-7 will understand immediately that Christ is not talking about any kind of earthly kingdom that can be realized and established here in the world. To mention but one thing, the citizens of the kingdom are described as those who are poor in spirit, who mourn, are meek, are hungry and thirsty for righteousness, are merciful, are pure in heart, are peacemakers, are persecuted, reviled, reproached, the objects of evil slander. What a strange kingdom it would be here upon earth where the citizens were all poor, constantly weeping, always hungry and thirsty. No, the kingdom is not like any earthly kingdom at all; this "Constitution" fits only a kingdom which is profoundly spiritual.

This was really the crux of the question which constantly existed between Jesus and His disciples while Jesus was on earth. The disciples were always looking for an earthly kingdom. They had visions of a kingdom which would be composed of the Jews, would extend once again to the boundaries which existed under Solomon, would be a mighty kingdom in which Jesus would lead the victorious armies of Israel into battle with the Romans to drive the hated heathen out of the land and restore the kingdom to Israel. This is why Jesus' life was such a great mystery to them. When the people of Galilee wanted to make

Jesus king, He flatly refused and, in fact, told them He would never be their King. The disciples simply could not understand this strange refusal of the Lord, for they thought it was the perfect opportunity for Christ to seize the throne of David. When the Lord repeatedly made no effort to gather the support of the influential Scribes and Pharisees in order to make preparation for a revolt against Rome, the disciples were puzzled and offended. Jesus' actions were always different from what they expected. He did not court popular approval and seemed rather to go out of His way to antagonize people. He did not make any pretensions of being a king in any earthly sense, but instead emphasized constantly His meekness and lowliness. When finally He rode triumphantly into Jerusalem and the people shouted, "Hosanna to the Son of David," Christ was riding on a donkey. No white and pawing stallion for Him; no retinue of courtly servants with trumpets and flags; only a donkey. And instead of shouting defiantly and rousing the people to battle, He sat quietly. In fact, if you could be distracted a moment from the tumultuous clamor of the multitude to look at the Lord, you would discover that He was weeping. Did you ever see such a king as this in all the earth?

Because the disciples were intent on an earthly kingdom they were constantly arguing about who was the greatest, for they coveted an important place in that kingdom. How biting then were the words of the Lord: "The kings of the Gentiles exercise lordship over them; and they that exercise authority upon them are called benefactors. But ye shall not be so: but he that is greatest among you, let him be as the younger; and he that is chief, as he that doth serve. For whether is greater, he that sitteth at meat, or he that serveth? is not he that sitteth at meat? but I am among you as he that serveth" (Luke 22:25-27). This same point was emphasized by the Lord at the time of the footwashing on the eve of the Lord's passion: "Ye call me Master and Lord: and ye say well; for so I am. If I then, your Lord and Master, have washed your feet; ye also ought to wash one another's feet. For I have given you an example, that ye should do as I have done to you. Verily, verily, I say unto you, The servant is not greater than his lord; neither he that is sent greater than he that sent him. If ye know these things, happy are ye if ye do them" (John 13:13-17). Strange words for an earthly king to speak.

This conception of an earthly kingdom was deeply rooted in the hearts of the disciples. They could not and did not shake it off until Pentecost, when the Spirit of Christ revealed to them the true nature of the kingdom. This is why Peter was prepared to fight to the death in the Garden of Gethsemane in the night of the Lord's betrayal. But because he was so wrong, Christ reprimanded him and told him to put his sword away. This is why the disciples could never understand the cross. Indeed, above that cross were the words of eternal truth: "This is Jesus of Nazareth, the King of the Jews." But whoever heard of a king dying a shameful and cursed death on a cross and remaining a king throughout? It was all wrong. The plaintive sob of the disciples can be heard in the words of the two men traveling to Emmaus: "But we trusted that it had been he which should have redeemed Israel" (Luke 24:21). And they meant to say, "But the cross has dashed into a thousand pieces all our hopes and dreams." How foolish they were! But they had no idea of the spiritual character of the kingdom.

Even when Christ finally ascended into heaven, the disciples still clung to that same idea. They asked the Lord on Mount Olivet: "Lord, wilt thou at this time restore the kingdom to Israel?" (Acts 1:6) Only after the Spirit was poured out, did they finally see and understand.

Beyond all doubt many today make the same mistake that the disciples made. And one can ask in all seriousness: do not these seekers for an earthly kingdom understand the work of Christ? Do not they have that same Spirit of Pentecost which enlightened the minds of the disciples?

The spiritual character of the kingdom is clearly evident in the history of that kingdom as described in the Scriptures.

When God first formed the earthly creation, He set man in the middle of it as king. Adam was appointed to the office of king so that he might, as a servant of God, rule in God's name over God's world as God's representative. He was ruler under God in God's house. He was not to rule as a sovereign monarch, but as a covenant friend-servant of God. He was called to rule over the entire creation in the service of his Maker and to praise and glorify Him Who was exalted over all.

We know that Adam failed in this calling. From the point of view of his kingship in the creation, we may describe Adam's fall as being an act of rebellion against the sovereign Lord. Rather than bow before his

God in humble submission while he ruled in God's name, he chose the alternative. He chose to become the representative of Satan in God's house to help Satan in his evil and nefarious scheme to make this creation the kingdom of sin and hell. He chose to occupy a position of servant-king under the devil rather than under God. This was, of course, the devil's purpose. Satan was intent on making this creation his own possession after he was banished from heaven. But in order to accomplish this, he needed man as his ally, for Satan, being a spirit, needed a representative who lived in the world, as a part of it, to work in the material and earthly creation. Satan needed someone who would agree with him and through whom he then could work to steal God's world from God and use it in the service of evil. By doing this, Satan determined to wrest God's creation from the Lord of heaven and earth, dethrone God, and establish himself as a ruler in God's place. It was a clever, hellish plan; and seemingly, it succeeded; for Adam bent a listening ear, agreed to the devil's plot and chose to stand against God on the side of the powers of darkness.

However, there are several points which need to be taken into consideration to understand this completely.

In the first place, as a result of the fall (and as the just punishment for sin) Adam was deposed from office. He could no longer serve God as king. He had forfeited his right to do this and had proved unworthy of this lofty position. He was dethroned. The creation was without a king.

In the second place, while it is true that Adam fell from the throne upon which God had placed him, nevertheless, this also was not outside the purpose of God. God had determined also this in His counsel. It was not a mistake in the purpose of the Most High which spoiled God's plan and forced the Lord to make a considerable number of alterations to accomplish His purpose.

This truth (which we have already discussed in another connection) has several important implications. On the one hand, this truth implies that the original creation in which Adam stood in rectitude was never intended by God to be the real kingdom. It was, of course, a kingdom. Adam as king ruled over the kingdom which included the entire creation. But it was not the final kingdom of God's purpose. Rather, the kingdom over which Adam ruled was only an earthly picture of another kingdom which God was determined to establish – i.e., the kingdom of our Lord Jesus Christ.

On the other hand, this also explains the purpose in God's decree of Adam's fall. Adam fell in order to make room for another King Who would rule in God's name over another kingdom. This other King of another kingdom is Christ Who rules in God's name over the kingdom of heaven.

Hence, immediately after the fall, God announced to our first parents (Genesis 3:15) that He would send this other King, Who would be the Seed of the woman, and Who would wage a fierce and bitter battle against Satan in the name of God so that the evil purpose of Satan would be utterly defeated and the kingdom of God realized.

But this kingdom was not to come immediately. It would come only when Christ Himself came into the flesh.

This does not mean that the old dispensation was not an important period of time. Although during all this time the kingdom of heaven was not yet come, nevertheless, it had all kinds of significance for the kingdom. The church which God gathered during this time was instructed in the truth of the kingdom. And it was instructed in the truth of the kingdom by means of the types and shadows of the law. But in every respect, these types and shadows pointed ahead to Christ.

As we noticed already, Christ as the fulfillment of all the types and shadows of the Old Testament, established the kingdom. He did so because of a number of aspects to His work on the cross. In the first place, He died as King, i.e., as God's appointed King in Whom it was God's purpose to establish the kingdom of heaven. In the second place, the fulfillment of the promise to our first parents took place on the cross, for Christ there and then crushed the head of the serpent and his seed. Paul writes to the Colossians: "And having spoiled principalities and powers, he made a shew of them openly, triumphing over them in it" (2:15). In the third place, He died for all the sins and guilt of His people by bearing it away in His perfect atoning sacrifice. He thus paid the price to satisfy the justice of God and to earn for His people the right and power to become once again the citizens of His kingdom. In the fourth place, the one chief characteristic of that kingdom is righteousness, and Christ earned that righteousness for the whole kingdom by the shedding of His blood.

The result of this perfect work of Christ is that He is ascended on high in order to take His place as the King of that kingdom at God's right hand. But all power is given to Him (Matthew 28:18) so that His rule is total and complete. He rules over all in the absolute sense of the word. He rules over all God's creation so that the sun rises and sets by His command; but He also rules over all men, devils, and angels. Nothing is outside His sovereign dominion. Just as God Himself is sovereign over all, the sovereign Creator and King of all, so now God rules through Jesus Christ, His own dear Son, so that all His purpose is accomplished. Paul makes this very clear in I Corinthians 15:27, 28: "For he hath put all things under his feet. But when he saith all things are put under him, it is manifest that he is excepted, which did put all things under him. And when all things are subdued unto him, then shall the Son also himself be subject unto him that put all things under him, that God may be all in all." The same truth is taught everywhere in the Scriptures. Perhaps one or two more passages will suffice to make the point. In Philippians 2:9-11, after Paul has discussed the humiliation of Christ even to the death of the cross, we read: "Wherefore God hath also highly exalted him, and given him a name which is above every name: that at the name of Jesus every knee should bow, of things in heaven, and things in earth, and things under the earth; and that every tongue should confess that Jesus Christ is Lord, to the glory of God the Father." Daniel saw a vision of this: "I saw in the night visions, and, behold, one like the Son of man came with the clouds of heaven, and came to the Ancient of days, and they brought him near before him. And there was given him dominion, and glory, and a kingdom, that all people, nations, and languages, should serve him: his dominion is an everlasting dominion, which shall not pass away, and his kingdom that which shall not be destroyed" (Daniel 7:13, 14).

But if it is true that the rule of Christ extends over all, the question is: What is the difference between the rule of Christ over the wicked and devils on the one hand, and the rule of Christ over His people on the other? And if it can be shown that there is a difference, what is the relationship between these two rules of Christ?

Christ carries out the sovereign rule of God. God alone, because He is the Creator of all, possesses alone the *right* to rule over all. This right is now that of Christ, under God.

The rule of Christ over His elect people is of a unique kind. For these elect of God (and for them alone) Christ died on the cross. For them He atoned with His blood. For them He arose again from the dead opening the way through the grave so that they too may follow Him into His everlasting kingdom. And now that He is exalted in heaven, it is for them that He rules over all the works of God.

But we are speaking specifically of the kingdom of heaven. And inasmuch as Christ's sovereign authority and rule is exercised within this kingdom, all this means that Christ is the sovereign Lord of His people. He rules over them. But He rules over them in such a way that they become the citizens of His kingdom. He rules over them by His grace and Holy Spirit. He rules over them by calling them irresistibly out of darkness – the darkness of sin and death, and bringing them into the kingdom of light. "Who hath delivered us from the power of darkness, and hath translated us into the kingdom of his dear Son" (Colossians 1:13). And the result of all this is that the elect become the willing subjects of His kingdom. They are made subjects so that they acknowledge Christ as their Lord. They are made citizens who bow before the sovereign rule of their king. They are brought into that heavenly kingdom by regeneration and conversion; and the result is that they live within that kingdom, give allegiance only to their Lord and Savior, and bow in all their life before King Jesus.

But Christ also rules over the wicked – men and devils. He it is Who sets kings upon their thrones and puts them down. He establishes princes in their domains, but He also removes them according to God's appointment. He rules over them, but also through them. His rule in all the affairs of men is of such a kind that these men do nothing else but accomplish God's eternal purpose. "The king's heart is in the hand of the Lord, as the rivers of water: he turneth it whithersoever he will" (Proverbs 21:1). But it ought to be immediately apparent that Christ does not rule over the wicked in the same way as He rules over His people. Obviously there is a difference, an important one. The wicked and the devils do not become the willing subjects of His kingdom. They hate Christ, oppose His rule, fight against Him, attempt with all their power to destroy Him, and engage all their life long in a frantic attempt to establish a kingdom of sin. This is the kingdom which is finally realized by Antichrist.

But Christ rules nonetheless. Only now He rules in such a way that the wicked, in spite of themselves, against their will, nevertheless serve the purpose of God. Christ rules over them through their evil, making their hatred, their warfare, their violent opposition serve His purpose. This then is the difference. Christ rules over His people, *making them the willing subjects of His kingdom.* But He rules over the wicked *in spite of their opposition and furious assaults upon Him.* He uses even their hatred and war against Him to serve His purpose. This is the whole point of Psalm 2, which had its historical realization in the kingdom of David: "Why do the heathen rage, and the people imagine a vain thing? The kings of the earth set themselves, and the rulers take counsel together, against the Lord, and against his anointed, saying, Let us break their bands asunder, and cast away their cords from us. He that sitteth in the heavens shall laugh: the Lord shall have them in derision. Then shall he speak unto them in his wrath, and vex them in his sore displeasure. Yet have I set my king upon my holy hill of Zion" (Psalm 2:1-6). (See also Revelation 5.)

Even here there is a point of contact that we must not miss. The rule of Christ over the wicked is a rule of sovereign supremacy. And it is such because, through His cross, He earned the *right* to rule over the wicked. But He rules over them, indeed against their will, also *for the sake of* His own kingdom. He makes their foul deeds and furious hatred serve His kingdom. He uses them, in His sovereign purpose, to establish the kingdom which shall continue forever. This is why He laughs and holds them in derision. There is a divine irony in that their raging against Him serves His purpose. He makes all they do help along in the realization of the salvation of His own so that they may inherit the glorious and eternal kingdom of heaven.

This is why *all things* work together for good to them that love God and are called according to His purpose. This is why no one can lay anything to the charge of God's elect. This is why, when God is for us, nothing can be against us. This is why we are *more than* conquerors through Him Who loved us. And this is why nothing can separate us from the love of God through Jesus Christ our Lord (Romans 8:28ff.).

The result of all this is that now, while we are still on this earth, the kingdom of heaven is within the hearts of God's people. They are citizens of that kingdom because they are brought into it by a spiritual wonder and are given the blessings of that kingdom in their hearts. Their citizenship in that kingdom is not to be identified with any earthly commonwealth. They are citizens of the kingdom of heaven. That is where their citizenship papers are to be found. And while they themselves are called to live here upon earth for a little while, they are pilgrims and strangers in the earth, walking an earthly sojourn as aliens in an alien land waiting for the day when they shall be brought into the kingdom of Jesus Christ. Throughout this present age therefore, Christ is working all things according to the will of God in order that His kingdom may come. The elect are being gathered; the events of the world are being fulfilled according to God's will – and are in this way signs of Christ's coming. (See Matthew 24.) The final preparations are being made for the coming of that kingdom in the day when Christ shall appear upon the clouds of heaven to establish His everlasting kingdom. Then the imperfect and typical theocracy of Israel will be perfectly realized. Then the kingdoms of this world shall be destroyed and shall become the kingdom of our Lord and of His Christ. Then all the new heavens and the new earth shall become a part of the glorious and heavenly kingdom over which Christ rules perfectly in the name of God, and all the elect shall be princes and princesses in the everlasting kingdom of heaven.

Yet the kingdom is not realized completely and perfectly as long as the history of this world continues. While Christ rules over all, the citizens of the kingdom of heaven live in the same world with the citizens of the kingdom of darkness. But the rule of Christ Jesus the Lord strikes into this world a deep antithesis between the two kingdoms and their respective citizens. Just because the rule of Christ is so basically different in the hearts of His own elect and in the lives of wicked men, a deep difference is struck between the wicked and the righteous. A chasm is created between the people of God and the citizens of Satan's kingdom. It is the chasm of the rule of Christ which affects every part of their lives. The people of God are in the world, but they are surely not of it. And nothing can bridge that chasm. I know, men are always trying to build a bridge across that chasm of the antithesis. They want to cooperate with the world. They want to build, e.g., the bridge of "common grace" and speak of areas of cooperation between the wicked and the people of God because of this grace operative in all men. They reach out across the chasm to join hands with the world in an effort to march to the drum-beat of sin. They set certain aims similar to the aims of the world as goals of their own life. And basically they do this whenever they seek to make this world a better place in which to live.

These efforts are always rooted in a denial of the fundamental distinction between the rule of Christ's grace of the elect and the rule of Christ's power over the wicked. All the rule of Christ is a rule of grace, so it is said, and the antithesis disappears in a misty vapor. And the result of this is that the kingdom of heaven becomes nothing but a kingdom realized here upon earth. All men are created in the image of God; all men possess that image; all men are therefore brothers united in one common brotherhood; this world must become a better place in which to live so that the kingdom of heaven is earthly and part of this history.

But really nothing can destroy the antithesis, for Christ preserves it. Many who nominally belong to the church may indeed destroy it in their own lives, but the result is that they go into the world and become worldly and carnal so that no spiritual difference exists any longer between them and the seed of the serpent. But God maintains the antithesis for all that. He maintains it because He preserves the cause of His kingdom in the world. And the result is that the people of God, though often sinful and in need of forgiveness, live in all their lives as citizens of the kingdom of heaven. Their lives are principally different from the lives of wicked men.

We must point out that this is not anabaptistic. The people of God must not engage in world-flight. This is never the calling of the church. The antithesis is not between nature and grace, as the Roman Catholics would have it. The antithesis is between sin and holiness, the power of evil and the power of grace. The church has never conceived of her calling to be one of isolation, waiting with folded hands on some lonely mountain top for the return of the Lord.

Nevertheless, the church lives in spiritual isolation and spiritual separation from the world. This antithesis cuts across the whole of life. He who is a citizen of the kingdom of heaven also marries and raises a family, just as the world does. But he marries and raises a family that his marriage may be a picture of the relation between Christ and His church and that he may bring forth the seed of God's covenant, the elect number of those who are destined to be saved.

The child of God goes to work each morning in order to earn his daily living. But he does this as a citizen of the kingdom of heaven even though he works at the side of a wicked man who hates God. But the reason why he works is to support the children God has entrusted to him and to promote the causes which manifest the kingdom of heaven in this world.

The elect believer sends his children off to school each morning. But he sends them to a school where they shall be taught the truth of the Scriptures so that "the man of God may be thoroughly equipped unto every good work." The citizen of the kingdom of Christ sends his boys off to service when his country calls; he too plods his way to the polls to vote on election day; he too gives his allegiance to those in authority over him. But he does all this in obedience to Christ Who rules over him even through wicked men and because he knows that all the kingdoms of this world must serve the purpose of the establishment of the the kingdom of Christ.

Through the whole of his life cuts the sharp line of the antithesis. Always he walks as a citizen of the kingdom of heaven. And as such a citizen, he seeks the kingdom of heaven in all that he does. "Seek ye first the kingdom of heaven and his righteousness" (Matthew 6:33). This is the fundamental principle of the whole of his life. He marches always as a soldier of the cross. He walks beneath the flying banners of Calvary. His warfare is against sin. He is of the party of the living God. And he always has the victory, for faith is the victory that overcomes the world.

We may well ask at this point what precisely does it mean to "seek the kingdom of heaven"? This question becomes especially urgent when we consider the fact that this kingdom is emphatically of heaven and not of this earth; while he who is called to seek it remains upon earth.

The answer to this question is not as difficult as it may first appear. To seek the kingdom of heaven means very definitely and concretely to seek the cause of God in the world, and that in distinction from the cause of the kingdoms of the world. The cause of God is represented by God's church where the gospel is preached. All that belongs to that cause of the church and the ministry of the gospel is part of that kingdom. And all that stands related to it belongs also to the manifestation of that kingdom here below. To this belongs the work of missions, the work of Christian education, the work of the home in the establishment of a covenant home, the work of every saint in his station and calling in life as he labors for the coming of the kingdom of Christ.

You see the importance of this. The child of God does not and cannot concern himself with the causes of the world. The efforts of the world are efforts put forth which are contrary to God's Word and are in the interests of establishing Satan's kingdom. How sad it is when the church of today piously and somewhat pompously hands out all kinds of advice to the government about how to solve the world's ills. How badly the church prostitutes her calling when she engages in social tasks for the betterment of mankind. How foolish when the church adopts the methods of the world to gain her ends, the methods of might and power, of marches and protests, of rebellion and numbers – when the Bible says emphatically, "Not by might, nor by power, but by my spirit, saith the Lord of hosts" (Zechariah 4:6). And if you say: Yes, but then we are always small and our voice insignificant and unheard in the raucous clamor of the enemy – so be it. "For who hath despised the day of small things?" (Zechariah 4:10) And we seek not a kingdom which is of this world.

The child of God is never *of* the world. He is *of* heaven. And it is always to heaven that he directs his thoughts and desires. Heaven is his home, his eternal destination as he walks his pilgrim pathway, the realization of the kingdom of which he is a part. The world goes to destruction and defeat. Only the kingdom of Christ endures. And of that kingdom he is a citizen by grace.

We have one final question to treat: What is the relationship between the kingdom of heaven and God's covenant?

That such a relationship exists is evident from many considerations.

In the first place, it ought to be obvious by now that those who belong to God's covenant are the same people as those who are the citizens of the kingdom of heaven. Christ, Who is the Head of the covenant is also the King of the kingdom. His cross was the realization of the covenant and the kingdom. His grace calls into the covenant and the kingdom. His power preserves both throughout all history. And these people, covenant people and citizens of the kingdom at the same time, are called to walk in the world in such a way that they represent both God's covenant and kingdom in all they do.

In the second place, this was the way things were in Paradise the first. Adam was created as king under God of all the creation, but he was also friend-servant of God who represented God's covenant in the creation, and himself lived in covenant fellowship with God.

In the third place, the final perfection of heaven is described in the Scriptures in terms of the full realization of both the covenant and the kingdom. It is the full perfection of the covenant because John saw "a new heaven and a new earth; for the first heaven and the first earth were passed away; and there was no more sea. And I John saw the holy city, new Jerusalem, coming down from God out of heaven, prepared as a bride adorned for her husband. And I heard a great voice out of heaven saying, Behold, the tabernacle of God is with men, and he will dwell with them, and they shall be his people, and God himself shall be with them, and be their God" (Revelation 21:1-3). And it is the full perfection of the kingdom because then the kingdoms of this world shall become the kingdom of our God and of His Christ.

Finally, there is one passage especially which clearly identifies the two, the passage with which we began our discussion. The passage is found in Psalm 89:19-37: "Then thou spakest in vision to thy holy one, and saidst, I have laid help upon one that is mighty; I have exalted one chosen out of the people. I have found David my servant; with my holy oil have I anointed him:. . . The enemy shall not exact upon him; nor the son of wickedness afflict him. And I will beat down his foes before his face, and plague them that hate him. But my faithfulness and my mercy shall be with him: and in my name shall his horn be exalted. I will set his hand also in the sea, and his right hand in the rivers. He shall cry unto me, Thou art my father, my God, and the rock of my salvation. Also I will make him my firstborn, higher than the kings of the earth. My mercy will I keep for him for evermore, and my covenant shall stand fast with him. His seed also will I make to endure for ever, and his throne as the days of heaven. If his children forsake my law, and walk not in my judgments; if they break my statutes, and keep not my commandments; then will I visit their transgression with the rod, and their iniquity with stripes. Nevertheless my lovingkindness will I not utterly take from him, nor suffer my faithfulness to fail. My covenant will I not break, nor alter the thing that is gone out of my lips. Once have I sworn by my holiness that I will not lie unto David. His seed shall endure for ever, and his throne as the sun before me. It shall be established for ever as the moon, and as a faithful witness in heaven."

While we cannot go into this beautiful and significant passage of Scripture in detail, there are several elements in it to which our attention must be called.

David had decided to build a house for the Lord in Jerusalem and had consulted the prophet Nathan, who had given David his blessing on the project (II Samuel 7:1-3). But the Lord sent Nathan back to David to tell him that he should not engage in this work, although his intentions were good. There were, evidently, two reasons for this. One was that David was a man of war who had subdued all Israel's enemies; and the other was that David was only a type of Christ so that he could not, in himself, depict Christ in all our Savior's work. It was for that reason that God promised David a son who would build this house: "And when thy days be fulfilled, and thou shalt sleep with thy fathers, I will set up thy seed after thee, which shall proceed out of thy bowels, and I will establish the throne of his kingdom for ever. I will be his father, and he shall be my son. If he commit iniquity, I will chasten him with the rod of men, and with the stripes of the children of men: but my mercy shall not depart away from him, as I took it from Saul, whom I put away before thee. And thy house and thy kingdom shall be established forever before thee: thy throne shall be established for ever" (II Samuel 7:12-16). It is to this word of God that David responds in Psalm 89.

The obvious historical reference to these words of God is to Solomon, David's son by Bathsheba, who did indeed build the glorious temple in Jerusalem. In him this prophecy was fulfilled historically and typically in the nation of Israel.

But it is immediately evident that this work of Solomon was by no means the full and complete fulfillment of the prophecy. It is true that all the words of Psalm 89 and II Samuel 7 were fulfilled in him: God beat down his foes before his face; God's faithfulness and mercy were with him; his hand was in the sea and his right hand in the rivers; he was higher than the kings of the earth; he and his seed did forsake

God's law and break God's statutes, and God did visit their transgression with the rod and their iniquity with stripes; and above all, God's lovingkindness was never utterly taken from him and God's faithfulness never failed; the covenant which God had sworn was never broken.

But while all these things were true, this prophecy was never completely realized in Solomon himself. God spoke of this with emphasis. God spoke of a mercy which He would keep for David *forevermore,* of a covenant which would *never* fail, of a seed that would endure *forever,* and of a kingdom which would be as permanent as the sun and moon. The very obvious reference is to Christ, the true Seed of David, Who performed the work which Solomon could not really do. And all the statements of God in the text apply to Christ.

All the emphasis in the text falls upon the fact that God is the One Who maintains His covenant. We have had occasion to observe before that the establishment of the covenant is God's work alone; that, therefore, the covenant could never be an agreement between God and man; that God does all that is necessary to realize His covenant with His people. But the same is true of the maintenance of that covenant. And the passage in Psalm 89 underscores this. It was after all true that Solomon and his seed did forsake God's law and did refuse to walk in God's judgments. They did break His statutes and did not keep His commandments. And God could very well have abandoned them and refused to keep them as His covenant people. And He did visit their transgression with the rod and their iniquity with stripes. This reached its climax in the captivity when the nation was brought to a foreign land. But even then God remained faithful to His covenant. He did not forget the oath which He had sworn. He did not alter the thing that had gone out of his lips. He kept His promise always even though His people were wholly unworthy.

That fulfillment was in Christ. Christ was the Seed of David and Solomon, Who established forever the throne of David and Who built the true house of God. He did this when God visited upon Him all the stripes of His anger against the sins of His people on the cross and Who beat His own Son with the rod of His fury. But by His perfect sacrifice on the cross, Christ established the perfect kingdom of righteousness and built the temple of God which is His body. This kingdom and temple are everlasting in the heavens. And in them both the covenant between God and His people is perfectly realized.

In Christ the kingdom and covenant are brought into perfect unity. The promise to David of an everlasting throne is at the same time a covenant promise, as is evident from the text. And in Christ, Who is both the King of an everlasting kingdom and the Head of the covenant of grace, both become one. The typical kingdom of Israel reaches its full realization in the "monarchy" of heaven. In its typical form, the kingdom had David and Solomon at its head with the temple at the very center. There God dwelt visibly in covenant fellowship with His people through all the types and shadows of the law. But in its fulfillment in Christ, its typical shadow passed away. Christ is the eternal King; but also in Him as His body is the temple raised to its everlasting perfection. He not only rules over His people sovereignly by the power of His grace, but He also takes them into His own covenant fellowship, and, through Him, into the covenant life which God lives in Himself.

All this is realized only in part in this life. It is true that already now Christ rules over us by His grace and Spirit in our hearts. He lives in us and we in Him. And the covenant is, therefore, within that kingdom, realized in principle. But it is not now perfect. We are still in this world, walking as pilgrims and strangers in the earth, and still in need of fighting the battle of faith, also against our own sins. We have not yet inherited the earth, as is Christ's promise to us. We are not yet clothed in the white garments of Christ's righteousness in perfection. We are still wicked and the covenant fellowship which we enjoy with God through Christ is not yet perfect. We do not walk perfectly as citizens of the kingdom of heaven.

But the day will come when all this shall be perfected. The promise made so long ago to Adam in Paradise that the head of the serpent would be crushed is then accomplished completely. Christ fundamentally accomplished this on the cross, but the devil still rages and storms, for he knows that he has but a little while (Revelation 12:12). But the time will come when he is cast into the lake of fire (Revelation 20:20). Then his evil power will be destroyed forever.

The promise made to Noah that the covenant would include in it the entire creation will then also be fulfilled. Now the creation still lives in the earnest expectation of the manifestation of the sons of God. It was made subject to vanity, but it shall also be delivered from the bondage of corruption. And while it waits, it groans and travails in pain (Romans 8:19-22). But presently this will be no more, for when Christ comes at the end of time, the entire creation shall be made new, for there shall be a new heavens and a new earth in which righteousness shall dwell (Revelation 21:1).

Then also shall all the true seed of Abraham, gathered from both Jews and Gentiles, elect according to the purpose of God, be brought into heaven. They shall be raised in their bodies from the dust of death to be made like unto the glorious body of Christ. They shall be there with their children as the covenant was established in the lines of continued generations (Hebrews 2:13). They shall be the heirs of the everlasting kingdom of heaven to rule with Christ as princes and princesses in the kingdom of God. And they shall be brought into the perfect fellowship of God's everlasting tabernacle where God Himself shall be with them and be their God, and where there shall be no more sin, no more suffering, no more pain and sorrow, for "God shall wipe away all tears from their eyes, and there shall be no more death, neither sorrow, nor crying, neither shall there be any more pain: for the former things are passed away" (Revelation 21:3, 4). We shall enter into the blessed and perfect life of God forever and ever, world without end.

But then all things will also be to the glory of God Himself. This has been the one dominant theme in all we have written. God is God. He must and will receive all the glory. He does all things for His own name's sake. All our salvation is the work of His sovereign grace through Jesus Christ. He realizes His kingdom. He establishes and maintains His covenant. It is all His work, never ours. He does it all that He may be glorified forever. And we, the redeemed covenant people, shall rejoice in Him, our God and Savior, through our Lord Jesus Christ.

Chapter 19

CONCLUSION

We have now reached the end of our study and we conclude with a brief review of what we have written.

Throughout our study we have emphasized that only a conception of God's everlasting covenant of grace which gives all glory to God and is faithful to the principles of His absolute sovereignty is a conception which is in keeping with the whole of the Scriptures. We have shown how throughout the history of the church from the time of the Reformation theologians have struggled with the problem of harmonizing the truths of sovereign grace, particularly sovereign predestination, with the truths of the covenant. We have shown how the difficulty in harmonizing these ideas was due to a wrong conception of the covenant, a conception which interpreted the covenant as an agreement or pact between God and man. And we have shown how the Scriptural idea of the covenant as a bond of friendship and fellowship between God and His people in Christ brings the whole truth of the covenant into beautiful harmony with the doctrines of sovereign and particular grace.

The triune God is in His own divine being a covenant God Who lives in perfect and gloriously happy covenant fellowship with Himself. God has eternally determined in His counsel to reveal His covenant life through Christ. He has done this by determining, according to the decree of sovereign election, to take into His covenant life a people, chosen in Christ, redeemed through the blood of His own Son. To that end Christ is eternally appointed to be the Head and Mediator of the covenant. In the fullness of time God sent forth His Son, Who took upon Himself the sins and the guilt of all His people. In dying the death of the cross, Christ made atonement for sin and earned for His people the right to be brought into God's covenant. Through Christ God's chosen people are made a covenant people, incorporated into the family of God, made heirs of the everlasting blessings of that covenant.

We have seen how the revelation of God's own blessed covenant life runs like a golden thread through the pages of the Scriptures and it has become a truth which has thrilled the hearts and enriched the lives of the saints throughout the ages. It has thrilled their hearts because of its rich beauty. It has enriched their lives because it has been itself their own blessed experience as God granted to them the unsearchable riches of Christ and the foretaste of the intimate communion of life with God in Christ as this will be realized in the glories of the new creation.

Adam was God's friend-servant, created in the image and likeness of God, made to know his God and to serve Him in love. God had prepared for him a home in Paradise where he constantly saw the beauties of the creation which revealed to him his God and where he walked with God and communed with Him in blessed communion of life.

Yet the first Paradise was still only a picture of the heavenly Paradise to come, and the first man Adam stood as king of the earthly creation and head of the human race as type and shadow of the second Adam. The first Adam was of the earth, earthy; the last Adam is the quickening Spirit and the Lord of all (I Corinthians 15:45, 47).

When Adam fell, God gave the promise of the seed of the woman in Whom God's covenant, dimly reflected in Paradise, would be perfectly realized. In the hope of the coming of this seed the believers of the Old Testament lived and died.

Enoch walked with God and was not, for God took him, to his everlasting home.

Noah found favor in God's sight, walked with God, saw the judgments of God poured out upon the first world of sinful mankind, but also saw the splendor of the rainbow that gave promise of a new creation in which heaven and earth would some day be united in one.

Abraham was the friend of God and father of all believers. To him was given the promise that Jehovah would be a God to him and to his seed after him forever (Genesis 17:7). At the height of his faith, when he showed his obedience to God by sacrificing his only son, he was given a glimpse of God's sacrifice of His only begotten Son for the sins of His people, and even saw from afar the resurrection from the dead (Hebrews 11:17-19).

Moses as the mediator of the old dispensation communed with God. He stood before the face of the Most High and the glory that he saw still shone on his face when he returned to the camp of Israel.

David was the man after God's heart, who was taken from the

sheepfold to be king over the theocracy of Israel. In this position he could write: "I will sing of the mercies of the Lord for ever: with my mouth will I make known thy faithfulness to all generations. For I have said, Mercy shall be built up for ever: thy faithfulness shalt thou establish in the very heavens. I have made a covenant with my chosen, I have sworn unto David my servant, thy seed will I establish for ever, and build up thy throne to all generations" (Psalm 89:1-4).

Solomon built God's house in Jerusalem, the city of the great king. God's house, typified by the temple proper, the Holy Place and the Holy of Holies, was the center of the shadow worship of the nation, for God dwelt typically among His people in covenant fellowship behind the veil. Israel had access to God through the priest, the altar of burnt offering and the sacrifices that lay smoldering on the altar. Only the high priest had the right to enter into God's presence, and that once a year with the blood of atonement for his own sins and the sins of the people. Yet there in that richly ornate house on Mount Zion, which was the joy of the whole earth, Israel lived in covenant fellowship with God and worshipped in the beauty of holiness.

"These all died in faith, not having received the promises, but having seen them afar off, and were persuaded of them, and embraced them, and confessed that they were strangers and pilgrims on the earth. For they that say such things declare plainly that they seek a country. And truly, if they had been mindful of that country from whence they came out, they might have had opportunity to have returned. But now they desire a better country, that is, an heavenly: wherefore God is not ashamed to be called their God: for he hath prepared for them a city" (Hebrews 11:13-16).

Throughout the dispensation of shadows the promises were increasingly enriched and the hopes and longings of the believers were intensified, for they all, along with father Abraham, longed to see His day (John 8:56). The prophet Isaiah, as an example of this, stood, as it were, at the very foot of the cross as he beheld in stunned amazement the Man of Sorrows, the suffering Servant of God, pouring out His soul as a sacrifice for the sins of His people (Isaiah 53).

And when the fullness of time came, God sent His Son, born of a woman, born under the law, Immanuel, God with us. John writes: "That which was from the beginning, which we have heard, which we have seen with our eyes, which we have looked upon, and our hands have handled, of the Word of life; . . . that declare we unto you, that ye also may have fellowship with us: and truly our fellowship is with the Father, and with his Son Jesus Christ" (I John 1:1-3).

God was in Christ reconciling the world unto Himself, nevermore to impute our sins to us. Never were heaven and earth closer than at that moment on Calvary when Christ's blood was shed as a perfect atonement for sin, when the Son of God in our flesh laid down His life for His sheep, given to Him of the Father.

Our Lord died and arose on the third day. He ascended to heaven to take our flesh into glory. There He lives and reigns, interceding for us and blessing us with every spiritual blessing until the day when He shall return with the clouds to make all things new.

On Pentecost Christ came to dwell with His church by His Spirit and by the Spirit the church becomes the temple of God in which God dwells through Christ in covenant fellowship. The tabernacle of God is with men. "Ye are the temple of the living God; as God hath said, I will dwell in them, and walk in them; and I will be their God, and they shall be my people" (I Corinthians 6:16).

God realizes all this sovereignly in history as He, through the Spirit of Christ, calls His people with a sovereign and irresistible call out of the darkness of sin and death, into the fellowship of His own life. He creates a covenant people by His own power and through the riches of His grace and mercy. He calls them to walk as His covenant people in the midst of the world and marks them with the sign of His covenant in baptism. He blesses them with all the blessings of His salvation and gives them the hope of everlasting life when the tabernacle of God shall be with men.

How beautiful this conception of the covenant is – especially when contrasted with the coldly mechanical view of a covenant as a formal agreement or pact. God is in Himself a family God: Father, Son, and Holy Spirit. This "family" life which God lives He reveals by taking His people into that blessed fellowship which He lives in Himself. In that family of our covenant God, God is the Father. As Father, He loves His family with an eternal and unchangeable love. He assumes all responsibility for the care of that family. He provides for all the needs of that family. He always, in all that He does to His children, seeks their good.

He prepares for them an inheritance which presently shall be their possession. And that inheritance is the great riches and treasures of salvation, finally bestowed upon His heirs in the new creation.

In that family, Christ is our Elder Brother. He is the Firstborn in God's eternal counsel. He is the One Who receives the birthright, the One Who has the "double portion" of His Father's possessions, the One Who has the rule over His brethren. He, as the Firstborn, not only prepared the way in the "womb" of God's counsel, but He also suffered and died on Calvary that a firm and lasting foundation of righteousness might be laid for that covenant. He is the Firstborn from the dead Who prepares the way in the "womb" of the grave, opening the door of the grave on heaven's side so that all His brethren might follow (Colossians 1:15-18).

And, in Christ, we are all a part of that family of God. We are the sons and daughters of our Father in heaven. We dwell together in one great family in the communion of the saints, in the unity of the body of Christ.

Thus we have the principle beginning of covenant blessedness while we are here on earth. God forms us into His covenant people and gives us already the beginnings of the riches of that covenant fellowship. He speaks to us through His Word and by His Spirit in the preaching of the gospel. And we speak to God in the intimacies of covenant fellowship. We speak to Him in our prayers, in our trust and reliance upon our heavenly Father. We seek all things at His hand, flee to Him for refuge in the storms of life, find in Him an ever present help in time of need, and tell Him of all our hopes and longings, our sorrows and griefs, our troubles and wants. In the truest and fullest sense of the word, we walk with God – as did Noah and Enoch. In a gloriously rich way we are the friends of God – as was Abraham. And through it all, we have the blessed privilege of walking in this present evil world as those who represent God's covenant and cause.

God's covenant covers every phase of our lives: our families, our place in God's church, our place in the world, our calling, our plans and purposes, our prayers, our very existence as living out of our God, through Him and unto Him. For we are His workmanship, created in Christ Jesus unto good works which God has before ordained that we should walk in them (Ephesians 2:10).

But all this can only be ours now in principle, for we are yet in our sins. We look in hope to the day when that covenant shall be perfected in all its glory and beauty in the new heavens and the new earth. Then shall be the marriage supper of the Lamb when the true covenant marriage of God and His people in Christ is realized, and when the whole family of God is gathered about the table of this marriage supper in the joy and laughter, the happiness and blessedness of the full perfection of heaven.

How beautifully the Scriptures speak of this in the conclusion of Holy Writ, the book of Revelation. "And a voice came out of the throne, saying, Praise our God, all ye his servants, and ye that fear him, both small and great. And I heard as it were the voice of a great multitude, and as the voice of many waters, and as the voice of mighty thunderings, saying, Alleluia: for the Lord God omnipotent reigneth. Let us be glad and rejoice, and give honour to him: for the marriage of the Lamb is come, and his wife hath made herself ready. And to her was granted that she should be arrayed in fine linen, clear and white: for the fine linen is the righteousness of saints. And he saith unto me, Write, Blessed are they which are called unto the marriage supper of the Lamb. And he saith unto me, These are the true sayings of God" (Revelation 19:5-9).

"And I saw a new heaven and a new earth: for the first heaven and the first earth were passed away; and there was no more sea. And I John saw the holy city, new Jerusalem, coming down from God out of heaven, prepared as a bride adorned for her husband. And I heard a great voice out of heaven saying, Behold, the tabernacle of God is with men, and he will dwell with them, and they shall be his people, and God himself shall be with them, and be their God. And God shall wipe away all tears from their eyes; and there shall be no more death, neither sorrow, nor crying, neither shall there be any more pain: for the former things are passed away" (Revelation 21:1-4).

"And he showed me a pure river of water of life, clear as crystal, proceeding out of the throne of God and of the Lamb. In the midst of the street of it, and on either side of the river, was there the tree of life, which bare twelve manner of fruits, and yielded her fruit every month: and the leaves of the tree were for the healing of the nations. And there shall be no more curse but the throne of God and of the

Lamb shall be in it; and his servants shall serve him: and they shall see his face; and his name shall be in their foreheads. And there shall be no night there; and they need no candle, neither light of the sun; for the Lord God giveth them light: and they shall reign for ever and ever" (Revelation 22:1-5).

It is by no means an exaggeration to say that God's covenant is the key to the interpretation of the whole of God's Word. It is a truth written large on every page of Holy Writ. It is a truth in the light of which the whole of the Scriptures must be interpreted. It is the central teaching of all that God has said in His infallible Word.

And at the same time it is the greatest possible comfort and hope for the child of God as he wends his weary way in the pilgrimage of this life. It is the truth which alone can sustain him, which can be a balm to his troubled soul, which can encourage him in life's disappointments and sufferings, which holds before him the hope of a blessedness which eye hath not seen, nor ear heard. It is his blessedness in this life and in the life to come.

And it is the truth that alone gives all glory to God. "For of him, and through him, and to him are all things: to whom be glory for ever" (Romans 11:36). "Even so, come, Lord Jesus" (Revelation 22:20b).

TEXTUAL INDEX